STALINGRAD
The Infernal Cauldron

STALINGRAD
The Infernal Cauldron
1942–1943

STEPHEN WALSH

amber
BOOKS

First published in 2000

This Amber edition printed in 2013

Copyright © 2013 Amber Books Ltd

Published by
Amber Books Ltd
74–77 White Lion Street
London
N1 9PF
United Kingdom
www.amberbooks.co.uk
Appstore: itunes.com/apps/amberbooksltd
Facebook: www.facebook.com/amberbooks
Twitter: @amberbooks

ISBN: 978-1-909160-58-3

Project editor: Charles Catton
Editor: Vanessa Unwin
Design: Brian Rust
Picture research: Lisa Wren
Additional picture research and caption translation: Lisa Mazura

Printed in China

PICTURE CREDITS

AKG:
8(t), 16, 22 (b), 23, 25, 34, 60(b), 75, 84, 85(b), 88, 94, 97(t), 104, 105(b), 110, 112(t), 115, 130–131, 137(t),
139, 142, 144(b), 150, 154, 159(t), 161(t), 162, 163(both).

Bundesarchiv:
6–7, 10(b), 14(b) 17(l), 33(b), 35(t), 36, 37(b), 40, 44, 45, 46, 50–51, 53(both), 54, 58, 59(b), 65, 70, 71(b)
74, 90, 91(both), 95(b), 99, 106(t), 107, 109(t), 112(b), 129(b).

Novosti:
22(t), 47(b), 52, 61, 63, 72, 78(t), 79, 93(b), 98(t), 102–103, 113, 114, 124, 134(t), 137(b), 140(r), 146(t),
148–149, 151(both), 153, 155, 157(both), 158, 159(b), 169(b).

The Robert Hunt Library:
13(t), 28–29, 57, 77, 111, 116, 121, 133, 141, 143.

TRH Pictures:
8(b), 10(t), 11, 12, 14(t), 18, 19, 20, 27(t), 30, 32, 37(t), 47(t), 55(both), 56, 59(t) (US National Archives),
62 (IWM), 66, 67(r), 68–69, 71(t), 76, 80, 81(both), 86–87, 89(t), 92, 93(t), 95(t), 98(b), 101, 105(t), 117, 122(both),
125(t) (IWM), 132, 134(b), 135, 136, 145, 146(b), 152(both), 156, 160, 161(b), 166(b), 167, 169(t).

Ukrainian Central State Archive of Cine-photo Documents:
9, 13, 15, 17(r), 21(both), 24(both), 26, 27(b), 31, 33(t), 35(b), 38, 39(both), 42, 43, 48, 49(both), 64, 67(l), 78(b), 82(both, 83, 85(t), 89(b),
97(b), 108, 109(b), 118–119, 120, 123, 125, 126, 127(both), 128, 129(t), 138(both), 140(l), 144(t), 147, 164–165, 166(t), 168.

Maps produced by András Bereznay

Colour insert illustrations:
All © Art-Tech except pages VIII, IX, X and XI (top) courtesy Engines of the Red Army in WW2 (www.o5m6.de/).

Contents

CHAPTER ONE

Operation 'Barbarossa'

The Invasion of the Soviet Union

When Hitler launched the invasion of the Soviet Union in June 1941, he anticipated a repeat of the Wehrmacht's earlier successes in defeating Poland, Norway and France in a single swift campaign. Instead, Germany found herself committed to a struggle that would lead to her utter defeat.

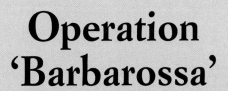

The battle of Stalingrad represents one of the most significant turning points of the twentieth century: the German Wehrmacht was defeated in a titanic struggle on the shores of the River Volga by a Red Army that, only a few months earlier, had appeared to be on the verge of complete defeat.

At the battle of Stalingrad, which lasted from 13 September 1942 until the final German surrender on 2 February 1943, the Russians – unlike at Berlin in April 1945 – were not fighting understrength formations full of old men and fanatically committed young boys. On the contrary, they engaged Germany's elite 300,000-strong 6th Army, commanded by Colonel-General Friedrich Paulus, one of Hitler's favourite generals. Stalingrad came to represent the resurrection of the Red Army and the spiritual tomb of the German Army. It may have taken another three years to come to fruition, but it was here

Left: German soldiers march across the Russian steppe under cloudless skies towards a date with destiny at Stalingrad. With the snows of winter behind them, their confidence was shared by the rest of the Wehrmacht.

that the fortunes of war began to turn against Germany on the Eastern Front.

The catastrophe at Stalingrad did not, of course, bring about the immediate defeat of Germany, but, after February 1943, few German officers genuinely believed in victory. Hitler, on the other hand, if secretly worried that victory in the east was slipping from his grasp, remained faithful to his belief in the idea of will and National Socialist ardour as the decisive factors in war. The defeat at Stalingrad finally completed the rupture of trust between Hitler and the army high command which began at the battle of Moscow in December 1941. To the Germans, Stalingrad was the single most catastrophic defeat of German arms since Napoleon's annihilation of the Prussian Army at Jena-Auerstadt in 1806. Germany was now engaged in a desperate war for survival against a resurgent and vengeful enemy upon whom she had inflicted the most savage and cruel war. To the Soviets, victory represented triumphant survival over the nightmare of adversity faced since the German invasion in June 1941.

At 0315 hours on 22 June 1941, the German army launched Operation 'Barbarossa', the largest single military operation of all time. The number of troops involved, the size of the operations, and the cruelty of the war both stagger and appal the imagination. This was a racial war of annihilation launched by

Above: The men responsible for Operation 'Barbarossa': Adolf Hitler (centre) poses with his field marshals and (to his right) Hermann Göring, head of the Luftwaffe, in the German Chancellory in 1940.

Hitler in pursuit of *Lebensraum* (living space) in the east. Success would acquire for Germany the agricultural and economic resources needed to secure immunity from Allied blockade and lay the foundations of the Thousand Year Reich. Simultaneously, it would destroy Hitler's ideological foe, the Communist Soviet Union, a state he believed to have

Right: A German soldier awaits the start of Operation 'Barbarossa' with a relaxed optimism. Few German soldiers believed the Red Army had the capacity to prevent the Wehrmacht winning a crushing victory.

been infiltrated by, and to be under the control of, the Jews. Furthermore, the destruction of the Soviet Union would, in Hitler's eyes, induce the unreasonably belligerent Churchill to make peace by acknowledging German control of Europe.

In Operation 'Barbarossa', the German Army would fight with remarkable skill, but nevertheless fail to defeat the Soviet Union in one campaign as Hitler had intended. Why did what succeeded so dramatically between September 1939 and November 1941 fail to secure complete victory by the end of 1941 and promise so much – but deliver so little – in 1942? Ironically, many of the reasons for the German failure on the Eastern Front, so emphatically confirmed at Stalingrad, lay in the nature of the German Army's approach to warfare and their fighting methods, commonly known as Blitzkrieg. The German Army's understanding of strategy was rooted in the nineteenth-century concept of the *Vernichtungschlacht* (strategic military victory in one single campaign). In accordance with this idea, it believed that destruction of the enemy army through tactical excellence in fighting would bring about strategic military victory in one single campaign, and thus automatically achieve the political objectives of the war. The German Army of the 1920s and 1930s drew many lessons from World War I, but refused to believe that the famous Schlieffen Plan of 1914 – perhaps the ultimate

expression of the *Vernichtungschlacht* – failed not because of tactical flaws in its execution by field commanders, but because it was unworkable unless the French and British adopted a suicidal strategic and tactical approach.

At first sight, Germany's remarkable victory in France between 10 May and 22 June 1940 appeared to justify the idea of the *Vernichtungschlacht*. In terms of manpower, armour and airpower, the two sides were approximately equal, yet, in those six weeks, Germany achieved what she had failed to do in four years between 1914 and 1918. Naturally, after June 1940, senior German officers concluded that *Vernichtungschlacht* during the modern industrialised era could be achieved through tactical excellence. However, the Wehrmacht won in France because the inferior French and British forces were unable to fight Germany's war of manoeuvre, and did not really provide a sufficiently stern test of German fighting prowess to validate the *Vernichtungschlacht* concept. The German belief – consciously or unconsciously – that it did helps to explain the failure of 'Barbarossa' in 1941 and Operation 'Blau' in 1942.

German fighting methods in World War II have become known as Blitzkrieg and are widely regarded

Below: German armour, carrying infantry, moves into a Soviet village. The lack of opposition was symptomatic of the the Red Army's collapse in the early days of Operation 'Barbarossa'.

as having constituted a revolutionary advance in the art of war. Yet, in November 1941, as the Germans approached Moscow, no less an individual than Hitler declared: 'I have never used the word Blitzkrieg, because it is a very silly word.' To German officers, the new word, one they did not use, simply described old fighting methods. Since the nineteenth century, German commanders had sought to destroy the enemy through the tactical encirclement and physical destruction of the enemy in a *Kesselschlacht* (cauldron battle of annihilation). This was the practical expression in the field of the strategic idea of *Vernichtungschlacht*. The means – that is, armour, airpower and motorisation – of carrying out the *Kesselschlacht* were new, but they served traditional aims. In effect, they were 'new wine in old bottles'. Of course, the number of encirclement and annihilation victories required to win the war in one campaign depended upon the size and skill of the opponent.

Between 1939 and 1942, the German Army absolutely endorsed the *Kesselschlacht* approach: indeed, their hallmark was the ability to encircle and annihilate their enemy. There was nothing unduly sophisticated about the idea. German methods did not focus on the 'brain of the enemy army' as a relatively bloodless method of victory: quite the opposite, the destruction of the enemy command was a by-product of a victory, not its catalyst. The other notable German characteristics were an

Above: A German infantryman carrying a heavy machine gun pauses for reflection. The slung weapon makes it clear he does not expect to be attacked by either Soviet airpower or ground troops.

Below: For thousands of Soviet soldiers, the war was already over. As prisoners, the future held little hope, for the Wehrmacht had neither the resources nor the inclination to cater for Soviet prisoners.

emphasis upon tactical creativity, boldness and flexibility, in conjunction with a superior understanding of the value of armour, airpower, radio and speed. In 1941, although the German Army's tactical ability to encircle and annihilate its opponents was raised to a new level of excellence, this did not achieve victory in one campaign. The Red Army survived Operation 'Barbarossa' because of its manpower resources and its ability to inflict a positional and attritional contest upon the Germans at the battle of Moscow from November to December 1941.

An invasion of the Soviet Union in 1941 posed problems that the Germans had not confronted in earlier campaigns. Three major factors – geography, distance and time – dominated calculations and their influence, implicit or explicit, was felt throughout 1941 and 1942. Geographically, western European Russia was dominated by the Pripet Marshes which ensured German operations in the south would be isolated until well into the Ukraine. Equally, the sheer size of the Soviet Union was a powerful influence upon the effective conduct of operations. German armoured units had suffered wear and tear in the short French campaign. It was only 322km (200 miles) from the Ardennes to the Atlantic, but it was 1609km (1000 miles) from Warsaw to Moscow and 1931km (1200 miles) from Leningrad to Rostov. Stalingrad was 3219km (2000 miles) east of Berlin. Once Hitler declared his intention to move east on 31 July 1940, planning was dominated by the desire to win in one campaign. Yet the Russian climate limited mobile warfare to between May and November, so time was a critical factor. Indeed, whether a state the size of the Soviet Union could be defeated in one campaign, no matter how accomplished the tactical prowess of the German Army, was very much open to question. It would require an unprecedented intensity of operations in a country whose backward infrastructure did not lend itself to rapid logistical provision. It was assumed Soviet forces could be annihilated in a series of *Kesselschlachts* wherever the Red Army was encountered. Whether the German Army could do this without suffering unsustainable attrition was a question rarely asked or answered – either in 1941 or 1942 – until it was too late.

Right: The speed of the advance committed German infantry to exhausting, if victorious, marches of 30 miles per day. Their lack of mobility is illustrated by this soldier's use of a bicycle.

Operation 'Barbarossa' evolved from the plan outlined by Major-General Marcks in August 1940. Marcks believed victory could be achieved in one campaign through the destruction of the Red Army in two phases. First, the Red Army's forces in European Russia would be annihilated in a series of *Kesselschlachts*. The battleground would be the land between the Soviet Union's 1939 and 1941 borders acquired as part of Hitler and Stalin's carve-up of Poland in August 1939. Marcks believed the agricultural and industrial value of these regions would compel the Red Army to stand and fight rather than adopting a strategy of trading space for time. It would be essential to prevent the Red Army's orderly withdrawal into the interior of Russia behind the line of the rivers Dvina and Dnepr. At all costs, the Germans had to avoid a positional campaign. Second, Marcks argued, the remaining Soviet armies could be defeated in a decisive battle of annihilation for Moscow. The loss of the political, intellectual, economic and communications heart of the Soviet Union, in conjunction with another

massive military defeat, would achieve strategic victory in one campaign.

This broad outline laid the foundations of Führer Directive 21 released on 18 December 1940. This was not a detailed campaign plan: indeed, it identified only the initial military objectives for the first phase of operations. Consequently, German planning would be characterised by argument and improvisation over the best way to defeat the Soviet Union in one campaign. Army Group Centre (AGC), commanded by Field Marshal Fedor von Bock, would lead the attack. Commissioned into the Reichswehr in 1898, Bock won Germany's highest military decoration, the Pour le Merite, as a battalion commander in World War I. He was the epitome of haughty Prussian military tradition and had commanded Army Group North (AGN) in the Polish campaign of September 1939 and directed Army Group B in the French campaign between May and June 1940. Under his control, AGC consisted of General Strauss' 9th Army and General von Kluge's 4th Army. AGC's striking power lay in General Hoth's 3rd Panzer Group under the operational control of 9th Army, and General Guderian's 2nd Panzer Group under 4th Army's command. AGC, led by 3rd Panzer on the northern wing with 2nd Panzer on the southern wing, was to create two *Kesselschlachts* at Bialystok and Minsk. The pockets would be annihilated by 9th Army and 4th Army, thus destroying Soviet forces in Belorussia. Air support, a critical dimension of German Blitzkrieg, was to be provided by Air Fleet 2, whose commander Field Marshal Kesselring told his officers to treat requests for close air support by army commanders as though they were his own. AGC's anticipated success in Belorussia was to be followed by its capture of the land bridge between the Dvina and Dnepr in the region of Mogilev–Vitebsk–Orsha. Its final objective in this first phase was Smolensk, the gateway to the Russian heartland. This would secure positions for a possible assault on Moscow. However, the aims of the second phase had not been clarified and Moscow had not been formally endorsed by Hitler as the specific objective of the campaign.

Field Marshal Wilhelm von Leeb commanded Army Group North (AGN). Leeb was an officer of ability and a strong, independent personality. He had played a minor role in crushing Hitler's 1923 Munich Beer Hall Putsch and was never one of Hitler's favourite generals. During the Polish campaign, Leeb

commanded Army Group C, guarding Germany's front with France, successfully leading the same formation in the French campaign, and taking the Maginot Line, an achievement for which he was promoted to field marshal in July 1940. AGN consisted of General von Kuechler's 18th Army on the left, Baltic flank and General Busch's 16th Army on the right adjoining Army Group Centre. AGN's strike force was Panzer Group 4 commanded by General Hoepner with air support provided by Air Fleet 1 under Colonel-General Keller. AGN would also receive support from 15 Finnish divisions committed to recapture territory north of Leningrad, annexed by Stalin following the Red Army's victory in the Winter War of November 1939 to March 1940. AGN's task was to destroy Soviet forces in the Baltic region, occupy the coast, and eventually capture Leningrad with, Directive 21 significantly envisaged, armoured forces diverted from Army Group Centre. At this stage, the Baltic and Leningrad were very much

Below: A German officer probes a building for Soviet troops. As the Wehrmacht advanced, the Red Army fell back, often bypassing Soviet units fighting their way back to their lines under cover of darkness.

Above: Field Marshal von Bock, commander of Army Group Centre, consults Colonel-General Herman Hoth of 3rd Panzer Group. By July 1941, many senior German officers assumed the Red Army was broken.

Below: A German light artillery/anti-tank team maintains a watchful air as German troops move into a Soviet town. The Red Army's opposition fluctuated from the negligible to the ferociously determined.

Hitler's preference, but not that of the Chief of the General Staff, Colonel-General Franz Halder. As in Poland and France, the course of the campaign, beyond the first phase, had not been determined: worse, there were two competing ideas, one held by Hitler and one by Halder – Moscow – on behalf of the army. This German failure to select and maintain a clear strategic objective would seriously undermine both the 1941 and 1942 campaigns.

Army Group South (AGS) deployed on the Polish–Ukrainian border was commanded by Field Marshal Gerd von Rundstedt. A Saxon, born in 1875, Rundstedt had an impeccable record. In 1914, he had distinguished himself in Alsace and as a divisional – and later corps – chief of staff on the Eastern Front. In October 1938, Rundstedt retired before returning to command AGS in the Polish campaign and the key Army Group A in France. The laconic Rundstedt was not convinced Germany could conquer Russia in one campaign and remained sceptical even after his appointment as the commander of AGS in March 1941. AGS consisted of General von Kleist's 1st Panzer Group, Field Marshal von Reichenau's 6th Army, General von Stulpnagel's 17th Army and General Schobert's 11th Army. The 1st Panzer was to reach the Dnepr at Kiev and move south-east, following the course of the river, to prevent the withdrawal of Soviet troops from the western Ukraine. The 17th Army would move east to act as the hammer to 1st Panzer's anvil, ensuring

Above: A German soldier, part of a mortar team, loads the weapon to suppress local Soviet infantry opposition. German units could also rely on the luxury of the Luftwaffe's complete air superiority.

Below: A German soldier shares a cigarette with a captured Russian. Such generosity was very much the exception to the rule in this war of ideology and annihilation.

Soviet destruction in a massive encirclement, while Reichenau's 6th Army was to guard AGS's northern flank along the Pripet Marshes. Schobert's 11th Army would cooperate with the Romanians on the Black Sea, the main objective being the capture of Odessa. Air support would be provided by Air Fleet 4, commanded by an Austrian, Colonel-General Alexander Lohr.

The German forces committed to 'Barbarossa' consisted of 3,050,000 men, 3350 armoured fighting vehicles, 600,000 motorised vehicles and, significantly, 625,000 horses mainly for resupply and artillery. These were organised into three army groups, seven armies and four panzer groups of army size, with seventeen panzer and thirteen motorised divisions supported by three motorised brigades. The main body of the army walked, exactly as their forefathers had done, made up of 153 'orthodox' infantry divisions. The Germans went to war in June 1941 with everything they could equip for combat yet, given the size of the task, the depth of the force was shallow. It simply could not become involved in prolonged positional and logistically consumptive fighting. If the battles between the 1939 to 1941 borders did not inflict a decisive blow, the attempt to defeat the Soviet Union in one campaign might destroy the Wehrmacht, not its opponents.

It is essential to understand the extent to which everything was dependent on a short decisive campaign of no more than four months. There were no serious contingency plans if the war dragged on into the winter, never mind the summer of 1942. There was some provision for conversion of the Russian railway gauge, but, given expectations of a quick victory, it was neither systematic nor adequate. It should not be assumed German commanders were unaware of potential supply problems caused by the poor infrastructure of the Soviet Union. However, the impact of Nazi ideology and the Wehrmacht's reasonable assumptions of its superiority over the Red Army combined to create a situation where expectations of victory were so contrived that Germany's fragile capacity to supply its forces in anything less than ideal combat circumstances was ignored. It was assumed German tactical brilliance would ensure the campaign's success before major difficulties were encountered. Equally, the Nazi belief of the Slavs as an inferior race produced a subtle and often unconscious perception among many highly competent military professionals that the Red Army

Above: A Red Army anti-tank team snatches some food while preparing to defend a Russian town. They are clearly not under attack, but their tense air indicates they are anticipating a German assault.

was incapable of a sufficiently effective defence seriously to trouble the Wehrmacht. This was a gamble of monumental proportions. In short, Operation 'Barbarossa' (and 'Blau' in 1942) repeated all the errors of that other German statement of faith in the *Vernichtungschlacht*, the Schlieffen Plan of August 1914. Operation 'Barbarossa' was just as unworkable unless the enemy fought in a suicidal manner, which, thanks to Stalin, it did. It is this, and the tactical brilliance of German battle commanders, that explains why the Germans came so close to victory in 1941. It was not because of the worthiness of the 'Barbarossa' plan.

Ironically, the successful tactical methods of 1939 and 1940 – namely the encirclement and annihilation of the opponent – in some ways appeared to undermine the German chances of victory in one campaign. In Poland and France, the panzer divisions had created the encirclements, reduced by the ordinary German infantry on foot with the help of the Luftwaffe. Naturally, armour and infantry moved at different speeds, so that in effect there were 'two' German armies: one on wheels and one that walked. In earlier campaigns, the problem had been contained, if not solved, due to the small distances and number of encirclements involved. Yet victory over the Red Army in one campaign would require more

and larger pockets, reduced quickly to prevent any Soviet troops not caught in the initial encirclements from withdrawing behind the Dvina-Dnepr line. The pockets would be so massive that leaving them to the infantry raised significant tactical problems. How could the infantry rapidly annihilate the pockets and keep up with the panzer groups as they dashed forwards to stop surviving Red Army forces retreating into the interior? In other words, forward tempo and the secure, rapid annihilation of the pockets were incompatible yet essential to winning in one campaign. A slower advance which would ensure the systematic destruction of the pockets was ruled out since it would invite an attritional struggle that could only favour the Soviet Union. The widespread mechanisation or motorisation of the infantry was beyond German means in 1941. In essence, the problem of the 'two' German armies was unsolvable, and would rear its head again in the 1942 campaign; however, on balance, the emphasis had to lie with the panzer groups, as Germany could not countenance a positional struggle. It was another monumental gamble. If it worked, a 1942 campaign was irrelevant; if it failed,

15

Germany would need a decisive victory in 1942 with fewer resources than those which had been insufficient in 1941. It is one of history's great ironies that the solution to these German strategic and tactical dilemmas lay with none other than Josef Stalin.

Stalin's policy in the 1930s had been to seek collective security with Britain and France against the rising power of Nazi Germany. Ignored at Munich in October 1938, however, Stalin cut a deal with Hitler in August 1939 known as the Nazi–Soviet Non Aggression Pact. This was done in the cynical expectation of a long war between the western capitalist powers which would create time to reform the Red Army, giving it the opportunity to capitalise on the exhaustion of the western powers. Nevertheless, Stalin did not possess a grand strategic master plan of Soviet aggression. Although ruthless in a way matched by few others, he was a cautious, calculating individual, with few of Hitler's gambling instincts. He was under no illusions as to Hitler's long-term intentions towards the Soviet Union, but Germany's astonishing success in 1940 came as a rude shock. Stalin knew the Red Army was in no position to defeat the Wehrmacht.

Below: German signallers lie flat whilst waiting to move up to an observation post. The Wehrmacht's artillery was as devastating to the Red Army as the Luftwaffe.

Although the Red Army prevailed over Finland in the Winter War of November 1939 to March 1940, it suffered 48,745 dead and 158,000 wounded amidst appalling military incompetence. The roots of this shambles lay in Stalin's murderous assault on the Red Army in the Great Purge between 1937 and 1938, as his paranoid mind sought to eliminate any potential threat to his power. At least 30,000 officers were imprisoned, tortured or executed, including 3 out of 5 marshals, 14 of 16 army commanders, 60 of 67 corps commanders, 136 of 199 divisional commanders, 221 of 397 brigade commanders and 50 per cent of all regimental commanders. The officer corps were destroyed, along with the modern ideas of deep battle and deep operations nurtured in the 1930s by men such as Marshal Mikhail Tukhachevsky, who was killed in June 1937 after signing a blood-splattered 'confession' about collusion with the German secret services. The Purge, which continued in a milder form until the eve of war, destroyed the Red Army's ability to confront an opponent as proficient as Germany. In 1936, General Kostring, the German military attaché to the Soviet Union, regarded the Red Army as a formidable force. By 1941, it was 'led' by incompetent or inexperienced officers rapidly promoted to replace purge victims. Their initiative was subdued into conformity by the threat of arrest. The failures in Finland had induced military

Right: Soviet soldiers pose for the camera. The relaxed air suggests that this picture was taken in June 1941, before the German attack descended upon the Red Army.

Below: German soldiers were very impressed by the power of the Luftwaffe. They did not want to become inadvertent victims, hence the clear identification of themselves as friend not foe.

reform and the release of many competent officers condemned in the Purge. In June 1941, however, the Soviets were caught in the middle of a transition and the benefits of reform were swept away by the suicidal military strategy imposed by Stalin.

At no stage did Stalin permit the Red Army to adopt a strategy of trading space for time. On the contrary, he committed it to a forward defence along the Soviet Union's western border. Marcks had foreseen and welcomed this for, if unable to engage in agile manoeuvre, the Red Army would be consumed in German *Kesselschlachts*. The Red Army of June 1941 was not capable of this level of defence, even if it had been allowed to try. Strategic command and control was dependent upon Stalin, while operational and tactical command was undermined by lack of radios. As independent initiative was neither encouraged nor tolerated in Stalin's Russia, paralysis and confusion were inevitable when confronted with the tactical speed and skill of the Wehrmacht. Stalin, fearful of provoking an attack he knew was coming,

denied the Red Army the chance to engage in effective reconnaissance and kept all intelligence to himself. He received countless warnings from his own sources and from the British whose information he dismissed as an attempt by Churchill to get the Soviet Union to fight Britain's war. No leader has ever been so well informed of what history has invariably described as a surprise attack, yet to the majority of the Red Army, the German assault on 22 June 1941 came as a complete shock.

Soviet armour, although huge in quantity, lacked quality in its machines, crew and training. In January 1940, the Red Army's all-arms tank corps were abolished and dispersed into an infantry support role. The German victory in the French campaign provoked a panic-stricken attempt to find an antidote to the panzer divisions and, in July 1940, the Red Army created the Soviet mechanised corps. An unwieldy force of two tank divisions and one motorised infantry division numbering 37,000, they were no match for the panzer divisions and panzer corps. By June 1941, there were 21 ill-prepared mechanised corps, instead of a smaller number of well-equipped and trained formations. They lacked radios, modern tanks, lorries for motorised infantry and effective air support. Of the Red Army's 14,000 tanks, only 1861 were modern KV-1 and T-34s, the rest being obsolete machines procured in the 1920s and 1930s. A similar picture emerged from the Soviet Air Force which, although it possessed 9500 aircraft in European Russia, was in no position to fight the

Above: A few hours of rain, even in high summer, seriously undermined German mobility. The German infantry found the mud tough work. For the retreating Red Army, such conditions provided respite.

Luftwaffe. Its aircraft were obsolete (some Soviet pilots flew biplanes), its organisation was chaotic, and its leadership, if anything, worse than the Army's, three successive heads of the airforce having been purged in the late 1930s. In 1941, the Red Army's greatest and perhaps only strengths, in contrast to later in the war, were its numbers and tenacity. The mobilised field strength of the Red Army in European Russia was about 3.5 million with its overall strength being 5 million before mobilisation of reserves. It was these manpower reserves which enabled the Soviets to survive 1941, as well as the chaotic tenacity of Soviet soldiers which inflicted cumulative attrition on the Wehrmacht.

In recent years it has been suggested – initially by the Soviet defector Viktor Rezun, writing as Viktor Suvorov – that in spring 1941 the Soviets were planning a pre-emptive war against Germany. A source of bitter historical controversy, particularly in Germany, the evidence lies in a document prepared by General Zhukov in May 1941 which discussed the possibility of an offensive. There is no doubt the proposal was made, but it was not a definite strategic decision to attack. It was one proposal among many written by the Soviet High Command with war imminent. Soviet troops were deploying along the border in the spring of 1941, not to attack, but to defend the Soviet Union's territory. Senior German officers involved in planning 'Barbarossa' – such as Marcks, Halder and Kostring – while aware of the

deployments, saw no prospect of a Red Army attack. Indeed, as late as 9 April 1941, Kostring's deputy, Colonel Hans Krebs, saw no enhanced preparations for war by the Red Army. Furthermore, it is clear from Stalin's craven desire not to provoke Germany that he wanted to avoid war. Equally, even if Stalin had wished to launch a pre-emptive attack, the Red Army of 1941 was incapable of conducting such an offensive. Stalin knew the weaknesses of the Red Army better than most: nobody had done more to create them.

The German attack on 22 June 1941 began with a massive strike by the Luftwaffe. It hit 66 Soviet airfields, destroying 1200 Soviet planes on the ground; those that managed to get airborne were easily shot down, enabling the Germans to acquire complete air superiority. The Luftwaffe made the life of Soviet units reeling under the German onslaught a miserable hell. Communications were smashed, movement was disrupted, supplies were chaotic, reserves were strafed and bombed, and coherent command was made virtually impossible. Soviet forces in the centre and north were smashed within hours, rendering the Soviet strategy of forward defence irrelevant. It was now a war of manoeuvre that only one side was capable of fighting. Army Group Centre (AGC) caught Soviet Western Front, commanded by General Dmitry Pavlov, entirely unprepared. Often mistakenly compared to a German army group, a Soviet Front was the basic Red Army operational formation. It was more variable in size and specifically task-oriented than a German army group, being more akin to a large German army such as the 300,000-strong 6th Army that would assault Stalingrad.

On Western Front's left, 2nd Panzer Group crossed the Bug at Brest-Litovsk, while, on AGC's other wing, 3rd Panzer Group crossed the Neman and reached Vilnius on 24 June. The two panzer groups turned inwards on 28 June to create a double envelopment near Minsk, with the inner encirclement executed further west at Bialystok by 4th Army in the south and 9th Army in the north. By 1 July, Western Front's four armies – 3rd, 10th, 4th and 13th – had been destroyed, losing 417,000 troops. On 22 July 1941, the unfortunate General Pavlov, summoned before Stalin for his 'crimes', paid with his life; however, thousands of Russians escaped eastwards, with 3rd Panzer forced to relinquish 12th Panzer Division to help 9th Army at Bialystok. Thus, at this early stage, the problem of the 'two' German armies made its presence felt. Nevertheless, on 1 July, AGC's armoured groups advanced across the Dnepr and Dvina towards Smolensk with the intention of creating another *Kesselschlacht*. The Soviet forces

were to be annihilated by 9th and 4th Army, to secure the 'land bridge' between Orsha and Vitebsk. General Halder believed this would induce Hitler to nominate Moscow – in line with his own wishes – as the campaign objective. The Soviets would be forced into a decisive battle of annihilation for the hub of their empire.

However, as Army Group North smashed through Soviet North-Western Front, commanded by Colonel-General Fedor I. Kuznctsov, Hitler was disinclined to change his ideas. The 8th and 11th Soviet Armies simply could not cope with the power and speed of the German forces. Led by General Reinhardt's 41st Panzer Corps, General Hoepner's Panzer Group 4 swept through Lithuania in 72 hours, while General von Manstein's 56th Panzer Corps crossed the Dvina at Daugavpils on 26 June. Indeed, such was the speed of the advance that a pause was ordered to enable 18th Army and 16th Army to catch up. The terrain prevented a *Kesselschlacht*, but in a matter of days the Soviet line had been wrecked and German troops were advancing towards Leningrad.

Once the initial surprise of the attack had worn off, however, Army Group South (AGS) faced

Below: A German MG34 heavy machine gun mounted for the sustained fire role. The soldier on the right uses binoculars to observe the effect of the machine-gun team's fire.

increasingly stiff resistance. The Soviet High Command had erroneously anticipated the Ukraine as the main German effort. As a result, South-Western Front, commanded by Colonel-General Mikhail P. Kirponos, contained some of the best Red Army units. The Russian line buckled, but did not break, and, as early as 27 June, AGS's orders were revised to envisage a less ambitious encirclement. Instead of advancing as far as Kiev, 1st Panzer Group would now turn south 161km (100 miles) west of the city. In mid-July, 1st Panzer, despite persistent harassment from General Potapov's 5th Army, finally broke through the northern flank of South-Western Front and duly turned south. Stalin would not permit a withdrawal of Soviet forces in central Ukraine and, in early August 1941 – in conjunction with 11th Army coming from the south-west and 17th Army to the west – 1st Panzer created the Uman *Kesselschlacht*. Its annihilation destroyed Soviet 6th, 12th and parts of 18th Army, netting 103,000 prisoners and tearing a gaping hole in South-Western Front's defences. Thus, by August 1941, the position of Rundstedt's AGS had improved considerably. However, it had not crossed the Dnepr and Hitler's concerns about its northern flank were about to exercise a vital influence upon the campaign.

By the end of July 1941, the Soviet position appeared hopeless. On 1 August, the Smolensk pocket's two-week resistance ended. The Germans were only 402km (250 miles) from Moscow and had killed, wounded or taken prisoner more than two million Red Army soldiers. Soviet defeat in one campaign seemed a matter of time, with the barriers of geography, distance and time now entirely overcome. General Halder, supported by the majority of army commanders, believed that, after a pause for replenishment, the main German effort should concentrate upon Moscow. He considered its importance would compel the Red Army to defend it, regardless of the situation elsewhere. The Red Army would be destroyed in a battle of encirclement and annihilation: Moscow was not an objective in itself, but a means to achieve German strategic victory. On 19 July, however, Hitler issued Directive 33, which diverted 3rd Panzer north to assist AGN in its assault on Leningrad, and 2nd Panzer south to assist AGS. This left only AGC's infantry to push on Moscow, undermining the very speed and tempo that had enabled the Germans to avoid positional war. In effect, Hitler rejected Halder's idea of making a decisive battle for Moscow the catalyst of a German *Vernichtungschlacht*. Indeed, on 30 July in Directive 34, Hitler officially rejected any attack on Moscow. These decisions caused an enormous row within the German high command at a time when the Red Army was in disarray. This argument arose in the middle of the campaign because no detailed operational campaign plan had been made at the outset. However well the Germans fought, they did not have the means to sustain the *Kesselschlacht* concept simultaneously across the entire front. To win in one campaign, the timing and location of the *Kesselschlachts* had to be carefully planned to husband German strength for the decisive battles. Hitler oscillated between the destruction of the Red Army and securing Leningrad or the Ukraine. Yet the latter were assets to secure Germany from economic blockade and would be a product of victory, not its catalyst. Hitler was endorsing objectives designed to fight a long war, while undermining German chances of winning in one campaign. The key issue was time: there is little doubt that, if the Germans had

Left: As the season moved from late summer into early autumn, Soviet resistance began to stiffen. These German infantrymen appear in some haste to consolidate their defensive position.

paused before launching an operation against Moscow in late August 1941, the Red Army, for all its bravery, could not have defeated the Germans. This row about an issue that should have been settled before the war started played a key role in saving the Soviet Union from defeat in one campaign.

Hitler got his way; one month after Directive 33, 2nd Panzer moved south on 21 August. In early September, Soviet commanders pleaded with Stalin to evacuate Kiev. He refused. On 16 September, 1st Panzer coming north met 2nd Panzer coming south at Lokhvitsa, east of Kiev, creating the outer encirclement, while 17th and 2nd Armies executed the inner encirclement. Stalin refused an immediate breakout and, after fierce fighting amid desperate scenes in which Colonel-General Kirponos was killed, 650,000 Soviet troops surrendered. As German forces moved south, Hitler issued Directive 35 on 6 September. It ordered a rapid strengthening of AGC with the aim of destroying Soviet troops east of Smolensk as a prelude to an advance on Moscow. However massive the German blow at Kiev, the very requirement for an offensive against Moscow indicated that it was not – and could not have been – a decisive blow.

Operation Typhoon, the attack of AGC on Moscow, began on 30 September 1941, nine weeks

Above: Confident and fresh German infantry advance further into Russia. Shirt sleeves and sunglasses have been replaced by great coats and balaclavas, but there is clearly plenty of fight left in these troops.

Below: The Wehrmacht's requisitioning of the harvest deepened the Soviet people's hatred of the invaders and consolidated Stalin's regime. Note the prevalence of horses and problems caused by rain and mud.

Above: Josef Stalin. By September 1941, he was under no illusions that the Soviet Union was on the verge of destruction, yet still ordered the Red Army to stand and fight the Wehrmacht.

Below: Soviet troops and armour counterattack in a burning town. The sustained resilience and tenacity of the Red Army in towns such as Smolensk dismayed German commanders and soldiers.

after the fall of Smolensk. The influence of distance and time was now increasingly apparent as the Germans raced against their own deadline, the Russian winter. On 2 October, reinforced by 4th Panzer as well as its own 2nd and 3rd panzers, AGC broke through the Soviet defences. In ten days at Vyazma, in a classical endorsement of their tactical methods, the Germans engulfed Soviet Western and Reserve Fronts, while, 241km (150 miles) to the south, Bryansk Front was destroyed by 2nd Panzer Group and 2nd Army. This was the moment of supreme crisis for the Red Army. It lost more than 600,000 troops in the Vyazma and Bryansk encirclements and its defences were shattered. It seemed to be just a matter of time before the Germans rolled into a panic-stricken Moscow; however, it started to rain, and within days the speed of the German pursuit slackened in the autumn mud. Here lies the true significance of the diversion of German combat power from Moscow in high summer. If the Germans had attacked Moscow in late August or early September 1941, there seems little doubt they would have still broken the Soviet line as in October, but, given better weather, would have been able to capitalise upon it. It is ironic that because of the time it took to complete, the Kiev encirclement – one of

the most impressive military victories in history – seriously undermined German chances of winning in one campaign. By the end of October 1941, the Soviets managed to impose some order and prepare for a battle of annihilation to defend Moscow in the depths of winter. This was a very different proposition to Halder's original idea of a fluid encirclement of Moscow by manoeuvre and the destruction of the Red Army by a fresh German Army.

Bock and Halder knew German troops were shattered and the panzers had already suffered serious mechanical wear and tear. The Germans did not possess the depth to fight a positional battle of attrition, yet found themselves in a situation where they had to in order to win in one campaign. During 'Barbarossa', the Red Army had proved unable to combine linear defence with depth. However, at Moscow, General Zhukov, appointed to command Western Front on 10 October in the wake of the Vyazma disaster, was helped by several factors which ensured this battle would be different. The terrain was punctuated by forests, marshland and numerous rivers which identified German assault axes, preventing them, especially in winter, from conducting the fluid armoured operations in which they had proved so superior to the Red Army. Equally, the obvious German objective made surprise difficult to achieve and intelligence easier to acquire. The Soviets correctly anticipated the German inclination to encircle and annihilate, so on their right wing General Rokossovsky's 16th Army was suitably reinforced, being 80,000-strong in positions 20km (12.4 miles) deep, while, on the left wing, Soviet 50th Army's positions around Tula were strengthened against Guderian's 2nd Panzer. These deployments forced the Germans into frontal assaults, enabling the Red Army to fight on something like equal terms for the first time in the war by combining depth and position.

In strategic terms, Soviet manpower resources enabled them to survive 1941, but, by early November 1941, the Red Army's strength in European Russia had fallen to 2.3 million, its lowest level of the war. However, when Stalin's master spy in Tokyo, the German Richard Sorge, indicated Japan's eyes were on the Pacific and not the eastern Soviet Union, Stalin permitted the secret transfer of 15 divisions from the Soviet interior. These were not wasted in piecemeal tactical commitment as Stalin finally permitted better commanders to control the Red Army.

Above: A German soldier pays the ultimate price of war. German casualties were less than those of the Red Army, but the steady attrition suffered by the Wehrmacht began to undermine its effectiveness.

Zhukov integrated some units into key positions in the line, but husbanded others in training inexperienced formations that were being rushed to the defence of Moscow. Moscow's pivotal position in the Soviet rail system was instrumental in this strategic redeployment and proved a major advantage in terms of tactical mobility during the battle. Soviet troops' movements were orchestrated with relative economy of effort, while the Germans thrashed around on unpaved roads in a sea of mud in shocking weather. Soviet commanders could rely on effective, if rough-and-ready, rear services, while German commanders endured irregular supply and movement. Their failure to provide adequately for the conversion of the Russian railway gauge – and thus to offset their crippling dependency on the roads – came to haunt them. If the Red Army was to fight a decisive battle of annihilation, then Moscow in the winter was the place to do it.

The final German assault began on 15 November 1941. The plan was to break through north and

Above: By November 1941, a group of resilient and talented Soviet commanders, who had endured the crucible of 'Barbarossa', emerged wiser and infinitely more experienced, to win the battle of Moscow.

south of Moscow, while Kluge's 4th Army fixed Soviet troops in the centre. To the south, Guderian's 2nd Panzer began its assault and, by 24 November, had taken Venev, 64.3km (40 miles) away, as it sought to encircle the city. Yet the crisis was developing to the north-west as Reinhardt's 3rd Panzer and Hoepner's 4th Panzer bore down across the frozen ground on the Soviet 30th and 16th Armies. On 23 November, 3rd Panzer took Klin 32km

(20 miles) north-west of Moscow, splitting the 30th and 16th Armies. The Soviet line groaned, but did not break as reserves forced the Germans to fight for every inch of ground. In desperate fighting, in nightmarish conditions, between 26 and 27 November, SS Das Reich clashed head on with 16th Army's 78th Siberian Division at Istra, north-west of Moscow, while on its flank 7th Panzer Division clawed its way over the Moscow-Volga Canal. On 28 November, Zhukov committed General Kuznetsov's 1st Shock Army which, with 16th Army, drove the Germans back over the canal. To the south, Soviet reserves halted 2nd Panzer at Tula and on the rivers Oka and Moskva. On 1 December, the temperature plunged to −35°C as 4th Army attacked west of Moscow. Although it succeeded in penetrating the flanks of Soviet 33rd Army to a depth of 24km (15 miles), it was brought to a grinding halt on 4 December 1941. The German assault had failed, yet, as German commanders contemplated their failure to win in one campaign, Zhukov stunned them by launching a counteroffensive on 5 December.

Its aim was to force the Germans away from Moscow. The retention of reserves enabled an overnight transition from defence to attack, surprising the German troops, who lacked proper defensive positions. The Moscow counteroffensive succeeded

Left: The famous T-34 was to prove the backbone of Soviet armour. Its armour, gun and cross-country ability made it a feared opponent for German infantry and armour.

despite Russian commanders' inexperience in offensive manoeuvre warfare. They did not match the tactical brilliance of their opponents, but inflicted a savage blow to German morale, which teetered on the verge of collapse. Although the Germans were driven back, Soviet mistakes narrowly prevented the encirclement of 4th German Army, which fought with a tenacity and skill born of desperation as catastrophe loomed. By 20 December, slowly but surely, the threat to Moscow had been removed. The Red Army developed its attack into an ambitious attempt to encircle and destroy Army Group Centre: General Konev's Kalinin Front attacked south-west from north of Moscow, while the left wing of Western Front moved north from south of Moscow. The aim was to meet at Vyazma. A crisis of confidence developed between Hitler and the German high command. On 17 December, Bock was removed on grounds of ill health to be replaced by Field Marshal von Kluge. On 19 December, Field Marshal von Brauchitsch was removed as commander-in-chief and replaced by Hitler. Hitler's order of 16 December, the *Haltebefehl* – to hold the line, lest withdrawal became a rout – clashed with the tactical flexibility which German field commanders requested and expected. In the next four weeks, as the fate of AGC hung in the balance, Hitler removed Guderian from 2nd Panzer (on 25 December), Hoepner from 4th Panzer, and Strauss from 9th Army. On 2 January 1942, Hitler ordered the line

held, regardless of the threat of encirclement. However, on 5 January, against the advice of Zhukov, Stalin ordered a general offensive across the entire Eastern Front. The concentrated power of the Soviet blow was dissipated and, although the Soviets achieved success elsewhere, the mortal threat to Army Group Centre slowly receded. By February 1942, the Soviet offensive began waning and, by March 1942, the German Army had recovered its confidence.

It had, however, been badly shaken, and not only west of Moscow. AGN's advance on Leningrad had been halted and, on 8 January 1942, it came under heavy attack in the Lake Illmen region. Nevertheless, although Army Group North incurred serious losses, by April 1942, it had survived the winter without a decisive Soviet breakthrough and still had Leningrad under merciless siege.

On 18 October, 1st Panzer received orders to advance on Rostov. Yet supply difficulties, which exercised an increasingly dominant influence over operations, ensured 1st Panzer did not begin its drive on Rostov until 5 November. The Soviet line broke, but, with torrential rain paralysing all movement, the attack was not resumed until 17 November. In temperatures of -20°C, Rostov fell on

Below: Soviet infantry on the outskirts of Moscow. The city environment and the wear and tear suffered by the Wehrmacht undermined its ability to defeat a resilient Red Army under better commanders.

20 November. However, Timoshenko's South-Western Front regrouped and, on 22 November, launched a fierce counterattack north of Rostov. On 28 November, under extreme pressure, 1st Panzer abandoned Rostov. Rundstedt approved Kleist's tactical decision and a further withdrawal 129km (80 miles) west to a winter defensive position behind the river Mius. Hitler ordered 1st Panzer to hold the line and, in the early hours of 1 December, relieved Rundstedt. Rundstedt was replaced by Field Marshal von Reichenau, an ardent Nazi, who confirmed Rundstedt's orders, a decision accepted by Hitler. On 25 October, Manstein's 11th Army broke through Soviet 51st Army into the Crimea across the Perekop Isthmus.

By 16 November, the Kerch Peninsula was in German hands, leaving only Sevastopol. The city's spirited defence led by General Petrov would defy 11th Army until May 1942. On 27 December, the Soviets transformed the situation in the eastern Crimea by landing elements of 51st and 44th Armies at Feodisya. The Germans found, as elsewhere on the Eastern Front, that they did not possess the means to drive the Soviets back and take Sevastopol. In the attempt to do both, they failed to achieve either. A stalemate had been reached, much to Hitler's chagrin. He regarded the Crimea as an essential condition of any German advance into the Caucasus, an advance intended for 1941 which would now be delayed until 1942.

By March 1942, the German Army had stabilised the front. Nevertheless, it had failed to defeat the Soviet Union in one campaign and its three army

Above: German infantry advance on Moscow. Despite bad weather, they remain cheerful and confident of victory; their lack of preparedness for the Russian winter and their limited mobility are evident.

groups were no longer capable of mounting simultaneous offensive operations. By 31 January 1942, the Eastern Army had suffered 917,985 casualties, nearly a third of the original force. It was impossible to replace them fully without inflicting serious damage on the German war economy. On 1 May 1942, units of Army Group South had only 50 per cent of their original infantry complement, with Army Group Centre and Army Group North down to 35 per cent. German armoured losses since June 1941 amounted to more than 4200 and, by 31 March 1942, the 16 panzer divisions in the east had only 140 operational tanks. Losses of motorised vehicles and horses – 101,529 and 207,943, respectively – had decisive consequences for mobility and supply. In 1942, while Army Group South waged an aggressive mobile war, Army Group Centre and Army Group North would engage the Soviets in defensive, positional war. Soviet losses in 1941 were horrific. It is estimated that, between 22 June 1941 and 31 December 1941, the Red Army suffered upwards of 6 million casualties, 3 million prisoners of war and tanks losses of 21,391. However shocking, they could be replaced and the Red Army retrained. It would take time, but the Red Army had survived.

The German Army had come within a whisker of defeating of the Soviet Union. Indeed, the first two months of the campaign could hardly have been more successful. Yet, the failure to win in one

campaign from this position underscores the German failure to appreciate that the Soviet Union could not be defeated in one campaign purely through accumulated tactical success. Victory in Poland, France and the Balkans naturally persuaded German commanders that tactical success achieved through the *Kesselschlacht* could be translated into strategic success in one campaign. In purely military terms, therefore, the Wehrmacht treated the invasion of the Soviet Union merely as the same war in a different place. As they would discover to their cost, however, it was very much a different war in a different place.

The *Vernichtungschlacht* was relevant to the Soviet Union only if the Wehrmacht's resources and tactical brilliance were used in a carefully calculated sequence of battles designed to maximise the Germans chances of winning in one campaign. This required a systematic, operational campaign approach, rather than a tactical, battle-centred one. However, the traditional beliefs of the German Army and its astonishing success between 1939 and 1941 prevented brilliant German officers from comprehending this development in the art of war. By March 1942, Hitler found himself in a position where Germany must achieve in 1942 what it had failed to achieve in 1941: the defeat of the Soviet Union in one campaign.

Above: A German artillery officer observes the German advance on Moscow. The sustained Soviet defence of Moscow brought Army Group Centre to the point of exhaustion.

Below: German troops retreat from Moscow pursued by the Red Army. The contrast in body language to the picture above left is quite marked; optimism has been replaced by dejection.

CHAPTER 2

The Advance to Stalingrad

28 June to 10 September

By March 1942, Hitler's Reich faced a new war. The European conflict of September 1939 to December 1941 had, with the entry of the United States and Japan, become a global conflict.

Hitler now found himself in prolonged total war of attrition against Great Britain, the largest empire in the world; the United States, the greatest economic power in the world; and the Soviet Union which, despite the mauling it had received in 1941, still possessed the largest army in the world. As Hitler knew well, Germany did not possess the manpower nor the economic resources to defeat such a coalition. Indeed, Hitler's entire grand strategy was based on short, decisive wars against isolated opponents in which German military supremacy would bring decisive victory, not overall economic and demographic resources. This was 'lightning war' (the literal translation of Blitzkrieg). In March 1942, it appeared imperative that Germany defeat the Soviet Union before turning west to confront Britain and America. If the Soviet Union was defeated, then her agricultural and economic assets would give Germany the ability to stand up to the naval and economic power of the Anglo-American alliance. Thus, in spring 1942, the defeat of the Soviet Union in one campaign – another monstrous gamble – appeared essential if Germany was to prevail in World War II. The 1942 campaign would pursue the *Vernichtungschlacht*, by means of the *Kesselschlacht*, as in 1941. While defeat in 1941 rocked the German Army, the failure of the 1942 campaign in the smouldering

Left: German infantry march across the steppe of southern Russia in early summer, 1942. By June, the Wehrmacht had recovered the initiative. Despite the setbacks of the winter, German soldiers were confident of ultimate victory.

cauldron of Stalingrad would shake the Third Reich and shatter German hopes of victory on the Eastern Front.

Hitler decided in Directive 41 of 5 April 1942 that the best way to defeat the Soviet Union in one campaign would be to destroy her armies in the south and simultaneously starve her of oil from the Caucasus region. The Volga would be cut above Stalingrad, not in it. This would render the Red Army immobile, making it easy prey for the Wehrmacht. The question of oil dominated Hitler's calculations. By March 1942, Germany's existing oil stocks could not sustain operations on the scale of 'Barbarossa', let alone a war of attrition against the Allies' coalition. Hitler was acutely aware of Germany's dependence upon the Romanian oilfields at Ploesti and believed it could only be offset by capturing the vast Soviet oilfields in the Caucasus. Maikop and Grozny together produced 10 per cent of Soviet oil, but the golden – if ominously distant – prize was Baku in Azerbaijan, which produced 80 per cent of all Soviet oil. On 30 June 1942, Hitler declared to the assembled officers of Army Group South: 'If I do not get the oil of Maikop and Grozny, then I must end this war.'

The objectives of the 1942 campaign were dominated by Hitler's inclinations to a greater extent than the objectives of 'Barbarossa'. After World War II German commanders conveniently blamed Hitler for Germany's defeat. Yet, in the spring of 1942, few German commanders, if any – with the exception of Halder – queried Hitler's designation of oil as the primary objective of the campaign. As a military strategist, Hitler was neither as talented as he thought nor as incompetent as others claimed. He was an inspired gambler, not a systematic military planner, but, following the apparent success of his *Haltbefehl* order of December 1941, he increasingly regarded his own judgment as infallible and his generals as lacking will and commitment to National Socialism. Yet the 1942 campaign's flaws were inherent in the German approach to war, and not just Hitler's.

Like 'Barbarossa', Directive 41 was a statement of strategic intent rather than a detailed campaign plan. It covered only the first phase of operations, in

Below: A German machine-gun crew in a bunker on the Eastern Front during March 1942. The permanence of the structure indicates that, by spring 1942, the Soviet counteroffensive had petered out.

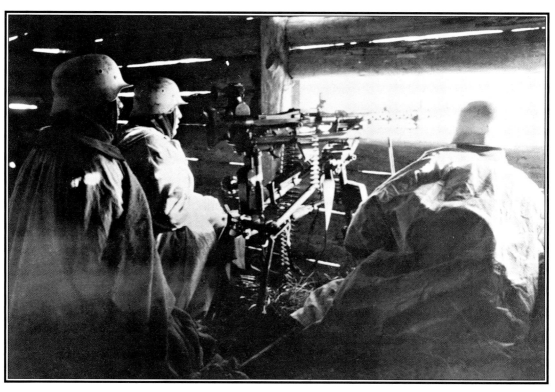

which, through a series of *Kesselschlachts* west of the river Don, the Red Army's forces in the south were to be destroyed. It is important to understand that Stalingrad, like Moscow, had not been designated the formal objective of the 1942 campaign. Stalingrad was a secondary objective to the destruction of the Red Army and the capture of Soviet oil resources. Oil, at least initially, was the purpose of the 1942 campaign. Operation 'Blau' was to be a three-stage offensive. The first stage would consist of a powerful drive east from the Kursk region by Group Von Weichs consisting of 2nd Army and 4th Panzer. The second stage would be undertaken directly to the south of this thrust by Paulus' 6th Army. The aim was to reach the banks of the upper Don in the Voronezh region and encircle the Red Army west of the Don. In stage 3, 4th Panzer would move south-east following the Don to trap and destroy Soviet forces driven east by General Ruoff's 17th Army advancing east from Rostov. After this second battle of annihilation, German forces would cut the river at Stalingrad and only then receive orders for the Caucasus campaign. The objectives were envisaged as Maikop, Grozny and a rapid advance down the Volga south of Stalingrad to Baku, the heart of the Soviet oil industry.

German planning for the 1942 campaign bore an ominous resemblance to that of 1941. The great nineteenth-century Prussian military philosopher Clausewitz believed that the art of war was the use of the available means for the predetermined end. Equally, he cautioned there must be a correlation or balance between means and ends. In 1941, Germany fielded three million men in search of the *Vernichtungschlacht* and failed largely because of the absence of an operational campaign plan. This ensured that German resources were wasted in brilliantly executed tactical encounters which made insufficient contribution to winning in one campaign. If there was a lack of correlation between ends and means in 1941, the disparity was even more alarming in 1942. During the winter of 1941–1942, the Germans struggled to hold the line, but now, with fewer troops, Hitler envisaged the conquest, occupation and exploitation of a massive area. Army Group South's frontage in June 1942 stretched 805km (500 miles) from Orel to Taganrog on the northern shore of the Sea of Azov. The salient of conquest Hitler foresaw from Orel to Stalingrad, south to Grozny and the Caucasus mountains, then

Above: The resilience and quality of the Wehrmacht was underestimated by Stalin and his commanders, who faced the summer campaign of 1942 with a misplaced optimism.

back to the sea of Azov measured 2091km (1300 miles). Baku was 322km (200 miles) from Grozny.

If the roads of European Russia were poor, those of the Caucasus and Don steppe were virtually non-existent. Nevertheless, the Germans remained heavily dependent on road supply, as the rail network consisted of a few single-line connections. The German offensive would be continually undermined by a lack of supply and that produced a fitful campaign entirely at odds with the concept of the *Vernichtungschlacht* and the bold, rapid envelopment of the enemy that was the hallmark of the German Army. As in 1941, the offensive began relatively late in the year, on 28 June 1942, which gave the Wehrmacht slightly more than four months to win a decisive victory. The difficulty of achieving a *Vernichtungschlacht* was complicated by the very objectives that Hitler had set for the campaign. In the spring of 1942, Hitler repeatedly emphasised the need for Germany to crush the Soviet Union before turning to confront the United States and Britain.

However, as in August 1941, Hitler's objectives were designed to acquire the resources to fight a long war in the west, which would undermine Germany's chances of bringing a quick end to the war in the east. German military power had to be directed at the objective most likely to achieve this: either the destruction of the Red Army or the taking of Moscow. As the 1941 campaign had demonstrated, it was far from clear whether, even at the peak of its strength and performance, the Wehrmacht had the capacity to achieve either of these objectives, let alone both. In the south, Hitler wanted both the destruction of the Red Army and the capture of the Soviet Union's oil resources. If the Wehrmacht had achieved both these aims, it is not certain that this would have induced the collapse of Stalin's empire. Although the Caucasus region accounted for 90 per cent of Soviet oil, which in 1941 amounted to nearly 38 million tons, the Soviet Union was not dependent on oil from this region. There were fields in the Urals and east of the Caspian Sea which could be tapped, if not in the same quantity, nevertheless

in considerable measure. The loss of oil resources and the destruction of Soviet forces in the south would have been a massive blow, but it is doubtful, given the Soviet will to continue the fight, that even the perfect execution of the German summer offensive of 1942 would have achieved the complete defeat of the Soviet Union. In conception as in execution, the 1942 campaign was flawed. It was simply unrealistic to expect that, with or without a definite operational campaign plan, German tactical brilliance could achieve such a decisive victory. The Wehrmacht remained an impressive fighting instrument, yet Hitler and his generals refused to accept that the limits of German national power had been reached. As in 1914 and 1941, the tactical prowess of the German Army was gambled in pursuit of aims that were too ambitious, with too few forces to achieve them, yet still too many forces to supply. There was, in short, a chronic lack of balance between ends and means.

The offensive was to be conducted by Army Group South (AGS), commanded by the rehabilitated Field Marshal von Bock, while Army Group Centre (AGC) and Army Group North (AGN) remained on the defensive. In 1942, the Wehrmacht could not undertake simultaneous offensive operations by all three army groups. Indeed, despite receiving 1.1 million reserves up to 1 May 1942, the German Army remained 625,000 under establishment. AGS received replacements, while the armoured units of AGC and AGN were cannibalised to replenish the panzer divisions of AGS. On the eve of 'Blau', AGS consisted of 46 infantry, 9 panzer, 4 light infantry, 5 motorised, 2 mountain and 2 SS divisions, a total of 68 divisions. These were supported by 25 allied divisions made up of General Gariboldi's 8th Italian, General Jany's 2nd Hungarian, General Dumitrescu's 3rd Romanian and General Constantinescu's 4th Romanian Armies. These allied armies were not of German quality, but they released German units for mobile offensive operations and, as such, were a useful strategic asset. However, when specifically targeted by the Red Army, their value declined as German units were broken up to stiffen their resistance. AGS was a powerful force of one million German and 300,000 allied troops. Air support would be provided by Air Fleet 4

Left: German reconnaissance troops advance quickly in the early stages of Operation 'Blau' in June 1942. 'Blau' began as impressively as 'Barbarossa', but very few prisoners were taken by the Germans.

Above: German self-propelled artillery and infantry advance across the steppe of southern Russian towards Stalingrad. This scene conveys some idea of the immense size of the Soviet Union.

Below: Heinrich Himmler was a infrequent and not completely welcome visitor to the Eastern Front. Himmler, like Hitler and Stalin, rarely ventured close to the front line.

commanded by Colonel-General Wolfram von Richthofen, which had 1500 aircraft.

The Soviet grand strategic priorities of summer 1942 were to exploit their new alliance with Britain and the United States, while repairing and re-establishing the shattered Soviet war economy. In a feat of extraordinary resilience, in the face of the German invasion of 1941, more than 1500 of the Soviet Union's most important war industries had been evacuated to new locations in the central and eastern Soviet Union. However, they had to be unloaded and re-assembled piece by piece before production could begin again. The Red Army, savaged if not destroyed by the Wehrmacht in 1941, was, as many senior commanders such as Zhukov recognised, in desperate need of retraining in the

arts of modern war under new commanders. It had substantial manpower resources, but they were not infinite and could not absorb losses and defeats on the scale of 1941. Soviet military strategy was directed by the Stavka or Soviet High Command. Stalin played a dominant if not dictatorial role: no one was in any doubt who was ultimately in charge. At the end of March 1942, Stavka met to discuss strategy for the summer campaign. Zhukov and Colonel-General Vasilevsky, the Deputy Chief of the General Staff, advocated a defensive strategic posture. However, Stalin insisted on a series of localised offensives

Below: German soldiers repair their motorbikes in Voronezh. The bitter fighting for Voronezh in July 1942 enraged Hitler, who had been advised by von Bock that Soviet resistance would be negligible.

Above: A German self-propelled gun advances cautiously through a Soviet hamlet. The nature of the terrain suggests this may be the Crimea in June 1942, although it is difficult to be certain.

Left: Soviet prisoners of war march across the steppe during September 1942. Due to changes in Soviet strategy in July 1942, these prisoners were very much the exception to the rule.

across the front designed to inflict strategic attrition on the Germans, whose skill and resilience he grossly underestimated. He seized upon Marshal Timoshenko's proposal to launch a major offensive east of Kharkov from the Soviet salient jutting westwards in to German lines south-east of the city.

Kharkov, the fourth biggest city in the Soviet Union and a major rail and road junction, was a valuable prize. The Soviet plan envisaged convergent attacks by South-Western Front. To the south-east of Kharkov, Lieutenant-General Gorodnyansky's 6th Soviet Army and 'Group Bobkin' would move north-west as the southern prong of the pincer. To the north, Lieutenant-General Ryabyshev's 28th Army, with flank support from Gordov's 21st and Moskalenko's 38th Armies, would move south-west and link up with 6th

Army west of Kharkov, trapping 6th German Army. Lieutenant-General Malinovksy's Southern Front had the task of securing South-Western Front's southern flank with Podlas' 57th and Kharitonov's 9th Armies. In total, Timoshenko deployed more than 640,000 troops, 13,000 guns, 1200 tanks, and 926 aircraft.

Yet, unbeknown to Stavka, the Germans were also preparing Operation 'Fredericus', the envelopment and destruction of the Soviet forces in the salient to secure jump-off positions for Operation 'Blau'. The German plan was familiar: from the north, Paulus' 6th Army would move south to meet Kleist's 1st Panzer Army coming north. However, on 12 May 1942, Timoshenko pre-empted all German considerations by launching a massive attack. The scale and ferocity of the assault forced 6th German Army to fight a desperate rearguard action. The Soviet 28th Army advanced 32km (20 miles) in the north, while Soviet 6th Army gained 24km (15 miles) in the south. By 14 May, a major Soviet victory seemed imminent, if Timoshenko's armoured reserves could convert tactical success into operational victory. Yet Timoshenko did not seize the moment and failed

to commit 21st Tank Corps. The Germans' response was dramatic.

Operation 'Fredericus' had been scheduled for the 18 May. Paulus' 6th Army could not fulfil its anticipated role, but, on 17 May, Bock ordered 1st Panzer to attack the southern wing of the Soviet thrust. With considerable air support from 4th Air Corps, 1st Panzer ripped into the weak and unsuspecting Soviet 9th and 57th Armies and, by the end of the first day, had advanced 40km (25 miles) into the rear of the Soviet thrust. The threat to Soviet lines of communication and supply, as well as encirclement, was obvious. Vasilevsky urged Stalin to terminate the offensive, but, dubiously reassured by Timoshenko that appropriate defensive measures had been taken, Stalin refused. By 19 May, Kharitonov's 9th Army had collapsed and an 80-km (50-mile) gash had been carved into the Soviet left flank. In turning to meet this mortal threat, Gorodnyansky's 6th Soviet Army released the pressure on Paulus' 6th Army, which now executed its role in the original – but now improvised – 'Fredericus'. On 23 May, 6th German Army met 1st Panzer, enveloping 6th and 57th Soviet Armies with elements of 9th and 38th Armies. The Soviet forces turned to confront their captors. In a series of desperate charges, often linking arms, Soviet troops, pulverised from the air, attacked the German

Below: German soldiers relax around an undamaged gramophone. It is difficult to be certain, but this may be 1st Panzer Army, part of Army Group A, celebrating the fall of Rostov, on 23 July 1942.

lines only to be decimated. By 28 May, having been cut to pieces, their resistance petered out. It was a shocking defeat snatched from the jaws of victory. Against 20,000 German casualties, 75,000 Soviet troops died and 239,000 were taken prisoner. Kharkov brutally demonstrated the gulf in tactical flair, air support and leadership at all levels between the Red Army and the Wehrmacht. The overcentralised Red Army, dominated by Stalin's misplaced faith in the offensive, was – as yet – no match for the German Army. It would take further disasters during May and June 1942 finally to persuade Stalin that, unless the Red Army was commanded by competent generals in a flexible and intelligent manner, the Soviet Union stood in grave danger of defeat.

As a prelude to 'Blau', Hitler ordered the capture of the Crimea. The Soviet position in the Crimea was a strong one. To the west, Sevastopol remained unconquered, while, to the east, the Soviets had a substantial defensive position covering the Kerch Peninsula. The Sevastopol garrison consisted of seven rifle divisions and three marine brigades led by the highly competent General Ivan Petrov. A former Tsarist officer, Petrov's career was plagued by political commissars, not least one Lev Mekhlis. A vicious crony of Stalin, Mekhlis was the political commissar of the Crimean Front commanded by the less-than-gifted Lieutenant-General Kozlov. By force of menacing personality and connections, he dominated the Crimean Front, but, against Manstein, he was unmasked. Operation 'Bustard Hunt', which began on 8 May, destroyed an apparently impregnable Soviet

Above: A German machine-gunner in action during August 1942. He is using the deadly MG-42 machine gun, a weapon feared by all who encountered it, and has a spare barrel strapped to his back.

Below: A happy, ebullient group of German soldiers announcing to the world that they are on the Caucasus road towards Stalingrad. The date is 6 August 1942.

position in the eastern Crimea. In a maelstrom of air and ground attack, Kozlov and Mekhlis lost 21 divisions of the 47th, 51st and 44th Armies. The evacuation of the Soviet forces across the Kerch Straits turned into a bloody disaster. The troops, caught on the beaches, were massacred by a rampant Luftwaffe and a massive artillery barrage. In just a week, the Soviets lost 176,000 troops, permitting Manstein to reunite the entire 11th Army for a final assault upon Sevastopol in Operation 'Sturgeon Catch'.

Sevastopol's defences were formidable, consisting of massive concrete emplacements, forts, tunnels, labyrinthine caves, trenches and interconnected pill-boxes. Manstein ordered five days of annihilation fire by huge mortars such as 'Karl' firing 2-tonne shells and guns such as 'Big Dora' with a range of 48km (30 miles). On 7 June, the final attack began, supported by a crushing aerial bombardment. German losses were heavy, but, on the night of 28 June, 54th Corps launched a daring and decisive amphibious assault across Severnaya Bay. Fighting continued for several days with Soviet resistance in the caves terminated by toxic smoke, in order to save German

Below: A Soviet sniper with camouflage and a specialist rifle. Soviet snipers would play an important part in the battle for Stalingrad, especially in picking off German air and artillery observers.

casualties. On 30 June, Stalin ordered the evacuation of Petrov, but the rescue of troops and civilians on the beaches was devastated by the Luftwaffe. It had been a brutal battle: German casualties were 24,000. However, in recognition of his victories at Kerch and Sevastopol, Manstein was promoted to Field Marshal. Now, instead of 11th Army moving across the Kerch Straits to take up blocking positions in the Kuban, as originally intended, Hitler ordered it north to undertake Operation 'Nordlicht', the reduction of Leningrad. As 11th Army moved north, Army Group South had already launched the great summer offensive.

'Blau', however, was nearly cancelled before it started. On 19 June, the operations officer of 23rd Panzer Division, Major Joachim Reichel, crash-landed behind Soviet lines. In flagrant contravention of Hitler's instructions, he was carrying orders outlining the role of 40th Panzer Corps, a key part of 4th Panzer. A German patrol found the aircraft and two graves, but only one body. The plans were in the hands of General Golikov, who was commanding the Bryansk Front. Golikov informed Stavka of the German intention to attack the Bryansk Front on 22 June and the first phase of 'Blau' had been completely compromised. However, 'Blau' was saved by Operation 'Kremlin', the German deception plan designed to persuade Stalin that the German objective was not the south, but Moscow. Its success and the Soviet prioritisation of Moscow was revealed in several ways. At the end of June 1942, Stavka deployed 28 armies between Leningrad in the far north and Tula to the south of Moscow, while only 18 – including the battered remnants of South-Western Front – were deployed between Tula and the Caucasus mountains. Golikov was told to forget Voronezh and prepare an attack on Orel in conjunction with Western Front's left flank. Stavka feared a German assault on Moscow from the south-west and wanted the Bryansk Front where it assumed the Germans were preparing to attack. It is impossible to prove if, as the political, economic and communications centre of the Soviet Union, Moscow was more valuable than Soviet oil, but, when faced with competing priorities in 1941 and 1942, Stalin chose the capital. Defeat in the south would be a massive blow, but to Stalin the loss of Moscow would be fatal.

Thus, Hitler's decision to move south in pursuit of a *Vernichchtungschlacht* appears flawed. Moscow's capture could not guarantee a decisive German

Right: A Soviet soldier is hit as he assaults a German position in May 1942. The defeat at Kharkov was a crushing setback for the Red Army, but would prove something of a blessing in disguise.

victory, but it was the Soviet centre of gravity. Golikov's protests that reconnaissance still indicated a major German build-up east of Kursk incurred Stalin's wrath. On 26 June, Stalin brutally informed Golikov, with the Reichel papers in front of him, that 'Blau' was a ruse designed to lure Soviet forces away from Moscow. As a chastened Golikov licked his wounds, the attack Stalin had contemptuously dismissed was about to descend on the Bryansk Front.

On 28 June, with massive air support from 8th Air Corps, General Hoth's 4th Panzer smashed into the junction of 13th and 40th Soviet Armies, while 2nd Army covered its left flank. On 30 June, Paulus' 6th Army attacked South-Western Front and crashed through Gordov's 21st Army and the remnants of Ryabyshev's 28th Army. That day, Golikov reported that, while the more northerly 13th Army was holding, Major-General Parsegov's 40th Army was crumbling. Stalin refused to authorise its tactical withdrawal and,

Below: Soviet commanders brief Red Army soldiers near Serafimovich in September 1942. The Soviet capture of this vital bridgehead would play a critical role in the outcome of the Stalingrad campaign.

controlling the battle from afar, despatched several tank corps to Bryansk Front without giving Golikov adequate control of their tactical deployment. Stalin's impatience ensured these reserves were committed, not as an organised force, but in a chaotic and piece-meal fashion. Hitler had emphasised the importance of destroying Soviet forces and, on 1 July, 2nd Army turned south to meet 6th Army at Stary Oskol. Only tough Soviet resistance enabled the majority of Soviet

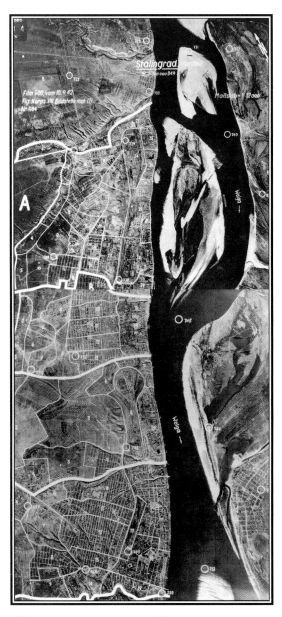

Left: A German reconnaissance photograph of Stalingrad taken four days before the first major German assault on the city. The shape of the city, the size of the Volga and the factories area are clearly visible.

with 800 modern tanks, but proved no match for experienced German formations. Its was pummelled by the Luftwaffe and, although the battle lasted until 8 July, the German advance towards Voronezh was not seriously disrupted. Indeed, while 2nd Army was under attack from 5th Tank Army, on its right flank, 4th Panzer forced the Don. In typically Stalinist fashion, Golikov was unfairly made the scapegoat for Stavka's blunders. He was replaced by Lieutenant-General Rokossovsky on 5 July as commander of the Bryansk Front and made Deputy Commander of the Voronezh Front.

Voronezh lay 4.8km (3 miles) east of the upper Don and was coveted by the Germans and Soviets for different reasons. Voronezh was a major road and rail junction between Moscow and the Don bend, and therefore Operation 'Blau' envisaged 2nd Army building a defensive front between Kursk and Voronezh to protect the rear of 4th Panzer and 6th Army as they moved south-east of Voronezh along the Don in accordance with stage 3 of 'Blau'. The city thus had a critical role to play in the successful execution of Operation 'Blau'. To the Soviets, Voronezh was essential for strategic mobility between the northern and southern regions of the Soviet Union. Its loss could act as a logistical springboard, either for a direct German assault on Moscow or an advance 161km (100 miles) east to cut the Stalingrad–Tambov–Moscow rail line. This would force a circuitous eastern detour to retain strategic lines of supply with the south regardless of whether the Germans swung north or south at Voronezh. In Hitler's mind, the key issue was that Voronezh did not delay the movement of 4th Panzer south-east. On 5 July, Bock advised Hitler that Voronezh appeared lightly defended and that its capture could be achieved. Hitler reluctantly consented to this arrangement as long as Bock immediately despatched 40th Panzer Corps south to be followed as soon as possible by the rest of 4th Panzer. To Hitler's fury, however, the Soviet forces defending Voronezh had been significantly underestimated and instead of a quick kill, 48th and 24th Panzer Corps became tied down in the city. It did not fall until 9 July.

'Blau' I was over, but Hitler was far from satisfied. German troops had conquered territory, but the

40th Army to escape eastwards before the pocket was closed on 2 July. Nevertheless, by 3 July, 4th Panzer's troops were on the upper Don west of Voronezh. A 64-km (40-mile) gap had opened up between the southern flank of the Bryansk Front and the northern flank of South-Western Front.

On 3 July, Stavka ordered Bryansk Front's 5th Tank Army commanded by Major-General Lizyukov to counterattack the German left flank held by 2nd Army. The 5th Tank Army was a powerful formation

Kesselschlacht west of the Don had taken only 40,000 prisoners. Equally, while a substantial portion of 4th Panzer was snarled up in Voronezh, the Soviet South-Western and Southern Fronts, aware of the danger of envelopment from the north, were already withdrawing east. 1st Panzer and 17th Army did not begin to move until 8 July and made slow progress against stubborn rearguard actions. On 9 July, Hitler made the first of several direct interventions in 'Blau' that were to have as much influence upon the campaign as Directive 33 of August 1941 had upon 'Barbarossa'. As expected, Army Group South was divided into Army Group A and Army Group B. Bock was dispensed with, having incurred Hitler's wrath over Voronezh. Army Group A (AGA), to be commanded by Field Marshal Wilhelm List, consisted of 1st Panzer, 17th Army, 3rd Romanian and 8th Italian. It was to advance east and link up with 4th Panzer before crushing the retreating Soviet armies in the major *Kesselschlacht* Hitler craved. It would then turn south to capture Rostov as a prelude to an advance into the Caucasus. Army Group B (AGB), under Field Marshal Maximilian von Weichs, was made up of 6th Army, 4th Panzer, 2nd Army and 2nd Hungarian. The Axis formations and 2nd German were to guard the northern flank, while 6th Army and 4th Panzer moved east to cut the Volga. The conquest of Stalingrad was not an objective. In addition, on 13 July, Hitler diverted 40th Panzer Corps south from 6th Army to execute an encirclement 161km (100 miles) north of Rostov at Millerovno. Yet, on 14 July, the Germans netted a paltry 14,000 prisoners. The Soviets had already withdrawn east in relatively good order. In contrast to 1941, the Red Army was no longer prepared to stand, fight and be slaughtered. On 6 July, Stalin had finally consented to a fundamental change in Soviet strategy by permitting the Red Army to trade space for time.

The crushing defeats of Kharkov, Kerch and the Crimea in May and June 1942 had cost the Red Army nearly 500,000 men. On 26 June, Colonel-General Vasilevsky had succeeded the ailing Marshal Shaposhinikov as Chief of the General Staff. Vasilevsky pleaded with Stalin for a change of strategy on two grounds. First, the Red Army remained tactically inferior to the Wehrmacht, therefore to stand and fight, as in 1941, would be suicidal. Secondly, the Red Army simply did not have the manpower to fight in the south and protect the Moscow approaches. The crushing defeat at Kharkov

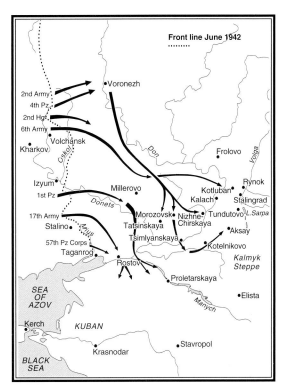

Above: Operation 'Blau' and the advance to Stalingrad by 6th Army in the late summer of 1942.

had left South-Western Front directly opposing 6th Army, and Southern Front engaged by 17th Army and 1st Panzer, desperately short of manpower that could not be replaced. South-Western Front's annihilation risked the exposure of Southern Front's northern flank and a complete collapse of the Soviet position between Voronezh and Rostov. On 6 July, Stalin directed Timoshenko's South-Western and Malinovsky's Southern Front to conduct a strategic retreat in order to escape the threat of encirclement as 4th Panzer came south. At a stroke, Stalin frustrated stage 3 of 'Blau', while Hitler's response to the opening stages of 'Blau' was about to transform the Stalingrad campaign.

On 16 July, Hitler diverted 4th Panzer south to AGA to act as the eastern arm of a great encirclement north-east of Rostov. Rostov was taken on 23 July, but again a major encirclement eluded Hitler; however, the consequences of his decision to divert 4th Panzer from AGB did not. Hitler's decision to rob Army Group B of its armoured forces is regarded by most historians as having the same significance as his diversion of Army Group Centre's armour from the Moscow Axis in August 1941. At a time when South-Western Front was in disarray, Hitler denied Army Group B, led by 6th Army, the very forces with the power and speed to drive on Stalingrad before the Soviets could organise its defences. The German Army was greatly superior to the Red Army in the speed and flexibility with which it waged manoeuvre war. However, the slowed 6th Army advance enabled Stavka to deploy three Soviet armies in the Don bend which, throughout late July and August 1942, engaged 6th Army in bitter attritional fighting. Nevertheless, despite the absence of prisoners, Hitler was convinced that Soviet resistance west of the Don had been broken. On 20 July, for the first time, Hitler formally ordered 6th Army to attack Stalingrad.

In Directive 45, issued on 23 July as Rostov fell, Hitler formally declared that the objectives of 'Blau' had been achieved. Hitler instructed List's Army Group A to cross the Don and capture the Caucasian oilfields and to follow this with an advance on Baku. However, a completely new objective was added, namely the conquest and occupation of the Black Sea coast. Army Group B was to move towards Stalingrad, followed by an advance down the Volga to Astrakhan. These objectives bore little relation to the realities of German strength and were based upon a gross underestimation of Soviet strategic reserves and will to fight. Hitler reversed his decision of 16 July and, on 30 July, removed 4th Panzer from Army Group A and returned it to Army Group B. It had already crossed the Don east of Rostov and now, after executing a left turn, would march up the southern bank of the Don in a north-easterly direction towards Stalingrad. Thus, while 6th Army was involved in bitter fighting west of Stalingrad, 4th Panzer was engaged in a separate advance, unable to provide mutual support and bedevilled by fuel shortages. Therefore the second stage of the German summer offensive was characterised by the same argument and improvisation over objectives as the 1941 campaign, again due to the lack of an operational campaign plan. The Red Army had once more been inadvertently reprieved as it struggled to prevent withdrawal turning into a rout.

Nevertheless, the Soviet position in early July was extremely serious. A 322-km (200-mile) gap had opened up between the Bryansk Front and South-Western Front, and Southern Front had lost contact

Above: Soviet troops destroyed the rail line behind them as they conducted a fighting withdrawal from July to September 1942. The southern Russian rail network was essential for mobility and supply.

with South-Western Front. On 12 July, Stavka Directive 170495 set up the Stalingrad Front under Timoshenko and, on 19 July, Stalin placed the city and its people on a war footing. The Stalingrad Front ran for 354km (220 miles) and, from north-west of Stalingrad, followed the Don south to its confluence with the River Chir south-west of the city. To the north-west was General Kuznetsov's 63rd Army, while to the west was General Kolpakchy's 62nd Army, with Chuikov's 64th Army to its left. Stalingrad Front's strength was illusory; 62nd and 63rd Armies had only 160,000 men, 400 tanks and 450 aircraft against the 300,000-strong 6th Army. Chuikov's 64th Army was a motley collection of divisions many with a strength of fewer than 2500 men. The Stalingrad Front was bolstered by the remnants of the defunct South-Western Front. General Danilov's 21st Army and Moskalenko's 38th Army deployed on the northern banks of the Don, while Kryuchenkin's 28th Army deployed behind 62nd Army. South-west of the city, Major-General Tolbukhin's 57th Army took up positions on the left flank of 64th Army. On 21 July, Timoshenko paid the price of South-Western Front's ignominious performance since May 1942. He was replaced as Stalingrad Front commander by Lieutenant V. N. Gordov, a capable if irascible commander.

On 23 July, Rostov fell to Army Group A. Soviet troops had put up a fierce struggle, but Stalin deliberately chose to depict the city as having fallen because of defeatists and fifth columnists. It is against this background that Stalin's infamous Order No. 227 proclaiming that the Red Army would not take 'one step back' must be judged. This was not only a vindictive dictator punishing 'defeatists' with murderous NKVD squads, but also an appeal to the Soviet people's survival instincts. In the darkest days of 1941, the Soviet authorities had not blushed in their attempt to stir the nation through patriotic appeal to the defence of mother Russia. Stalin's order reminded his people that there was nowhere to retreat to once the Volga and the Caucasus mountains were reached. The destiny of the nation was at stake and it was the duty of every citizen to defend his or her future. It was, in short, a call to total war, for the people to rise up and throw back the invader. It was buttressed by the menacing presence of the NKVD, who would not hesitate to dispense a brutal and arbitrary 'justice' to those deemed insufficiently committed to the struggle. It is easy to depict the Red Army as committed to the fight at Stalingrad because they had no choice, caught as

Below: Soviet infantry disembark from a T-34. As a main battle tank, the T-34 was invaluable, but also played a key role in the combat mobility of Soviet infantry.

they were between two dictators involved in a brutal struggle to annihilate each other. Yet more fought to repel the bestial savagery of a hated invader than through fear of the Stalinist regime.

On 25 July, Army Group A swept across the Don into the Kuban steppe. On the German right, 17th Army drove back the 18th and 12th Soviet Armies and, by 9 August, had reached the outskirts of Krasnodar, a major Soviet oil-refining centre. On the left flank, 1st Panzer broke through 37th Army of the North Caucasus Front, which was commanded by Stalin's sycophantic compatriot from the Russian Civil War, Marshal Semyon Budenny. By 9 August, 1st Panzer had reached Maikop in the Caucasus foothills, south-east of Krasnodar. Hitler's delight turned to dismay as Soviet forces had completely wrecked Maikop's oil production and storage facilities. Such was the damage that hardly a barrel of Soviet oil would ever be used by the Wehrmacht. After Maikop, Soviet resistance began to increase and the pace of Army Group A's advance, dependent as it was on the Luftwaffe, slowed to a crawl. Army Group A found itself in bitter fighting, bereft of air support and supplies, and without the means to achieve objectives that were massively beyond its capability. The speed of its assault declined in proportion to Hitler's escalating obsession with Stalingrad as Army Group B moved towards a date with destiny.

As Army Group A spluttered to a halt, the battle for Stalingrad was joined in earnest. On 23 July, 6th Army smashed through the right flank of Kolpakchy's 62nd Army. Stavka had hoped to buy time by engaging the Germans west of the Don, but, as at Vyazma in October 1941, the Soviet line had been penetrated with ease. On 25 July, Chuikov's 64th Army came under severe attack and began to crumble. It was defending the critical bridge over the confluence of the Don and Chir at Niznhe-Chirskaya. The bridge was of the utmost tactical, operational and strategic significance, but, on the evening of the 26 July, Chuikov was forced to order a retreat across the Don, blowing up the bridge in the face of the Germans. The junction of the 62nd and 64th Armies was collapsing and a thoroughly alarmed Stalin ordered Vasilevsky to take charge of the defence of the city. The right wing of 62nd Army was encircled and its annihilation would destroy the entire Soviet operational position west of Stalingrad. Vasilevsky saw no other option but to launch a hastily prepared attack on 6th Army's left and right flanks to rescue 62nd Army. The 1st Tank Army would attack 6th

Below: German soldiers receive their pay outside Stalingrad in September 1942. The weather is perfect and the air of relaxed confidence is unmistakable.

Army's left flank while, from the south, 4th Tank Army would attack its right flank. Danilov's 21st Army would attack 6th Army's left rear flank.

Once again, the apparent strength of this Soviet counterattack hid serious deficiencies in the forces about to undertake it. Commanded by Major-General Moskalenko, 1st Tank Army was the old 38th Army replenished with inexperienced reservists, while Major-General Kryuchenkin's 4th Tank was the former 28th Army which, like 38th Army, had been mauled by the Germans as part of South-Western Front. This improvised counterattack undertaken without adequate reconnaissance or air support had a dreadful whiff of 1941 about it. Vasilevsky, a thoughtful and talented man, was not a slaughterer of troops, but he knew the momentum of 6th Army's attack had to be broken. It was to be a tactical sacrifice to try to retain some degree of operational control. On 27 July, 1st Tank Army assaulted 6th Army's left wing, but 4th Army's simultaneous assault was delayed by 48 hours as it struggled to cross to the Don under furious attack from the Luftwaffe. Nevertheless, by 29 July, the two tank armies began to crawl their way across the steppe, threatening the 6th Army from the north and south. In the pocket, 62nd Army's trapped formations – two divisions and a tank corps – battled furiously against their captiv-

Above: German artillery bombards Soviet positions in and around Stalingrad during September 1942. They appear well supplied and unpeturbed about Soviet retaliation from the air or on the ground.

ity. By 1 August, 6th Army had been forced on the defensive. It still retained the initiative, but no longer possessed the strength to bounce the Soviet line west of Stalingrad. It was bogged down in attritional fighting: Vasilevsky had stabilised the position, at least temporarily.

As one crisis subsided, Gordov – in command of Stalingrad Front – confronted another on his left flank. On 31 July, General Hoth's 4th Panzer began its assault on Stalingrad. It easily brushed aside Major-General Trufanov's 51st Army, but came under fierce attack on the Aksai river from the left wing of Chuikov's 64th Army. The 4th Panzer regrouped and, on 5 August, attacked the junction between 64th Army and Tolbukin's 57th Army, which had its left flank anchored on the Volga directly south of Stalingrad. After initial success, 4th Panzer was brought to a standstill by 57th and 64th Armies. These battles bring home the significance of Hitler's July 1942 decisions, which were as pernicious in their undermining of German chances of victory in one campaign as those of July 1941. Hitler's diversion of 4th Panzer had released the pressure as surely as his diversion of 2nd Panzer in August 1941. Now, as before Moscow in 1941, the Germans found themselves trapped in bitter attritional fighting, as both 6th Army and 4th Panzer – the latter conducting a south-western approach on Stalingrad disturbingly similar to that of 2nd Panzer's failed assault on Moscow – found themselves unable

to overcome their opposition. As a consequence, although it reached Stalingrad during September 1942, Army Group B did so only after fierce fighting. At Stalingrad, as at Moscow, the Red Army would inflict a battle of attrition upon the Wehrmacht, but one whose scale and horror would destroy the Germans in a cauldron of their own making.

The stalemate of the first days of August provoked a reassessment on both sides. On 5 August, Vasilevsky reorganised the Soviet defence of Stalingrad. The unwieldy Stalingrad Front was divided up: Gordov retained control of 63rd, 21st, 1st Tank, 4th Tank, 24th and 66th Armies. To the south, Colonel-General Yeremenko took charge of the new South-Eastern Front, which encompassed 62nd, 64th, 57th and 51st Armies. The demarcation line between the two fronts was the river Tsaritsa, which ran right through the centre of Stalingrad. Field Marshal von Weichs instructed 6th Army and 4th Panzer to launch a concentric attack on the Soviet forces west of Stalingrad; 6th Army was to cross the Don and advance eastwards; and 4th Panzer Army was to break through 64th Army's defences south of Stalingrad and reach the Volga. On 7 August, 6th Army sliced through 62nd Army. Paulus ordered a

Above: Stalingrad before the assault: the tree-lined avenues of Stalingrad come under aerial attack. On 23 August and afterwards, Richthofen's Air Fleet 4 would pulverize it into smouldering ruins.

bold advance to the Don's most easterly point at Vertyachy. However, the marshy terrain and the attentions of 1st Tank Army ensured that 6th Army was unable to capitalise upon its success. In an uncharacteristically bold move, Paulus refused to allow 6th Army to become involved in positional fighting against 1st Tank Army. On 23 August, supported by the full power of the Luftwaffe, 6th Army's 51st Corps launched a dawn crossing of the Don in the teeth of fierce Soviet opposition. General von Wietersheim's 14th Panzer Corps burst through 62nd Army's defences and, with massive close air support, Major-General Hube's 16th Panzer Division charged 80km (50 miles) across the Don-Volga land bridge and reached the Volga north of Stalingrad. The river was cut, thus fulfilling the original mission outlined in Directive 45, but 16th Panzer came under fierce attack from 62nd Army, workers' militia battalions and Soviet tanks straight off the assembly lines of the Stalingrad Tractor Factory. As 16th Panzer battled for its life on the Volga, von Wietersheim implored Paulus to withdraw. Paulus held firm and 6th Army's position was boosted by a massive Luftwaffe terror raid on Stalingrad.

Between 23 and 24 August, Lieutenant-General Fiebig's 8th Air Corps rained death from the skies, as thousands of bombers obliterated the city. The bombing smashed rail and road communication and made civic government virtually impossible for days. The deliberate use of incendiaries on wooden residential areas created a burning hell. Panic and demoralisation spread, as fires burned out of control and buildings collapsed.

Hospitals and industrial plants alike were destroyed as burning oil set the Volga alight. Black smoke rose thousands of feet and Richthofen described the city as 'a fantastic sight'. Lieutenant-General Chuikov, soon to acquire immortality as the defender of Stalingrad, observed 'the huge city, stretching for nearly 35 miles [56km] along the Volga, was enveloped in flames. Everything was blazing, collapsing. Death and disaster descended on thousands of families.' It is estimated that more than 30,000 people lost their lives under the bombardment, but still Stalin refused

Above: As Hube's 16th Panzer Division reached the Volga to the north of Stalingrad on 23 August 1942, Soviet workers in militia groups left their factories to confront the Wehrmacht.

Below: The deadly impact of the Luftwaffe is revealed in this dramatic photograph. The Stalingrad-1 railway station is burning in the background. The symbolism of the sculpture would soon become apparent.

to order a mass evacuation, as he believed the troops would fight better for a 'living city'.

The right wing of 6th Army faced bitter resistance from the 62nd Army's left wing as it clawed its way over the Volga towards Karpovka west of Stalingrad. German officers noticed an ominous stiffening of Soviet resistance: the fighting was hard and progress slow. The 16th Panzer anticipated relief from 4th Panzer's south-western thrust designed to link up with 6th Army and envelop 64th and 62nd Armies in a *Kesselschlacht* between the Don and Stalingrad. However, General Werner Kempf's 48th Panzer Corps met fierce resistance from Chuikov's 64th Army, dug in on the Tinguta hills south-west of Stalingrad. Hoth broke off the attack and regrouped his forces. While German infantry fixed their opponents, in a brilliant tactical move 32km (20 miles) to the left, Kempf's 48th Panzer broke through on 31 August. Weichs ordered 4th Panzer to close the ring with 6th Army at Pitomnik 16km (10 miles) west of Stalingrad. Yet Soviet 62nd and 64th Armies rapidly withdrew to the outskirts of the city, once again frustrating the German desire for a major *Kesselschlacht*. Weichs, mistakenly believing this to be a sign that Soviet resistance had finally broken, ordered 4th Panzer to advance alone into the city, following the easterly course of the Tsaritsa river. It was met by determined resistance, as was 6th Army to the north. Nevertheless, the Germans were now at the gates of

Above: The grim, tense determination of the Red Army's soldiers to defy the Wehrmacht is clearly shown in this scene. A German assault on the Soviet defences on the outskirts of Stalingrad is imminent.

Stalingrad and remained confident that the city was in their grasp.

Stalin also feared the city's imminent fall. On 26 August, three days after 16th Panzer had breasted the Volga, he made Zhukov Deputy Supreme Commander in Chief. Zhukov was a talented, if ruthless, commander, who had defied the Germans at Leningrad and Moscow in 1941. He arrived at the front on 29 August and informed Moskalenko – now commanding 1st Guards Army north of Stalingrad – that 'we've been fighting already for two years, and now it's time we learned to do it properly'. Stalin badgered Zhukov to launch an attack on 6th Army's left flank. The plan was for 1st Guards, 24th Army and 66th Army to break 6th Army's left wing and divert its relentless advance to the city. On 3 September, Zhukov informed Stalin a delay was necessary unless the assault was to be a pointless failure. Despite sarcastically observing, 'Do you think the enemy will wait until you bestir yourselves?' Stalin reluctantly agreed. He had a point: on 28 August, after five days of desperate fighting, General Hube told his officers 'the shortage of ammunition and fuel is such that our only chance is to break through to the west. I absolutely refuse to fight a pointless battle that must end in the annihilation of my troops and I therefore order a break-out to the west.' Hube acknowledged he was disobeying orders: indeed, he specifically absolved his officers from their oath of loyalty to Hitler. However, Hube, the one-armed general who was one of Hitler's

favourite commanders, was saved from his wrath when 3rd Motorised Division broke through to 16th Panzer. By 31 August, the remainder of 6th Army had finally closed up to the Volga and the Soviet chance had gone. At 0630 hours on 5 September, 1st Guards attacked, followed by 24th Army and 66th Army. The attack was met by artillery, armour and airpower, its deepest penetration being only 3657m (4000 yds). Stalin ordered continued attacks and for a week the Stalingrad Front engaged the 6th Army's left flank. On 10 September. Zhukov informed Stalin that 'with the forces which are available to the Stalingrad Front we are not able to break through the corridor and link up with the troops of the South Eastern Front in the city'. He told Stalin that he considered further isolated attacks pointless. By early September, Major-General Strecker's 11th and Major-General Heitz's 8th Corps had secured 6th Army's position. By 10 September, 4th Panzer had advanced into the southern outskirts of the city and linked up with General von Seydlitz-Kurbach's 51st Corps. The weary 62nd Army fell back into the city.

The battle of Stalingrad was about to begin. Hitler was confident that after a short but futile struggle the defenders of the city would be put to the sword. Stalingrad was increasingly taking on a massive psychological significance for both sides. To the

Right: Soviet troops in rudimentary fortifications defend their position against a German attack. German commanders noticed a significant stiffening in the Red Army's resistance in August and September 1942.

Germans, its conquest became the rod that would finally break the back of Soviet resistance and pave the way to complete victory on the Eastern Front. To the Red Army, Stalingrad became a symbol of their defiance of Nazi Germany. As the battle wore on, it became tinged with an anxious desperation that defeat in such a titanic struggle would represent an unsustainable blow. Nazi Germany appeared at the zenith of its power. Its armies controlled Europe and had marched to the borders of Asia on the Volga and in the Caucasus.

Yet, as in 1941, the Wehrmacht found itself committed to a decisive battle of annihilation where its great superiority in manoeuvre warfare could not be exploited. The rubble-strewn terrain, the positional nature of the fighting, and the extended German supply lines ensured that, like Moscow, Stalingrad was fought on terms where the Red Army stood some chance of success. In the words of Professor John Erickson, 'Stalin had committed himself, the Red Army and the Russians at large to one of the

most terrible battles in the whole history of war.' Hitler's invasion of the Soviet Union in June 1941 had given rise to possibly the most savage, cruel war in history. In 1941, Hitler's gamble had failed, but, in September 1942, the tactical brilliance of the Wehrmacht appeared to have brought German victory within reach. However, while the Volga had been cut, the Soviet oilfields had not been captured. The Wehrmacht had won several impressive victories, but the Red Army had not been destroyed.

Below: The Red Army's capacity for improvisation in the face of river obstacles became legendary during World War II. Soviet troops man-handle a lorry with an anti-aircraft gun bolted on across the Don.

CHAPTER 3

The First Battle of Stalingrad

14–26 September 1942

As the German 6th Army began its preparations for the attack on Stalingrad, few of the commanders and men on both sides could have envisaged how long the struggle would last for this unusual and symbolic Soviet city on the banks of the Volga.

Stalingrad, originally called Tsaritsyn and now Volgograd, was no ordinary Soviet city. Tsaritsyn had flourished during the nineteenth century as a key trading post on the Volga linking the northern and southern extremities of the Romanov empire. It was intimately linked with the mythology surrounding the Bolshevik Revolution of October 1917 and the subsequent civil war of 1918–21. It had been the scene of one of the Red Army's most decisive victories over the White counter-revolutionary forces of General Denikin. After Stalin achieved supreme power in 1925, the history of the revolutionary struggle and his role in it was rewritten. He had actually played a minor role in the Bolshevik seizure of power, but now Comrade Stalin was credited as playing a decisive role in the Soviet triumph at Tsaritsyn. The city's place in Soviet history and Stalin's role in its heroic defence were cemented when he named the city for himself in 1925, a fact that was most certainly not lost on Adolf Hitler. In fact as a representative of the inner sanctum of the Bolshevik party in the field, Stalin had few military skills and made little constructive contribution to

Left: German armour moves forwards to the outskirts of Stalingrad. The panzers were a key instrument of German warfare in open country, but struggled to have the same impact within the confines of the city.

the Red Army's victory. He was a constantly disruptive influence, undermining military professionalism and former Tsarist officers fighting for the Reds. Rarely visiting the front, he remained at headquarters as a malevolent influence, instilling proletarian discipline and revolutionary retribution. He surrounded himself with cronies such as Kliment Voroshilov, a militarily useless lickspittle with a shared talent for intrigue whom Stalin would make Defence Commissar of the Soviet Union during the 1930s. Stalin had a wicked memory: virtually anyone who crossed him during the civil war – such as Tukhachevsky in 1920 – was eliminated in the Great Purge of 1937–38. Stalin had considerably less military ability than Hitler, but shared with him a contempt for human suffering and casualties, as well as a belief that will and ideological fervour were the decisive forces in war.

After Lenin's death in 1924, Stalingrad was designated a beacon of revolutionary endeavour. It was a showpiece city of 600,000 people and played a key role in Stalin's drive for industrialisation in the 1930s. Its presence on the Volga made it an important part

of the Soviet oil industry and, once war broke out, its factories were an instrumental part of the war economy. As an economic, military and psychological target, it was of considerable value, but its capture would not have induced the Soviet Union's collapse. It was also an ideal place to fight a battle of annihilation. As at Moscow, the terrain west of Stalingrad, littered with gullies and ravines, was hardly conducive to rapid manoeuvre. The urban character of the city with its towering factories and sprawling worker settlements impeded the effective coordination of airpower, armour and infantry which lay at the heart of the Wehrmacht's brilliance. The pursuit of the German's favourite tactical method, the *Kesselschlacht*, was also undermined by Stalingrad's peculiar shape. The city stretched virtually 40.2km (25 miles) in a north–south direction along the western bank of the Volga, but was only a maximum of 6.4–8km (4–5 miles) in depth, while the Volga, 1.6km (1 mile) wide at this point, more or less ensured the city could not be completely enveloped, thus forcing the Germans into a frontal assault. It was, in short, a formidable defensive position. The city centre was dominated by an ancient Tartar burial mound, the Mamayev Kurgan, marked on all military maps as Point 102.0. The Mamayev Kurgan would become the scene of weeks of bitter encounters, to the extent that the usual 1m (3 ft) of snow which normally settled during the winter did not due to the intensity of the fighting. The northern end of Stalingrad was dominated by its famous factories: the Dzerzhinsky Tractor Factory, the Barrikady Ordnance Factory and the Red October Steel Plant. To the south of the Red October lay the Lazur Chemical Plant, while directly in front of the Barrikady was the Silikat Factory. In conjunction with their workers' settlements, these factories amounted to a massive interconnected, fortified position. They would become the scene of endless, vicious battles as the Germans sought to annihilate the right-wing bulwark of the Soviet defence, the destruction wrought by the Luftwaffe reducing the area to an unrecognisable, tangled nightmare of trenches, cellars and ruins.

The southern end of the city was divided from the north by the River Tsaritsa, which flowed east into

Left: Lieutenant-General Vasily I. Chuikov: appointed to command the 62nd Soviet Army on 12 September 1942, he would prove an inspired choice. Chuikov would gain lasting fame as the defender of Stalingrad.

Above: A German 88mm anti-aircraft gun in action outside Stalingrad in September 1942. In the background, Stalingrad burns under the impact of the Luftwaffe's incessant bombardment.

Below: A German forward observer consults his charts, before passing information to artillery crews via the field telephone. In the battle for the city, such men would become prime targets for Soviet snipers.

the Volga directly to the south of the Stalingrad No. 1 railway station. To the south of the Tsaritsa lay the suburbs of Minina and Yelshanka, where General Shumilov's 64th Army protected the left flank of 62nd Army. To the east of Stalingrad-1 was a landing stage connecting Soviet forces on the western bank to reserves and supplies on the eastern shore at Krasnaya Sloboda. The mighty Volga loomed over the battlefield. It was both the threat of a watery grave and a source of survival for Soviet troops fighting in

the city. In fact, the German failure to cut the flow of men and matériel into the city and the evacuation of casualties and spent units across the Volga would be instrumental in the Soviet triumph. However, in early September 1942, the only outcome that appeared likely at Stalingrad, whatever its properties as a defensive position, was a crushing German victory. In their hearts, many Soviet commanders secretly shared this fear, including General Lopatin, the commander of 62nd Army. Lopatin, a brave but broken man, had commanded 62nd Army in the bitter fighting west of Stalingrad, but, on 12 September, he was replaced by the man who would become synonymous with the Soviet triumph at Stalingrad: Lieutenant-General Vasily Chuikov.

Chuikov, aged 42, had fought in the Russian Civil War, but, since the outbreak of war in the east in June 1941, he had been the Soviet military attaché to China. He had returned to the front in June 1942, briefly commanding 64th Army and a shock group which administered a bloody nose to 4th Panzer in August 1942. Chuikov had not been infected with the despairing resignation of endless defeats that had broken many Soviet commanders and, with his back to the wall in Stalingrad, he was to prove an inspired choice. He was stocky, outspoken and a notoriously scruffy character, but – in contrast to the

Below: German tank men examine a Soviet T-34 at close quarters. It was not just German tanks which struggled to manoeuvre in the close city environment.

more studious Paulus – a born scrapper. Chuikov was tough, optimistic and bloody-minded, although such was the stress of battle that he suffered from dreadful eczema. However, the bandaged hands of this natural fighter came out fists clenched to lead his men to a remarkable victory. Chuikov's nerve held in the darkest moments of the struggle, even if his fierce temper did not, as he showed – with his long-suffering men – the natural wits and guts to frustrate the 6th Army.

Chuikov had been studying German tactical methods and felt that he had discerned a weakness of great relevance to Stalingrad. He acknowledged the Germans' ability to integrate airpower, armour and infantry in a way that no other army had been able to do. However, until their airpower went in, the armour rarely attacked, while the infantry followed the armour. On the wide open spaces of the Don steppe, this was the secret of German success. Yet, as Chuikov understood, such tactical methods would be less than easy to implement in the close confines

Above: A dramatic picture of a Soviet T-34 exploding under the impact of a direct hit. It does not take much imagination to consider the fate of the crew within such an inferno.

Below: German infantry move forwards in Stalingrad. Their pensive expression reveals how vulnerable they feel crossing open ground: it is a dash for cover, a pause for breath, followed by another dash for safety.

of the city. He knew he had to break the chain of German operations and stop the Luftwaffe, which had already annihilated the city, sweeping across the skies of Stalingrad in its usual style and numbers. As he himself commented in his memoirs: 'The enemy had firm mastery in the air. This dispirited our troops more than anything, and we feverishly thought about how to take this trump card out of the enemy's hand.' Chuikov's solution to this problem was to order Soviet infantry to 'hug' the lines of their German counterparts as closely as possible, preferably no further apart than a hand-grenade throw. The Luftwaffe's bombing accuracy had already begun to suffer in the difficult urban environment, but the fear of hitting frontline German, as well as Soviet, troops seriously undermined its capacity to give the intimate close-air support to which German units had become accustomed. It still paralysed all daytime movement and smashed communications, but its influence on the battle was not as great as it might have been. Indeed, the rubble-strewn nature of the city helped the Soviet defenders more than the Germans. Thus, German armour and German infantry, which would find it increasingly difficult to manoeuvre en masse, would have to fight their own

way forward at close quarters, a task they were unaccustomed to and disliked. This meant that, although Stalingrad was to prove a torturous experience for 62nd Army, it was fought on terms where they stood some chance of success. However, the days when Chuikov could sit back and tell himself, sure in the knowledge of victory, what a fine job he had done were a long way off. On 14 September, the Germans launched a thunderous assault on the city: the battle of Stalingrad had begun.

On the eve of the German attempt to storm Stalingrad, 6th Army and 4th Panzer Army faced a total of nine Soviet armies along a 643-km (400-mile) frontage under the command of Gordov's Stalingrad Front and Yeremenko's South-Eastern Front. The South-Eastern Front comprised 62nd, 64th, 57th and 51st Armies, with Chuikov's 62nd Army deployed in the city. It was 54,000-strong with 900 guns, many of which were on the eastern shore, and 100 tanks. The German 6th Army contained 15 divisions. To the north-west, four divisions of Strecker's 11th Corps monitored the 21st Soviet Army and the 4th Tank Army deployed on the northern banks of the Don. To the right of 11th Corps, directly north of Stalingrad, were two infantry divisions of Heitz's 8th Corps along with 14th Panzer Corps. To the west, five divisions of von Seydlitz-Kurbach's 51st Corps prepared to storm the city, supported on their left flank by 60th Motorised Division. To the south of the Tsaritsa in Stalingrad's southern suburbs lay General Hoth's 4th Panzer Army. Four divisions – 94th

Above: A German machine-gun crew dug in on the streets of Stalingrad. The sandbags, the ample supply of ammunition and the spare barrel indicate they intend to hold their position.

Infantry, 29th Motorised, 14th Panzer and 24th Panzer – faced 62nd Army's left flank, while 4th Panzer's two remaining divisions – 297th and 371st Infantry – deployed on the right flank against Shumilov's 64th Army. The basic Soviet military units of army, corps, division and brigade were considerably smaller than their German counterparts. In Soviet terms, the 300,000-strong 6th Army was a front. A Soviet army was about the size of a German army corps, roughly 60,000–70,000, although on both sides this was far from an exact figure. A full-strength panzer division was 18,000-strong and considerably more than the equivalent of a 1942 Soviet tank or mechanised corps. By July 1942, a typical Soviet tank corps consisted of three tank brigades of 53 tanks each, containing 32 T-34s and 21 light T-70 tanks, one motorised rifle brigade, a reconnaissance battalion, a mortar battalion and an artillery battalion. Additional supporting units of engineers, signallers and supply troops gave an authorised strength of 7800 men, roughly equivalent to a panzer regiment. The 39,000-strong mechanised corps savaged in 'Barbarossa' had been replaced with smaller, better balanced units. By September 1942, a Soviet mechanised corps contained three mechanised brigades, each with a tank regiment, plus one or two tank brigades. In total, with supporting units, its authorised strength was 13,559 men with 100 T-34s, plus 104 other tanks made up of heavy KV-1s and light T-70s. The new mechanised corps were designed to counter a panzer division, but, due to scarcity of resources, only eight were formed during 1942. Finally, a full-strength Soviet infantry division numbered 10,500, approximately two-thirds the size of its German counter-part, although few on either side were up to strength at Stalingrad.

On 14 September, Lieutenant-General von Seydlitz-Kurbach's 51st Corps was launched against the city, directed by General Friedrich Paulus. Paulus and his commanders were confident – perhaps too confident – of victory. Tall and of neat appearance, Paulus had been an excellent chief of staff to 6th Army during the 1941 campaign until taking over command in January 1942, following the death of Field Marshal von Reichenau. Paulus was conformist, but nurtured a quiet and intense ambition. He had been promoted to command 6th Army with Hitler's approval, an admiration that was reciprocated by Paulus, who thought the Führer's instinctive military

Below: German artillery in the Minina suburbs on the southern side of the Tsaritsa river, showing the grain elevator: its defence, in which 50 Soviet soldiers defied three German divisions, would become legendary.

talents greater than many of his military contemporaries acknowledged. He was an industrious and capable man who had done well at Kharkov in May 1942 and during the advance to Stalingrad. However, he was not an instinctive fighter with the natural tactical flair of Chuikov. The defeat at Stalingrad and his own surrender on 31 January 1943 would weigh heavily upon Paulus during his captivity, which endured until 1953. He returned to Dresden in East Germany and died aged 67 an unhappy man, of motor neurone disease in 1957.

Defeat, however, was not in Paulus' mind on 14 September 1942. At 0630 hours, hundreds of German guns, aircraft and tanks hurtled towards 62nd Soviet Army. Chuikov had actually intended a small series of counterattacks himself, but was beaten to the punch by 51st Corps which began a two-pronged assault in the north and centre of the city. South of the Tsaritsa, 4th Panzer attacked Shumilov's 64th Army. Infantry divisions 71st, 76th and 295th led the south-easterly assault of 51st Corps, while immediately to the south of the Tsaritsa 24th Panzer and 94th Infantry Division attacked through the Minina suburbs. On their right, 14th Panzer and 29th Motorised Division drove for the Volga in the Yelshanka district. The two-pronged nature of the

German assault revealed their natural proclivity to seek the encirclement of the enemy, even within the confines of the city. The aim of the offensive was for 4th Panzer's forces south of the river to create their own small encirclement south of the Tsaritsa and reach the Volga. The 51st Corps would do the same to the north and conquer the Mamayev Kurgan. The German forces would then combine and drive along the banks of the Tsaritsa to the central landing stage. Its conquest would isolate 62nd Army on the western bank from its lines of supply on the eastern shore.

By mid-afternoon, Chuikov's command post on top of the Mamayev Kurgan had been knocked out, leaving 62nd Army with no effective command and control. As the full fury of the German assault descended on them, Soviet troops fell back into the buildings before ambushing isolated German armoured units or engaging marauding German infantry in hand-to-hand struggles. However, the Germans rolled on block by block, advancing towards the Volga over the Mamayev Kurgan towards Stalingrad-1 railway station and the ultimate prize of the landing stages. The Soviet artillery ranged on the eastern bank fired salvos over the Volga to disrupt the Germans, but to no avail. Chuikov was in danger

of losing control of the battle and, under a smoke screen laid by the Soviet gunners, removed his headquarters to what became known as the 'Tsaritsyn Bunker' on the northern bank of the Tsaritsa. The 62nd Army's headquarters was actually in front of many of its divisional command posts but from there Chuikov was able to gauge the weight of the German offensive and recognised the desperate nature of the battle. If the Germans were able to capture the landing stages and sustain the isolation of 62nd Army, then the battle for Stalingrad would be over before it had really begun. Chuikov committed his last tactical reserves, a tank brigade with only 19 tanks, to block the German advance. At dusk, Chuikov pleaded with South-Eastern Front's commander, Colonel-General Yeremenko, to send Major-General Aleksandr Rodimstev's 13th Guards Division across the Volga under cover of darkness.

This was no time for mistakes. As they lined up on the eastern shore at Krasnaya Sloboda, none of Rodimstev's men could be under any illusions as to what awaited them. The city was silhouetted by flame and fire as the sounds of battle echoed across the river. The division was 10,000-strong, but lacking in heavy weapons. At 1900 hours, Chuikov told Rodimstev to ready his men. The 13th Guards were to storm the shore, secure the landing stages and retake the Mamayev Kurgan and Stalingrad-1 railway station. These objectives were too ambitious, but this mattered little to Lieutenant Chervyakhov as he led the 1st battalion of the 42nd Regiment of 13th Guards into battle. As the boats beached, Chervyakhov's men hacked, punched and wrestled the initiative from the Germans to create a bridgehead. The rest of 13th Guards moved quickly through the city streets to take up positions on the left flank of the Mamayev Kurgan and around the station. At dawn, 13th Guards were attacked by the 71st and 295th German divisions, while 4th Panzer continued its advance south of the Tsaritsa. The fighting for the station raged back and forth during 15 September, as 13th Guards met the German assault head on. The station changed hands four times during the day, but was in Russian hands again by nightfall. It would change hands 15 times by 19 September. On 16 September, 13th Guards temporarily wrested the initiative from

Left: German soldiers take on food and supplies to sustain them through the fighting. The lavish supply pictured here would be a distant memory by November 1942.

the 71st Division and cleared the landing stages and the surrounding area, as well as recapturing the station. However, the balance tipped in the German's favour on 17 September as 76th Division was committed. The Germans gradually gained the upper hand and, by 19 September, had secured the station and brought the landing stages under sustained fire. By 20 September, 13th Guards – at dawn on 15 September standing at 10,000-strong – had been decimated. It now stood barely 2700-strong, but there is little doubt it had saved the city. It had slowed down the German advance and given Chuikov time to reshuffle his troops and bring more reserves across the Volga.

The fighting for the Mamayev Kurgan was equally intense. On 14 September, the German 295th Division made a supreme effort to take this most vital of positions. By 15 September, it had destroyed Chuikov's command post on the Mamayev Kurgan and brought the summit under fire. The left-wing Colonel Solugub's 112th Division, the 9th Motorised

Below: As German casualties mounted, the Wehrmacht was no longer as cocky in its expectations of rapid victory as it had been in summer 1942. Nevertheless, in September 1942, the weather remains ideal.

Above: By 26 September 1942, Paulus declared the south and centre of the city won. The swastika was raised over his headquarters, the Univermag department store near Stalingrad-1 railway station.

Right: The first German attack on Stalingrad, showing the front line before and after the attack, and notable locations in the city.

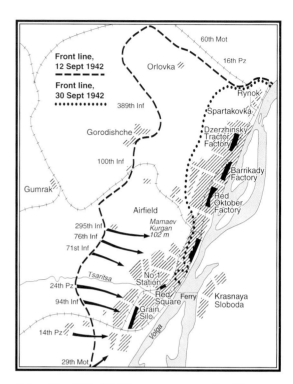

Infantry Brigade, was fighting for its life and in desperate need of reinforcement. This was an exceptionally important tactical position: its summit would enable clear observation of both the right and left wings of 62nd Army's defences, as well as the movement of reserves and supplies from the eastern shore. Its capture would facilitate accurate, targeted artillery fire and air support, usually so difficult in urban encounters because of the close and congested nature of the struggle. A sustained and directed bombardment of the Volga crossings would have severe consequences for 62nd Army and its ability to hold the 6th Army at bay. The Mamayev Kurgan heights also had psychological significance for both German and Soviet troops fighting down in the city: neither wanted the other looking down on them. The Mamayev Kurgan's importance is revealed in Chuikov's memoirs. He recalled of the night of 15–16 September: 'that night we were all concerned about the fate of the Mamayev Kurgan. If the enemy took it he could command the whole city and the Volga.'

At dawn on 16 September, Chuikov ordered two regiments – 42nd of 13th Guards and 46th of Colonel

Solugub's 112th Division – to storm the Mamayev Kurgan and hold it at any price. After a ten-minute barrage, 42nd attacked the northern side of the summit and 46th the north-eastern. Despite heavy casualties, the Soviet troops fought their way to the summit, but were immediately hit by the Luftwaffe and German counterattacks. For the duration of the battle of Stalingrad, the Germans repeatedly attacked the summit in grim but inconclusive fighting, characterised by bayonet duels and the use of grenades at close quarters. Chuikov vowed 'that we would hold on to Mamayev Kurgan whatever happened'. He would keep his promise, but, by 17 September, with the Germans on the Mamayev Kurgan and 13th Guards' position beginning to crack, 62nd Army desperately needed help.

Nevertheless, dawn on 18 September brought no respite and began as usual with a massive Luftwaffe attack. The remains of Solugub's 112th and 42nd Regiments continued their murderous struggle on the Mamayev Kurgan, but, at 0800 hours, to Chuikov's amazement, the Luftwaffe disappeared. It had gone

Left: A Soviet infantry squad dashes across open ground within the city. The relatively undamaged nature of the buildings in the background suggests this is quite early in the battle for Stalingrad.

to fight off the offensive Zhukov had launched against the left flank of 6th Army between the Don and the Volga. On 12 September, Zhukov informed Stalin that he considered it 'obligatory for us even in these grave circumstances to continue our offensive operations, to grind down the enemy, who no less than us, is taking losses, and simultaneously we will prepare a more organised and powerful blow'. The more powerful blow would trap 6th Army in November 1942, but the situation in the city demanded a more urgent contribution. Moskalenko's 1st Guards, Kozlov's 24th Army, and Malinovsky's 66th Army launched their attack against the German 8th Infantry and 14th Panzer Corps on a 32-km (20-mile) front, with the main assault delivered by 1st Guards and 24th Army. The dual aim was to relieve

Below: An heroic pose for posterity on the summit of the Mamayev Kurgan. It was taken after the Soviet triumph in February 1943, but clearly indicates the extent to which the Kurgan dominated the city.

the pressure on 62nd Army and link up with its right flank. At 0530 hours, after an artillery barrage, 1st Guards and 24th Army attacked the Germans, who retained the tactical advantage of the high ground. The Soviet barrage failed and the assaulting troops were met by a hail of artillery, anti-tank and machine-gun fire. Soviet cooperation between armour, artillery and infantry was poor, as tightly concentrated units reeled under a concerted German counterattack spearheaded by the Luftwaffe. Stalingrad Front ploughed on for five days amidst horrendous losses for little tactical gain and a merely temporary diversion of the Luftwaffe. However, Chuikov pronounced himself grateful for a six-hour respite from the Luftwaffe. Chuikov asked Yeremenko for two full divisions, but got two brigades. He deployed the 92nd Naval Infantry Brigade on the left flank, south of the Tsaritsa, and the 137th Tank Brigade to the right of the Mamayev Kurgan. At 1800 hours on 18 September, Yeremenko

ordered Chuikov to conduct a counterattack. The aim was as follows: '62nd Army Command, after creating a shock group of not less than 3 infantry divisions and one armoured brigade in the area of Mamayev Kurgan, will launch at attack towards the north-west outskirts of Stalingrad, with the aim of destroying the enemy in this area.' This was an over-ambitious task designed to complement the Stalingrad Front's renewed assault, but Solugub's 112th Division failed to capture the summit.

To the left of the Mamayev Kurgan, the 13th Guards was losing its fight for the railway station. On 19 September, the Germans secured Stalingrad-1 and, by 21 September, had surrounded the 1st battalion of

Below: A graphic illustration of the carnage wrought by the fighting in the city. The air of nervous expectation is palpable as German soldiers scan the rubble for the merest hint of enemy activity.

13th Guards. As the guards fell back, moving from house to house, the battalion was cut off. It had to fight its way out of encirclement in fierce hand-to-hand fighting as buildings collapsed around it. The men took up positions barely 274m (300 yds) from the central landing stage. Lieutenant-General Hartman's crack 71st Division continued its advance towards the river and by evening had the landing stage under direct fire. The aim was to reach the Volga and roll up the 13th Guards' left flank, isolating 62nd Army in the centre and north of the city. The Germans would then crush 13th Guards in a minor *Kessel*, with 71st Division moving north to link up with 76th and 295th Divisions moving south-east. The left flank of Chuikov's 62nd Army was in danger of collapse and in the small hours of 23 September, 2000 men of Lieutenant-Colonel Nikolai Batyuk's 284th Siberian Division crossed the Volga into the city. As

Above: A plume of thick, black smoke rises thousands of feet into the air as the Luftwaffe pummels Stalingrad. The Soviet 62nd Army feared the Luftwaffe like nothing else.

Batyuk's men landed, German infantry encroached within 137m (150 yds) of the Volga, while a dawn raid by the Luftwaffe hit oil drums on the river bank. The river burned, and the smoke mingled with the half-light of dawn to protect Batyuk's men as they approached the bank. The lead regiment of 284th Siberian went straight into action, clearing a path for the division which moved through the burning city to bolster the left flank of 13th Guards and support Gorshny's 95th Division on the south-eastern slopes of the Mamayev Kurgan. The primary objective of 284th Siberian was to shore up 13th Guards, clear the area surrounding the landing stage, and drive on to the northern banks of the Tsaritsa. At 1000 hours on 23 September, the Siberians and 13th Guards counterattacked 71st Division and checked its proposed northern drive up the Volga. However, although 62nd Army's left was stabilised, the recapture of the landing stage and Stalingrad-1 proved beyond Chuikov's men. Yet, if the situation north of the Tsaritsa was under control, the battle south of the river was in danger of spinning out of it.

The German attack south of the Tsaritsa aimed to reach the Volga and divide the left flank of 62nd Army from the right wing of Shumilov's 64th Army. On the right flank of 4th Panzer, 14th Panzer and 29th Motorised Division advanced rapidly towards the Volga, completing the isolation of Chuikov's 62nd Army. To their left on the southern banks of the Tsaritsa, 24th Panzer and 94th Division moved through the Minina suburb, defended by 35th Guards Division and the 42nd Infantry Brigade. On 17 September, they were joined by the 92nd Naval Infantry Brigade, as a ferocious struggle developed over the enormous concrete grain elevator on the shores of the Volga. The grain elevator was all that stood between the union of the two wings of 4th Panzer's attack and the complete destruction of the Soviet position south of the Tsaritsa. The Soviet defence was conducted by 30 naval marines and 20 guardsmen, and its staggering ferocity dismayed the Germans. Wilhelm Hoffman of the 94th Division recorded his impressions of the struggle as his battalion, part of 267th Regiment, attacked the grain elevator. 'Our battalion, plus tanks, is attacking the elevator, from which smoke is pouring – the grain in it is burning, the Russians seem to have set light to it themselves. Barbarism. The battalion is suffering heavy losses. There are not more than sixty men left in each company. The elevator is occupied not by men but by devils that no flames or bullets can destroy.' The battle for the elevator continued until 22 September, dragging in elements of three German divisions. It proved a microcosm of the battle of Stalingrad. In this battle of annihilation, things did not move quickly as on the open steppe. A single

*Above: The trauma of the Luftwaffe's indiscriminate destruction
of Stalingrad is revealed in the expressions of these young women.
However, the Luftwaffe proved unable to break the will of the people.*

building could hold up a regiment or division for hours as the fighting moved from floor to floor and room to room. Soviet troops fought for every building and street, conceding ground inch by inch as they were forced back to the Volga. On 20 September, Hoffman reported 'the battle for the elevator is still going on. The Russians are firing from all sides. We stay in our cellar; you can't go out into the street.' The battle raged for another 48 hours, but, on 22 September, a relieved Hoffman believed that 'Russian resistance in the elevator has been broken. Our troops are advancing towards the Volga. We found about 40 Russian dead in the elevator building ... the whole of our battalion has as many men as a regular company. Our old soldiers have never experienced such bitter fighting before.'

The tenacity of the defenders was matched by the attackers, but the Germans were being dragged into a battle of attrition day after day and night after night. Nevertheless, Paulus, Hoth and the ordinary German soldier continued to believe in final victory. The 6th Army had never been defeated and was the strongest field army the Wehrmacht could muster. Defeat at the hands of a 62nd Army they had chased into Stalingrad was simply unthinkable and not even considered. As the 94th Division finally conquered

the grain elevator, the Soviet position south of the Tsaritsa began to deteriorate. The 35th Guards Division had been ground to pieces and the depleted naval marines of the 92nd Brigade had joined forces with the 42nd Infantry Brigade, whose commander was killed in a Luftwaffe air raid on 23 September. Chuikov's knowledge of the battle south of the Tsaritsa was naturally dependent upon information provided by commanders on the spot. However, on 24 September, under the pressure of battle, the new acting commander of 42nd Brigade removed himself from the western bank to Golodnyi Island in the middle of the Volga, where he continued to send Chuikov false reports. This duplicity was not discovered until 25 September, but by then the battle south of the river had already been lost. The new commander of 42nd Brigade reported to Chuikov in the midst of the fighting that its men were short of ammunition, food and water, and could not hold out much longer. Hoffman's diary for 26 September complained 'our regiment is involved in constant fighting. After the elevator was taken the Russians continued to defend themselves stubbornly. You don't see them at all, they have established themselves in houses and cellars and are firing on all sides, including from our rear – barbarians they use gangster methods.' However, late on 26 September, Hoffman's men acquired merciful respite. The 92nd Brigade crumbled under the combined assault of 24th Panzer and 94th Division. The 24th Panzer reached the Volga and brought the central landing stage under fire from south of the Tsaritsa as the broken remnants of 92nd Brigade and 42nd Brigade were evacuated across the Volga.

Chuikov's 62nd Army had survived the first onslaught, but there was little doubt the Germans had won a significant tactical victory. The 4th Panzer had reached the Volga on an 8-km (5-mile) front from the Tsaritsa to the southern suburb of Kuprosnoye. The Germans had the central landing stage west of Krasnaya Sloboda under fire, while the Luftwaffe kept up a constant attack on the small armada of boats that ferried men and matériel back and forth across the Volga. In the centre of the city, the Germans had secured the railway station and driven the Russians off the summit of the Mamayev Kurgan, even if they had not taken it. Soviet counterattacks on the 6th Army's northern flank had been comprehensively rebuffed and 62nd Army's bridgehead reduced to the industrial area at the northern end of

Stalingrad. Yet it did not feel like a victory. The strength of Soviet resistance dismayed many German soldiers. The Germans no longer displayed their customary cockiness and contempt for the soldierly qualities of their Soviet opponents. The German soldier knew within hours of the battle commencing that he was not in his natural habitat, but began to harbour an uneasy suspicion that his Russian counterpart was at home in this alien environment. Hoffman recorded in his diary on 28 September that his regiment and division were celebrating victory. 'Together with our tank crews we have taken the southern part of the city and reached the Volga. We paid dearly for our victory. In three weeks we have occupied about five and a half square miles. The commander has congratulated us on our victory … when on earth is the war going to finish? When will the Russian forces in Stalingrad be exhausted? Will this blood bath be over by Christmas?'

German soldiers quickly realised this was a very different battle and christened fighting in Stalingrad as *Rattenkrieg* (war of the rats). The German command struggled to come to terms with the anarchic nature of street fighting. Its claustrophobic character suffocated flexible manoeuvre, as well as the integration of airpower, armour and infantry. In his 1955 book, *The March on Stalingrad*, Major-General Hans Doerr, who took part in the campaign, described the

scene as one in which 'the time for conducting large scale operations was gone forever; from the wide expanses of the steppe land, the war moved into the jagged gullies of the Volga hills with their copses and ravines, into the factory area of Stalingrad, spread out over uneven, pitted, rugged country, covered with iron, concrete and stone buildings.' The German Army had carried all before it through the simultaneous application of airpower, panzer divisions and infantry. In open-manoeuvre warfare, the Wehrmacht was rarely surpassed in its tactical ability to implement the *Kesselschlacht*. Yet, at Stalingrad, in what they recognised as a very different battle – as before Moscow – the German command sought to apply familiar but inappropriate methods. The Luftwaffe would bomb, groups of panzers would lunge forwards followed by infantry in pursuit of minor *Kesselschlachts*. However, the close, congested nature of the streets strewn with rubble made the rapid multi-unit operations necessary to encircle and annihilate the enemy virtually impossible. The execution of the *Kesselschlacht* was dependent upon flexible tactical command by divisional commanders, but, if flexibility was to be retained in the chaotic

Below: Stalin permitted the evacuation of civilians as the fighting in the city intensified. Soviet citizens cram everything they can into lorries that will bring them to safety across the Volga, as the battle rages on.

battle for Stalingrad, command had to be devolved at the very least down to regimental level, possibly even lower to battalion commanders. However, this level of command was incompatible with the coherent, large-unit actions the likes of which Paulus, Hoth and most other commanders deemed necessary to destroy quickly significant numbers of Red Army troops.

The battle for Stalingrad had descended into hundreds of minor but murderous tactical confrontations fought out at platoon, company and battalion level, yet the planning of senior German officers remained centred on the division. In their attempt to apply the remarkable tactical flexibility of German command methods in open war, commanders robbed their units of the very flexibility, upon which they prided themselves. They were in pursuit of victories on a scale that was not on offer in Stalingrad. The tempo of German attacks was undermined, thus reinforcing the attritional nature of the battle that German commanders were trying to escape. This battle of attrition was fought by the infantry with the support of armour and airpower. Likewise, the heavily centralised Soviet command system, based as it was around the idea of a 'managed battlefield', had completely failed

Above: A German machine-gun crew positioned behind a wall with a clear field of fire over the outskirts of the city. The MG34 was capable of firing 800–900 rounds a minute.

to cope with the speed and flexibility of German manoeuvre war in both 1941 and 1942. It is therefore deeply ironic that, almost in spite of themselves at Stalingrad, the Russians, particularly 62nd Army, adapted far better than their German counterparts. The isolation of 62nd Army on the western bank helped considerably, as flexible, devolved command did not come naturally to an officer corps that was battered into submission by Stalin in the 1930s. However much Stalin might rant and threaten from Moscow, however much Zhukov might admonish and Yeremenko interfere, in the final analysis, Chuikov was master in his own house, even as it crumbled around him. No other Soviet army commander, either before or after Stalingrad, ever had as much tactical freedom in the execution of superior orders as Chuikov. He understood that close command and control of the entire battle, even if desirable, was not possible because of the city's shape, the frenzied nature of the fighting, and the paucity of effective communications. Chuikov dispensed with the conventional organisational units of division, brigade, battalion and company when planning and executing operations. The basic Soviet fighting units at Stalingrad became the shock group. Chuikov and his commanders formulated plans which were implemented by flexible ad hoc units of between 50 and 100 men which were specifically tailored to the mission. In defence and attack, Soviet troops seemed to move with a greater speed, stealth and agility than German soldiers. Soviet armour, in contrast to German panzers, was not required to indulge in complex tactical manoeuvre, but was used as defensive firepower, often deliberately buried and camouflaged within the rubble of a collapsed building. In conjunction with the Soviet artillery on the eastern bank of the Volga, Chuikov's flexible tactics frustrated 6th Army as it battered itself against 62nd Army.

Nevertheless, on 26 September 1942, Paulus declared the southern outskirts and the city centre won. Although concerned about the Soviet's unexpected tenacity and the inability of the Luftwaffe to close the Volga lifeline, the German commander remained quietly confident of eventual victory. The arrogant assumption of victory had gone and was now replaced by a sober expectation of success.

As Soviet reconnaissance detected the redeployment of 4th Panzer's 14th Panzer and 94th Infantry to the north and centre of the city, the crucible of battle shifted. German and Soviet troops would now fight for the monuments of Stalin's brutal policy of industrialisation during the 1930s: the Dzherzinsky Tractor Factory, the Barrikady Ordnance Factory and the Red October. As the battlefield diminished, the intensity of the fighting increased. The 6th Army was in a duel to the death such as it had never known. However, as Chuikov's sorely tried men wilted under the full might of the second German attack, launched at dawn on 27 September 1942, German victory appeared imminent.

Below: The scale of destruction in the city tells its own story. A German anti-tank unit in action during October 1942. The men's attention is fixed on some distant action.

Below: A German soldier – still looking cheerful despite the setbacks encountered by the 6th Army – and his vehicle, both bearing the scars of recent confrontations.

CHAPTER 4

The Second German Assault on the City

27 September to 7 October

By 26 September 1942, General Paulus was now hopeful rather than confident. Although he had declared the south and centre of the city won, the sustained ferocity of Russian resistance had taken him aback and unnerved his commanders.

Paulus knew his men were struggling to come to terms with the savage intimacy of close combat. His army, schooled to an unprecedented degree of excellence in manoeuvre war, was failing to adapt to a world of rubble, improvised squads, sewers, buildings, bayonets, daggers and grenades. The strain was beginning to tell on Paulus. As Chuikov struggled with eczema, German staff officers noted that Paulus was increasingly withdrawn and suffered from intermittent bouts of dysentery. The nervous twitch on his left cheek that he occasionally displayed became a more obvious companion. He was not helped by Hitler and the Nazi party hierarchy's persistent underestimation of the task that confronted 6th Army. How could the undefeated 6th Army, with two corps of the 4th Panzer Army under its command, totalling nearly 300,000 men, possibly fail? German propagandists had presented the fall of Stalin's city as imminent for several weeks, but still it did not capitulate.

Left: A German mortar team prepares to support an attack in the ruins of Stalingrad. The scale of the destruction caused by endless Luftwaffe raids, shelling and hand-to-hand fighting can clearly be seen in the background.

The strained relations between Hitler and the Chief of the German General Staff, Halder, snapped on 24 September. Halder was sacked and replaced by Major-General Kurt Zeitzler, formerly chief of staff to the German armies stationed in France and the Low Countries. Hitler and Halder had fundamentally disagreed about the direction – or lack of it – of the 1941 campaign, and over the 1942 campaign. Halder remained convinced that, if Germany was to win the quick victory her grand strategic situation and lack of resources demanded, the focus of operations had to be on the Moscow axis. He also sought to defend the traditional independence of the general staff over operational matters in the field. Since the crisis of December 1941, an uneasy tension existed between Hitler's role as head of state and commander in chief of the Army and the freedom Halder perceived to be both his right and that of his fellow officers. Aloof and austere, he barely concealed his irritation and contempt for what he regarded as Hitler's amateurish meddling in professional military affairs. The more Halder criticised the military madness of fighting a positional battle of annihilation such as Stalingrad – which in his opinion could not be decisive – the more blindly obsessed Hitler became with

victory at any price. The Führer increasingly valued National Socialist commitment as the main criteria of generalship, and not objective military thought. Stalingrad was to be taken, however long it took: that was Hitler's strategy. Victory would demonstrate the superior will and racial qualities of the Germanic peoples and bring about the collapse of Stalin's Bolshevist empire. Ironically, as Hitler began to micro-manage the German Army, often interfering in the smallest tactical detail, Stalin finally began to accept the advice of commanders such as Zhukov and Vasilevsky. The increasing freedom enjoyed by Red Army commanders in the planning and execution of operations – in contrast to the ideologically driven straitjacket that Hitler's mind imposed upon the Wehrmacht – would play a vital role in condemning 6th Army to the cauldron.

If early September was late summer, then late September, as all German officers knew to their cost, was unmistakably autumn. Since it often took a

These pages: A German infantry unit in the same location as the mortar unit surveys the ground, decides on its course of action and advances from behind its temporary cover. Despite the Luftwaffe's attentions, all movement was fraught with danger.

Above: Chuikov's 62nd Army forced the German 6th Army to battle for every yard of the city. Here, in a rubble-strewn trench, a Soviet soldier is in the act of throwing a grenade.

battalion a day to secure a single building, Paulus and his officers appreciated that there was little time to lose. As the battle in the south of the city began to subside, Paulus regrouped his depleted formations for an immediate assault on the industrial heartland of Stalingrad.

To the north of the Mamayev Kurgan, Stalingrad's gigantic factories and workers' settlements acted as an enormous fortified bulwark of the Soviet 62nd Army's precarious existence. The main German attacks would concentrate on the Mamayev Kurgan and the Red October Steel Plant at the southern end of the factory complex and, in the north of the city, from the Gorodische area, on the Dzerzhinsky Tractor Factory. The aim was familiar and predictable. The two thrusts were to break through Soviet lines to reach the Volga, turn inwards, and advance down the shoreline to encircle Soviets troops caught to the west of them, fixed by German thrusts on the Barrikady settlement. The Soviet defence was to be splintered, encircled and annihilated.

The highly effective reconnaissance network that Chuikov's 62nd Army maintained within the city quickly detected German preparations to move north. Chuikov regrouped his forces from his head-quarters on the riverbank behind the Barrikady Factory. He instructed his commanders to pay particular attention to strengthening anti-tank defences and the laying of mines, while buildings were to be prepared for defence, inside and out. Batyuk's 284th Siberian was integrated into the line on Chuikov's left between the slopes of Mamayev Kurgan and the Red October plant. As the main landing stage where the Tsaritsa flowed into the Volga came under attack, Chuikov's men improvised three more crossing points in the north and centre of the city. They also constructed a rickety bridge, lashed together with a motley collection of materials, to sustain the flow of men and matériel in and out of the city. These landing stages played a key role in Stavka's basic strategy at Stalingrad. In stark contrast to the Germans, who increasingly threw every division they could spare into the battle for the city, Stavka and Yermenko's South-Eastern Front deployed only as many troops as they thought necessary to hold the line and fix 6th Army in the city.

As 6th Army bled, Chuikov's 62nd Army was drip-fed sufficient resources and men as could be put into the firing line. The defence of the factory area which protected the western bank of the Volga with its landing stages was critical if the Soviets were to survive inside the unearthly ordeal that was Stalingrad. By mid-September, the organisation of the landing stages was under military command, with definite procedures for loading, evacuation and operations. The western priority was ammunition, men, and food – that being the order of their importance – while easterly traffic focused on the evacuation of the wounded and hapless German prisoners. Chuikov's staff instructed the landing areas to establish officers responsible for the reception and distribution of supplies, while military engineers undertook maintenance of the thousands of small craft which ran the gauntlet across the Volga. This was the lifeline of the 62nd Army's existence in the battle for the city and gave it the ability to play its role in the wider operational and strategic plans being formulated by the Red Army. If the landing stages were lost, or traffic across the Volga permanently halted, German victory was inevitable. This, more than anything else, was the centre of gravity of the battle of Stalingrad. The failure of the 6th Army to isolate the battle on the western shore from the source of Soviet fighting power on the eastern bank lay at the heart of its defeat.

The lifeline was sustained by Rear Admiral Rogachev's naval flotilla, which also took under its command hundreds of civilian fishermen and their vessels. These crews transported the men of 13th Guards and 284th into battle, enduring the attentions of the German artillery. To undertake crossings by day invited disaster, but night crossings without lights risked collision with the other craft scurrying back and forth before dawn exposed them to the small mercies of the Luftwaffe. The dark currents of the Volga concealed the shifting wrecks of earlier German victims and, unless the crew could free the craft before dawn, their fate acquired a cruel inevitability. Rogachev's men shipped thousands of tonnes of food, ammunition and men while fighting a constant war of attrition with German aircraft preying on the Volga. The collection of steamers, barges, armoured gunboats, minesweepers, floating anti-aircraft platforms and rowing boats also evacuated more than 200,000 civilians once Stalin gave permission at the end of August.

German artillery and small arms fire was a major problem for the Soviet vessels approaching the western bank, but their main foe was the Luftwaffe. Formed in 1934 to provide close air support for ground operations, the Luftwaffe was a formidable instrument of war and a key German asset. Its principles of flexibility, concentration of force, boldness and shock were essentially those of the panzer divisions. It had played a key role in the 1940 campaign and savaged the obsolete Red Air Force in 1941. Air support for the German campaign was provided by Air Fleet 4, commanded by the arrogant but competent Colonel-General Wolfram von Richthofen. Richthofen, a nephew of the illustrious Red Baron of World War I, was regarded as the Luftwaffe's leading expert on divebombing and had acquired international notoriety in 1937 when his Condor Legion had pulverised the Basque town of Guernica, in the Spanish Civil War of 1936–39, an event immortalised by Picasso's painting.

Air Fleet 4 was divided into two air corps. Air Corps 4, commanded by Lieutenant-General Kurt Pflugbeil, supported Army Group A's advance in to

Below: The second German assault on Stalingrad, showing the position of the front line on 26 September and 13 October.

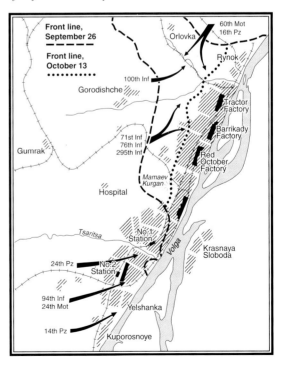

the Caucasus, while Lieutenant-General Martin Fiebig's 8th Air Corps supported Army Group B's march on Stalingrad. If the Luftwaffe maintained tactical air superiority over Stalingrad in strategic terms, however, it suffered from the same lack of correlation between ends and means that plagued the German Army's 1942 campaign. Air Fleet 4 began Operation 'Blau' with 1500 aircraft, of which 1150 were operational, but, within three months, such was the wear-and-tear of constant operations that, by the end of September, the fleet's strength had declined by 40 per cent. In simple terms, the Luftwaffe, like the Army, did not have the resources to conduct two separate and diverging thrusts over an enormous area into the Caucasus and over Stalingrad. By the end of September, Army Group A's support had become periodic and intermittent as Hitler, regardless of his earlier prioritisation of oil, switched the focus of German operations to Stalingrad. The Luftwaffe maintained air superiority over Stalingrad despite the brave, if outclassed, efforts of Major-General Khyrukin's 8th Air Army. Yet, by then the combined but depleted resources of Air Corps 8 and 4 were insufficient to provide both close air support and isolate the western bank from Soviet resources on the eastern shore. The Luftwaffe

Below: General Paulus surveys the fighting at Stalingrad through field glasses. Paulus had been shocked by the tenacity of the Red Army's defence of the city, but was determined to push 62nd Army into the Volga.

had devastated the city and was a constant thorn in 62nd Army's side, but proved incapable of breaking its will to fight. Equally, despite its tactical superiority, it could not deliver a killer blow in the decisive battle of attrition with Rogachev's naval flotilla. As Richthofen recognised, Air Fleet 4's diminishing resources simply could not saturate the area, while the ever-increasing demands on men and machines increased the attritional wear-and-tear on its resources. No less than 6th Army, the Luftwaffe was in a battle of attrition which it had to win quickly or risk defeat. In late August and early September 1942, Stalingrad's air defences were shockingly insufficient, both on the ground and in the air. The city possessed four anti-aircraft guns in mid-August 1942, but by October they had increased substantially. The arrival of the head of the Soviet Air Force, Colonel-General Alexsandr Novikov, led to a steady improvement in the performance of Soviet airpower, while the Luftwaffe's inability to dedicate sufficient resources to undertake a sustained interdiction programme of the railway network meant that anti-aircraft resources flowed into the region. As with the German army in 1941 and 1942, the Luftwaffe was still scoring tactical victories and remained technically superior to its opponents, but, even with the means at its disposal, could not achieve a decisive victory. The effort to do so inflicted a degree of attrition that would bring Air Fleet 4 to the point of collapse.

Nevertheless, the Luftwaffe remained a feared opponent. As Chuikov commented: 'The Luftwaffe literally hammered anything they saw in the streets into the ground.' Therefore Chuikov's regrouping to face the expected German assault in the north of the city had to be undertaken with great care yet speed at night, whereas German units remained more or less immune to air attack at this stage. However, Chuikov's men were increasingly familiar with the city environment and quickly adapted to the nature of combat in the city. Having received intelligence on the likely area and objectives of the German attack, Chuikov quickly appreciated that, if the Germans were able to secure the Kurgan in the early stages of the attack and use it as a fire base, then the situation of the defenders below assailed from their left and right would become intolerable. In line with Clausewitz's belief that defence must be active, not passive, Chuikov planned a pre-emptive tactical assault on the Mamayev Kurgan. He instructed Rodimtsev's 13th Guards on the left to attack towards

Above: Soviet oil storage units burn out of control following a Luftwaffe attack. By hiding Soviet daytime movements in the city, the smoke, visible 40 miles away, proved a blessing in disguise.

the station, while to its right Batyuk's 284th would attack the southern end of the Kurgan. At the same time, Gorshny's 95th Infantry Division would assault the eastern slopes of the Mamayev Kurgan. The attack was to begin at 0600 hours on 27 September after an hour-long artillery barrage. Significantly, Chuikov's Order No. 166 finished with the following exhortation: 'I again warn the commanders of all units and formations not to carry out operations in battle by whole units like companies and battalions. The offensive should be organised chiefly on the basis of small groups, with tommy-guns, hand grenades, bottles of incendiary mixture and anti-tank rifles.' The contrast with German commanders who, although they began to urge their men to form 'storm groups', continued to think in divisional and regimental terms, is quite remarkable.

As Chuikov had instructed his men to keep the fighting at close quarters, it was almost inevitable

that, when one side was attacking, the other must be actively defending. The defenders quickly appreciated the defensive value of rubble, trenches and especially fortification of strong points within buildings. As the Germans discovered to their cost, the congested nature of street fighting severely curtailed the ability of large formations to undertake coherent sustained operations. Chuikov instinctively understood that the very nature of such fighting meant its conduct must be dominated by small, heavily armed groups of infantry capable of swift, flexible action in both defence and attack. At Stalingrad, the shock group was the basic Soviet unit and, in Chuikov's eyes, evolved naturally from the chaotic nature of street fighting. The shock group was to act independently in pursuit of objectives laid down by a divisional commander, who in turn received orders from Chuikov. The idea was to make 62nd Army's pursuit of its objectives compatible with the decentralised flexibility necessary to fight with the speed and stealth that the conditions within the city demanded, especially with the looming menace of the Luftwaffe. The shock group of between 50 and 80 men was broken down

into three interdependent units: the storm group, the reinforcement group and the reserve group.

Comprised of between eight and ten men, the storm group was the cutting edge of the shock group. Its role was to infiltrate the enemy's position, be it a trench system or building, and destroy the enemy. The men were armed with machine guns, grenades, daggers and a short-handled shovel to be used as an axe at close quarters. The commander of the storm group, also in overall command of the shock group, was equipped with a signal rocket to be fired as soon as the storm group was inside the enemy position. This would trigger the reinforce-ment group, whose job was to finish off the enemy and secure the immediate area against enemy counter-attacks, then prepare the immediate tactical defence of the captured objective. This group was usually about between 20- and 25-strong, and heavily armed with light and heavy machine guns, anti-tank rifles, picks, shovels, mortars and explosives. The reinforce-ment group always contained combat engineers who played a critical role in both defence and attack. The reserve group, between 30- and 50-strong, was used initially as a blocking force against potential attack and as an immediate source of reserves should the first two sections encounter tough resis-tance. The soldiers alternated between service in each group to acquire an automatic understanding of the shock group as a whole. Reconnaissance, surprise and speed at close quarters were the ingre-dients of success and defeat. Reconnaissance was

Above: A German infantry and mortar unit moves quickly across desolate open ground. Their sense of urgency and vulnerability are clearly evident from their demeanour.

essential to identify minefields and enemy firing points or blindspots, as well as to find bearings in night fighting among the tangled maze of trenches, rubble and shattered buildings. Surprise and speed were heavily influenced by Chuikov's hand-grenade rule, which laid down that the distance to be covered should be no greater than 27m (30 yds), the distance of a grenade throw. Chuikov also trained his men on the basis of a three-minute timetable to attack, clear, secure and reinforce the position.

Equally, the men of 62nd Army were instructed to defend the position, as well as take it, without reliance on supplies and communication from their parent unit for at least 24 hours. The men of the rein-forcement and reserve groups were responsible for establishing an all-round defence. At first, machine gunners, mortar and anti-tank rifle crews would deploy on the ground floor, but, as the reserve group secured the area, they would then move up the building to acquire greater observation and fields of fire. The engineers would then lay mines to channel any enemy attack into a prepared killing zone, while the reserve group ensured the delivery of food and ammunition. If the area could be held for 24 hours, it was usually possible to relieve the shock group and integrate the position into the overall regimental, brigade or divisional position. Chuikov's 62nd Army would then inform the artillery commanders on the eastern shore, so that if the area came under major attack it could receive support. This was the method by which 62nd Army fought the battle of Stalingrad and, if inexperienced units could survive their dangerous early days in the city, they quickly became semi-independent fighting units skilled at infiltration and night fighting. They had to be in order to survive. The 6th Army was a powerful and resilient opponent, while the Luftwaffe ruled the day, making all movement fraught with danger. Nevertheless, Chuikov's tactical instructions ensured that, despite 62nd Army's terrible casualties, its men were trained for and understood the nature of the fight they were underaking at Stalingrad, in a way that German infantrymen did not.

However, as Clausewitz said, it is easier to defend something than to acquire it. Chuikov's pre-emptive attack of 27 September was met at 0800 hours by a devastating intervention by Fiebig's 8th Air Corps. The 62nd Army was pinned down for two hours. Gorshny's 95th Division – whose men had fought their way almost to the top of the Mamayev Kurgan – was now destroyed, while Batyuk's 284th Siberians made little progress and 13th Guards' assault was easily held. At 1030 hours, 6th Army delivered a devastating riposte which left 62nd Army reeling back towards the Volga. Chuikov's men faced 11 German divisions under the command of 6th Army, consisting of three panzer divisions (14th, 24th and 16th), two motorised divisions (29th and 60th), and six infantry divisions (71st, 79th, 94th, 100th Jager, 295th and 389th). The 16th Panzer was on Chuikov's far right in the Rynok suburbs, while the fresh 389th division attacked south-east towards the Tractor Factory from the north-western suburb of Gorodische.

On its right, 24th Panzer moved towards the Barrikady, while 100th Jager advanced on the Red October plant. The 295th Division renewed its tussle with the Soviet 95th Division for the Mamayev Kurgan. The 76th Division guarded the railway station, while, from the south, the 71st Division's objective was to move north behind 13th Guards and make a southerly approach to the area of the Red October. Meanwhile, the 14th Panzer and the 94th Division remained in the southern reaches of

the city, consolidating the German position south of the Tsaritsa.

The Luftwaffe ranged over the battlefield with devastating effect, destroying 62nd Army headquarters' communications with units bearing the brunt of the German assault. By the evening of 27 September, Chuikov understood the gravity of the situation. The left flank of Solugub's 112th Division defended by the 189th Tank Brigade had suffered a severe tactical reverse at the hands of 24th Panzer and had been driven back 1.6km (1 mile) towards the outskirts of the Barrikady settlement. On 24th Panzer's left, 389th Division had made excellent progress against the right wing of 112th Soviet Division towards the Tractor Factory flanked on its left by the River Mechetka. To the right of 24th Panzer, the 100th Jager had also driven the Soviet 23rd Tank Corps back to the western edges of the Red October workers' settlement. The 95th Division, pounded incessantly by a combination of German artillery, airpower and the attentions of 295th Division, was barely denying the Germans complete control of the Mamayev Kurgan. Chuikov commented in his diary that night: 'One more day like this and we will be in the Volga.' He knew full well that the following day would bring no respite, but an intensification of German attacks. In summary, by the evening of 27

Right: A German infantry section in the ruins of the workers' settlement west of the Red October factory. The improvised helmet camouflage is a testimony to the psychological impact of Soviet snipers.

Above: As the fighting continued in Stalingrad, while the Luftwaffe was diverted north of the city, the 62nd Army raced to get fresh men and supplies into the city using a variety of landing stages.

Above: Joining the Party: should a soldier (or sailor) who was a member of the Communist Party die, his family would automatically be officially notified. Non-members' families were often not contacted.

September, a day begun with a Soviet counterattack, the Germans had advanced nearly 2743m (3000 yds) and had more or less destroyed two Soviet divisions, the 112th and 95th. In response to the German shift to the north of the city, Stavka abandoned the division of responsibility for the city between Stalingrad Front to the north under Gordov, and Yeremenko's South-Eastern Front. On 28 September, Yeremenko's command was renamed the Stalingrad Front with responsibility for fighting in the city, while Gordov's old Stalingrad Front was disbanded and replaced in the same area north of the city by Lieutenant-General Rokossovsky's Don Front, which retained the mission of launching diversionary attacks on 6th Army's left flank. In his report to his superiors, on the evening of 27 September, Chuikov outlined the gravity of the situation, indicating the scale of the Germans' success in one day's fighting and his urgent need for reserves and above all relief from the Luftwaffe. He appealed to Nikita Khruschev (future General Secretary of the Soviet Union and denouncer of Stalin's crimes in 1956, but in September 1942 the Stalingrad Front's political commissar) for help. 'I make no complaint about our air force, which is fighting heroically, but the enemy has mastery in the air. His air force is his unbeatable trump card in attack. I therefore ask for increased help in this sphere – to give us cover from the air, if only for a few hours a day.' In the following days, Rokossovsky's Don Front would launch hastily prepared and bloody assaults on 6th Army's flank, but these provided little relief for 62nd Army.

During the night of 27–28 September, Rogachev's men ferried the men of Colonel Smekhotvorov's 193rd Rifle Division across the Volga into the city. There they deployed in the early hours among the cooking houses and outbuildings of the Red October workers' settlement and the southern edge of the Barrikady plant to meet 24th Panzer's attack. At dawn, Chuikov ordered a counterattack on the Mamayev Kurgan with two regiments of Batyuk's 284th Siberian and the one remaining regiment of Gorshny's 95th Division. The Soviet artillery on the eastern bank had been ordered to shell the summit of the Mamayev Kurgan throughout the night to prevent the Germans consolidating their temporary victory over 95th Division. As the barrage intensified, the Soviet troops attacked with the support of 8th Air Army and, in fierce fighting, battled their way to the summit. However, in the face of German counterattacks, they were unable to capture it. The Siberians lost 300 dead in this encounter, but, along with the shattered 95th Division, refused to be driven off the hill, denying control of it to the Germans. On 28 September, Chuikov's men defended their positions with more success and Chuikov felt that the German assault lacked the fluidity and cohesion between armour, infantry and airpower that had characterised the brilliant attack of 27 September. Indeed, more by instinct than judgment, Chuikov was correct: the Germans had suffered serious casualties where it mattered most in this kind of fighting – among the junior officers and senior NCOs. The Germans battered away at the 62nd Army on the Mamayev Kurgan and to the west of Red October and the Barrikady throughout 28 September, but with relatively little success. Keen to sustain the general momentum of the German attack rather than allowing the fighting to subside into trench warfare, Paulus switched the German *Schwerpunkt* (main thrust point) to the north-west of the city, to the Orlovka salient.

The Orlovka salient lay to the north of the Gorodische district. It protruded several miles into the German lines north-west of the Mechetka river, which met the south-easterly flow of the Orlovka river before both flowed into the Volga north of the Dzerzhinsky Tractor Factory. This lay immediately to the south of Stalingrad's northern suburbs of Spartanovka and Rynok. The salient was surrounded by German units: to the north on the Volga (occupying the positions it had taken on 23 August 1942) was Hube's 16th Panzer, with Major-General Kohlermann's 60th Motorised Division to its right. At the north-western tip of the salient between Gorodische and the village of Orlovka lay Major-General Magnus' 389th Division, with the left wing of Lieutenant-General Sanne's 100th Jager covering the salient from the village of Gorodische. The Soviet salient measured only 8km by 3.2km (5 miles by 2 miles) and was lightly defended by four regiments of Colonel Andryusenko's 115th Rifle Brigade and a single composite battalion, all that remained of Solugub's 112th Division. It was a natural *Kesselschlacht* and Paulus committed 16th Panzer and 60th Motorised from the north and 389th and 100th Jager from the south on 29 September. The pincers met on 30 September, securing an easy victory and reducing the Soviet positions in the north to a narrow bridgehead bordered by the Mechetka and the Spartanovka settlement. The Tractor Factory was now directly threatened from the north and north-west, but Chuikov resisted the temptation to weaken the Soviet defences elsewhere to rescue a lost cause in the Orlovka salient. Andryusenko's men continued to battle it out for seven days within the encirclement, as they fought their way south-east to the Soviet line. Simultaneously, the left wing of 6th Army beat off another attack from the Don Front, but despite maintaining the momentum of the German assault, it is difficult to see what Paulus had achieved through this operation. It was an easy victory in a city where such things did not exist.

On the evening of 28 September, within the city Chuikov urged his commanders 'to act with all possible haste in carrying out the engineering work to strengthen their positions, in building anti-tank and anti-infantry obstacles at the front and in depth, and in preparing buildings for defence action in the event of street fighting.' On 29 September, as German troops attacked the Orlovka salient, 24th Panzer crashed on towards the Barrikady and Red October settlement. The smashed units of Solugub's 112th Division retreated to the Silikat Factory under

Right: Two Soviet mortar men check their targets before ranging in their weapons. The high-angle, close-range tactical fire of weapons such as mortars was critical to both sides.

fierce attack, while to the west of the Red October settlement, the Germans succeeded in driving a deep wedge between the right flank of 193rd Division and the 112th Division's left flank on the southern edge of the Barrikady Factory. The German attack drove on, seeking to break the Soviet line and reach the Volga. The riverbank was but 1.6km (1 mile) away; if the Germans reached it, the 62nd Army would be broken in two and the Red October landing stage would be destroyed. Furthermore, if it breasted the shore, 24th Panzer would have the choice of turning right to link up with 71st Division or moving north up the riverbank behind the Barrikady, threatening Chuikov's headquarters and settling in position to meet German units moving south from the proposed assault on the Tractor Factory. In chaotic fighting, Smekhotvorov's 193rd threw in everything it could to stem 24th Panzer's attack, losing three regimental commanders and three battalion commanders in a single day. But it held the line. On the Soviet left, inconclusive, bitter fighting continued for the Mamayev Kurgan.

The night of 29–30 September was one of feverish activity. The Soviets worked frantically throughout the night to bolster shaky units before the Germans renewed their assault at dawn. The 42 Rifle Brigade under Colonel Gorshkov was deployed in the north-west of the city in the Rynok area. At the same time,

Above: German infantry amidst the rubble and destruction of Stalingrad's buildings and factories. It could take a battalion a whole day to secure a single building.

Major-General Stepan Guriev's 39th Guards Division – one of the toughest units in the Red Army raised from the 5th Parachute Corps – was deployed in positions directly to the west of the Red October on the right of 193rd Division and Batyuk's 284th Siberian. The Soviet reinforcement was completed by Major-General L. N. Gurtiev's 308th Division which was moved in behind Smekhotvorov's 193rd between the Red October and Barrikady, while its right wing held the south-western corner of the Barrikady Factory itself. These units were all under-strength like their German counterparts, but the Red Army's ability to ship nearly 10,000 men across the Volga at a time when German units appeared on the edge of victory underscores the significance of the German failure to cut off the battle in the city from the eastern bank.

On 1 October, 6th Army continued its attack along 62nd Army's perimeter. Concentrating its firepower on 193rd Division, and intensifying the pressure on 284th Siberian and 13th Guards, its aim was to splinter the Soviet defence further and reach the Volga before rolling up the broken pockets. It is a moot point as to whether Paulus would have been better advised to concentrate German power on one single thrust against 193rd Division, whose position buckled, but did not break. Paulus was trying to spread the Soviet defence to create room to bring the full weight of 6th Army's overwhelming numerical superiority to bear. Yet Chuikov, perhaps because he had so few men to spare as through any great tactical insight, refused to take the bait, and concentrated his forces squarely in the centre of Stalingrad in the area between Stalingrad-1 and the Tractor Factory. It was desperately important that 62nd Army's defensive perimeter retained some depth. This permitted the protection of the landing stages behind the factories and also the rapid movement of tactical reserves from dormant sectors to active ones. This was presumably what Paulus was trying to frustrate by committing Soviet troops along the line. During the night of 1–2 October, 100 enterprising men of the 295th German division worked their way south of the Mamayev Kurgan through the main Stalingrad sewer behind 13th Guards' position. It was only through a rapid counterattack that Rodimtsev's men repaired the breach.

By 2 October, 62nd Army held a 19.3-km (12-mile) bridgehead which fluctuated in depth from a maximum of 2500m (2734 yds) to a minimum of 500m (547 yds). As the battle moved north towards the Tractor Factory on 2 October, Chuikov was nearly

Above: A German infantry squad in Stalingrad's industrial district. The confusion of tangled metal and rubble helped the defenders, and each new part conquered required thorough checking.

Below: When fighting through the ruined factories of Stalingrad, the Wehrmacht came across some items of machinery supplied by German firms, evidence of the previous good relations between the two countries.

Top: Soviet bunkers dug deep into the west bank of the Volga, built to provide shelter from the constant German shelling and air attacks. Chuikov spent much of his time in bunkers such as these.

Above: While a machine-gunner keeps watch, three Red Army soldiers seize the chance for a meal in the ruins of the city. All supplies for the soldiers had to be brought across the Volga.

Above: A Soviet commissar inspects the defences outside Stalingrad itself. In the background, a Soviet mortar team pose for the camera. Mortars could be moved quickly, thus avoiding retaliatory air attack.

killed in a Luftwaffe bombing raid which hit his headquarters on the Volga. On the cliff above them, the bunker oil-drums, presumed empty by Chuikov's staff, were set on fire by German incendiaries. Thick, black, choking smoke and oozing, boiling oil threatened to asphyxiate or burn alive his men. As his staff fainted from the effects of smoke, Chuikov temporarily lost control of the battle, but, once order and communication with the outside world was re-established, the raging fire on the cliffs above was to prove something of a blessing in disguise. The Luftwaffe, convinced nothing could function beneath the billowing black smoke and fire, left Chuikov's headquarters relatively unmolested only 700m (765 yds) away from the heaviest fighting, as the battle for the Tractor Factory began on 4 October.

It was clear that the Germans were planning a major thrust on the Tractor Factory and the northern reaches of the Barrikady complex. During the night of 2–3 October, Yeremenko sent 62nd Army Major-General Viktor Zholudev's crack 37th Naval Guards Division. These commandos had been specifically trained in street fighting and were deployed on the western approaches to the Tractor Factory, with 308th Division to its left in front of the Barrikady, while between these two relatively fresh units the

remnants of Gorshny's 95th Division acted as a minor tactical reserve. The 37th Guards were followed across the river by the 84th Tank Brigade. Its 49 tanks, made up of 5 heavy KV-1s, 24 T-34s and 20 T-70s, were deployed on the right wing north of the Tractor Factory to bolster the 112th Divison. German divisions were also on the move: on 3 October, 14th Panzer and Hoffman's 94th Division were brought north. In the face of heavy attack by 389th and 60th Motorised, Solugub's 112th Division was forced to retreat over the Mechetka river towards the Tractor Factory. To the south of 112th Division, after 12 hours' fighting, Gurtiev's 308th finally conceded ground to 24th Panzer and withdrew to the gates of the Barrikady, incorporating into their position the Silikat Factory. On 308th's left flank, Smekhotvorov's seemingly indestructible 193rd fought off German attacks all day to the west of the Red October and, although forced to give ground, its line was not broken.

By 4 October, Chuikov estimated there were three German infantry and two panzer divisions fighting on a frontage of 5000m (5468 yds). The 14th Panzer had been brought into the line between the north-west corner of the Barrikady and the Mechetka river. It was to drive north-east on the Tractor Factory against Zholudev's 37th Guards. Hoffman's 94th Division had been deployed in the area between the Barrikady and the Red October. It was clear that the Germans were planning a major effort in this area against the Soviet 193rd and 308th Divisions, as the German 389th and 100th Jager divisions were on 94th Division's left. On 3 October, Hoffman recorded: 'We have entered a new area. It was night but we saw many crosses with our helmets on top. Have we really lost so many men? Damn this Stalingrad!' On 4 October, Hoffman wrote: 'Our regiment is attacking the Barrikady settlement. A lot of Russian tommy-gunners have appeared. Where are they bringing them from?'

On 5 October, the Germans made a supreme effort. Chuikov's staff estimated the Luftwaffe made 700 attacks on the Tractor Factory alone and a further 2000 in the general area. Fierce fighting developed between 14th Panzer and 37th Guards, with the Guards giving no quarter, but being slowly driven back. The 14th Panzer captured the Silikat Factory and cut off the 6th Tank Brigade on the Mechetka river north-west of the Barrikady.

Below: Stalingrad was defended by all able-bodied men. Here members of a workers' militia battalion observe the fighting in the distance during October 1942.

Nevertheless, elsewhere Soviet resistance held firm, as Hoffman complained: 'Our battalion has gone into the attack four times, and got stopped each time. Russian snipers hit anyone who shows himself carelessly from behind shelter.' As the Germans lined up a final decisive thrust between the Barrikady and the Tractor Factory, a crushing 40-minute bombardment from the 62nd Army's artillery massed on the eastern bank delivered a stinging riposte. The German attack was delayed and, in Chuikov's words, 'October 6 passed without any particular enemy infantry and tank activity.'

At the insistence of Stalingrad Front's command, Chuikov ordered a counterattack for 7 October by Zholudev's 37th Guards and, on its left, Gurtiev's 308th Division. It was forestalled by a renewed German offensive undertaken by 14th Panzer and 60th Motorised. The Germans broke into the workers' settlement west of the Tractor Factory itself. To save the position, Chuikov quickly ordered the trucks carrying 62nd Army's Katyusha rockets to reverse their rear wheels over the cliffs of the Volga's western bank to acquire the necessary elevation to hit the approaching enemy. As the Germans moved across the Mechetka, the screaming salvos of Katyushas wiped out nearly two battalions at the junction of 37th Guards right-wing and the sorely tried 112th Division. To the south, 193rd Division continued to defy the Germans, and on 8 October something of a lull descended upon the fighting for the city.

The 62nd Army had been driven back and was on its knees, but once again it had endured all the 6th Army and the Luftwaffe could throw at it. Paulus sacked von Wietersheim as the commander of the 14th Panzer Corps and von Schwedler from the 4th Army Corps for criticising his conduct of the battle. A visit from Hitler's personal adjutant, General Schmundt, boosted Paulus' morale. Hints were made that the Führer had great things in mind for him should he succeed at Stalingrad: Paulus would replace Jodl as Chief of the Wehrmacht Staff, while von Seydlitz-Kurbach was rumoured as Paulus' successor. This appeared to revive the flagging 6th Army's commander, who requested three fresh divisions for his 'final assault'. Although he received only four specialist combat engineer battalions, he set about planning the final offensive and regrouping his existing formations. Hitler was more and more obsessed with the conquest of Stalingrad, despite the fact that Zeitler's first act as Halder's replacement as Chief of the General Staff was to recommend that the battle for the city be terminated.

Chuikov's army had survived, but knew the battle was far from over. It was race against time to repair 62nd Army's defences. On 14 October, in a desperate frenzy driven by the approach of winter, 6th Army launched itself once more against the 62nd Army. The critical stage of the battle of Stalingrad was about to begin.

Above: In the middle of man's inhumanity to man, animals sometimes found a curious peace. The Wehrmacht was very dependent upon horses for artillery and supply. By December 1942, they would be eating them.

Below: By early October 1942, Paulus's 6th Army controlled 75 per cent of the city. The swastika flew in central Stalingrad, but 6th Army could not destroy Chuikov's 62nd Army.

CHAPTER 5

The Third German Assault on Stalingrad

14–29 October 1942

A lull of four days settled upon the city. Neither side was under any illusions about the scale of the task that confronted them when, not if, the fighting was renewed.

German commanders viewed the coming of winter with a despondent eye, while Chuikov wondered if his men could stand up to another assault. The approach of winter also threatened 62nd Army's lifeline to the eastern bank of the Volga. Once the river froze, supply across the ice would be relatively straightforward. However, as it was in the process was freezing, which would take several weeks, Rear Admiral Rogachev's ships would be threatened by massive ice floes, especially as crossings had to be undertaken at night without lights. Isolated from reserves, supplies and ammunition, Chuikov's army would not stand up to the 6th Army for long, no matter how bruised and bewildered the German troops felt in this city that had long since ceased to bear any resemblance to a place fit for human habitation.

Hitler focused upon Stalingrad with a maniacal intensity to the exclusion of the original purpose of the German summer offensive of 1942, the Caucasian oil resources. Stalin had always understood Stalingrad's significance, but increasingly the Red Army's heroic defiance against 6th Army took on global importance as a living symbol of the Allies' determination to subjugate Hitler's Third

Left: A disabled German tank with the bodies of four German soldiers. The tank has just been in combat with a Soviet T-34. German tanks suffered heavy casualties in the city, where they found it virtually impossible to manoeuvre.

Reich. On 14 October 1942, Hitler issued Operations Order No. 1, which halted all German operations elsewhere on the eastern front save for the Caucasus and Stalingrad. Stalingrad was now the objective by which German success or failure in the 1942 campaign was to be judged. As Clausewitz believed, war was fundamentally a moral contest of wills fought by intellectual and physical means. He warned that 'battle should not be considered as mutual murder, its effect is rather a killing of the enemy spirit than his men'. Paulus knew he had to break the will of Chuikov's 62nd Army, while Hitler believed – because he had to – that defeat at Stalingrad would destroy the spirit of the Soviet Union. The 6th Army was about to make a supreme effort, one that would take it and Chuikov's 62nd Army to the limits of human endurance.

Below: A Red Army counterattack on the outskirts of Stalingrad is supported by mortar fire. Constant minor attacks such as these wore down the Germans' morale.

As the fury of the second German assault died down, Yeremenko ordered Chuikov to improve the 62nd Army's position by launching a counterattack. The aim was to upset German preparations for a new offensive and to increase the depth of the Soviet position. All that separated German troops from victory was 3.2km (2 miles). If Chuikov was to defend Stalingrad, tactical mobility behind Soviet lines was critical in order that reserves were deployed effectively to parry German attacks. On 12 October, Major-General Zholudev's 37th Guards Division, in conjunction with one regiment of Colonel Gorshny's 95th Division, attacked the western outskirts of the Tractor Factory. In a city where progress was increasingly measured in feet and inches, it was a remarkable success. Zholudev's crack commandos, following an artillery barrage, advanced more than 274m (300 yds), while 95th Division moved forwards 183m (200 yds). The attack caught the 6th Army by surprise, but on 13 October Chuikov's men were

Below: Red Army SU-76 self-propelled guns parked under the treeline for protection from German reconnaissance aircraft. By October, the Russians were gathering material in preparation for a major offensive.

Above: As the battle for Stalingrad progressed, the Red Army brought more and more artillery pieces into action against the Germans. Here a gun team are receiving firing orders from a forward observer.

firmly rebuffed. Paulus was planning his retaliation and the temporary nature of 37th Guards' tactical supremacy became brutally apparent on 14 October.

At 0800 hours, the Germans launched a frenzied assault on the Soviet lines. The Germans regarded this as as a dawn assault, for Hitler insisted that the 6th Army operate on German, not Soviet, time. Three infantry divisions (Hoffman's 94th, 389th and 100th Jäger), two panzer divisions (14th and 24th) and four fresh, specialist combat engineer battalions – in total 90,000 men and 300 tanks on a 3-mile front with massive air support – plunged towards the 62nd Army. This was the day of reckoning for the 62nd Army as it reeled back at the hands of German units who were keen to avenge their recent reversals at the hands of 37th Guards. The initial German aim was to break through to the Volga between the Tractor Factory and the Barrikady Factory, pitting 14th Panzer against Zholudev's 37th Guards. On 37th Guards' right was 112th Soviet Division on the eastern bank of the Mechetka, with its right flank anchored on the Orlovka river as it moved to the Volga, north of the Tractor Factory. On the northern

side of the Orlovka, in the Spartanovka suburb, lay Colonel Gorokhov's 124th Rifle Brigade. On 37th Guards' left, Major-General Gurtiev's 308th Division was deployed in the Sculpture Park, directly in front of the Barrikady, while Gorshny's 95th was dug in behind the junction of 37th Guards and 308th Division as an immediate tactical reserve. To the south of 308th Division lay Smekhotvorov's battered 193rd Division, guarding the area between the Barrikady and the northern end of the Red October; to their left, east of the Mamayev Kurgan, was Batyuk's 284th, an opponent feared and respected by all German troops. Chuikov's extreme left flank, north of the Tsaritsa, was still held by Rodimtsev's 13th Guards.

The German attack was of a scale and intensity such as even this most cruel of encounters had not yet witnessed. Chuikov's staff counted 3000 attacks by the Luftwaffe, followed in by German infantry and armour. The main assault was on Zholudev's 37th Guards, Solugub's 112th and the right flank of Gurtiev's 308th. An apocalyptic scene developed as explosions merged into explosions, masonry tumbled, aircraft screamed overhead and German tanks ground their way forwards. Chuikov described the

Above: A German officer occupying a ramshackle fortified position in Stalingrad. He is armed with the Soviet PPSh-41 submachine gun, a robust weapon ideal for fighting in urban areas.

days fighting as of 'unprecedented ferocity'. In their slit trenches, the men of 37th Guards and 95th, 112th and 308th divisions sheltered as best they could from a rampant Luftwaffe. On the ground, the junction of 37th Guards' left and 308th's right was being pounded by the combined might of 14th Panzer, 100th Jager and 389th Division. At 1130 hours, by Chuikov's own admission, some 180 tanks belonging to 14th Panzer broke through Zholudev's 37th Guards advancing in the general direction of the Tractor and Barrikady factories. 14th Panzer's left wing swung north-east towards the Orlovka river through the workers' settlement of the Tractor Factory. By the afternoon of 14 October, Solugub's 112th found itself enveloped by 14th Panzer's breakthrough and fixed frontally by 60th Motorised on the opposite bank of the Mechetka. As in earlier encounters within the city, German commanders revealed their natural inclination to encircle and annihilate their opponent in a *Kesselschlacht*. It was both their greatest strength and their greatest weakness. As

112th fought on, 14th Panzer moved east to complete the isolation of Gorskhov's 124th Brigade north of the Orlovka in Spartanovka. The Soviet position was deteriorating by the hour under the incessant attacks of the Luftwaffe and 6th Army. Major-General Zholudev was buried alive and, although rescued, he was distraught at the destruction of his division. Gurtiev's 308th was in a perilous position. Its right bulwark, 37th Guards, had crumbled, while, to the west, 308th was engaged to its front by 389th and assaulted on its left flank by 100th Jager. If, or when, 14th Panzer moved south, 308th Division was vulnerable to encirclement.

By midnight on 14 October, it was clear that the Germans had won a significant tactical victory. The Tractor Factory was surrounded on three sides and German assault groups had made it to the Volga, splitting the 62nd Army once again. The German 6th Army had broken the 37th Guards Division and 112th Division, while Colonel Gorokhov took command of the remnants of 115th and 149th rifle brigades and merged them with his own 124th Rifle Brigade in Spartanovka. During the night of 14–15 October, 62nd Army shipped 3500 wounded men across to the eastern bank of the Volga. Chuikov was now faced with a critical decision. Should he commit his forces into holding the Tractor Factory, the loss of which could lead to the complete collapse of 62nd Army's right wing, but leave the 62nd Army exposed in all other areas of the city? On the other hand, dare he rely on the tenacity of Soviet troops in position to force the Germans to battle for every square foot of the Tractor Factory and slow their southern advance down the Volga? Chuikov's knowledge of, and the predictable nature of, the German tactical modus operandi, the *Kesselschlacht*, resolved the dilemma. He gambled that German attacks on the northern end of the Soviet bridgehead would be followed by powerful German thrusts in the south against Soviet positions weakened by troop redeployments designed to bolster the Tractor Factory. In each encounter thus far, the Germans had sought to reach the Volga and roll up the Soviet flanks. In his memoirs, Chuikov claimed: 'Paulus tactics were clear: he was trying to lure our main forces to the factory area and, paralysing them there, at the same time surreptitiously prepare an attack on a new sector.' Chuikov's ramshackle, if effective, reconnaissance network led him to believe a German concentration was emerging west of the Red October. Thus, he did

Above: German soldiers in a wrecked building. The strain on the soldier nearest the camera is clear. The man in the background appears to be wearing Russian uniform.

Above: A Romanian soldier bandages the hand of a wounded colleague. Romanian units were not of comparable quality to German formations, but often fought well when properly led and equipped.

Left: A Soviet light mortar unit deployed between two buildings. This shot conveys an excellent impression of the claustrophobic nature of street fighting and the limited observation available.

fighting was chaotic with no clearly defined front lines. It crept closer and closer to 62nd Army's command post behind the Barrikady Factory. Indeed, at one point, a small group of German soldiers infiltrated the Soviet defences and brought Chuikov's command post under fire. By the end of 15 October, 37th Guards and 95th Division had suffered 75 per cent casualties in 48 hours. The 62nd Army had once again been forced to concede ground in the north, but the rate of German advance was nothing compared to the 1828m (2000 yds) they had gained, in a matter of hours, on 14 October.

On the night of 15–16 October, Chuikov received reinforcements for the first time since the renewed German assault. However, a single regiment of Colonel Ivan Lyudnikov's 138th Siberian Division could not redeem the calamity that had befallen Chuikov's units. The 114th Regiment of Zholudev's 37th Guards numbered fewer than 200, while its sister regiment, 117th, had fewer than 50 men in its ranks. Chuikov's men were hardly able to confront the renewed German offensive in the early hours of 16 October. The assault involved five German divisions, three divisions – 14th Panzer on the riverbank, 100th Jager on its right and 305th Division behind them – moving south to the Barrikady. To the south and south-west, respectively, 94th Infantry and 24th Panzer would move on the area between the Barrikady and Red October. As the tired men of 37th Guards and Gorshny's 95th wilted under the combined air and ground assault of 100th Jager and 14th Panzer, the main burden of the northern assault fell on the 84th Tank Brigade. The left wing of 14th Panzer advanced on the northern approaches to the Barrikady, but 84th Tank Brigade's dug-in and superbly camouflaged T-34s opened fire at less than 91m (100 yds) and stabilised the Soviet position, at least temporarily, on the riverbank. The German assault groups milling around under heavy fire to reorganise their attack were then brought under devastating fire by the Soviet artillery over the Volga. Shells and rockets rained down on confined and exposed German units. However, to the west of the Barrikady, Gurtiev's 308th was under fierce pressure, trying to hold together 62nd Army's right. Further south, Smekhotvorov's 193rd and Major-General

not fall into the trap Paulus had laid for him, but that did not mean Chuikov's men could prevent Paulus from implementing 6th Army's plan.

The timely committal of reserves and ammunition had been, and was, critical to the survival of 62nd Army. Yet such was the intensity of the German assault by ground and air that nothing could be ferried into the city. The Luftwaffe had finally managed to halt the flow of men and matériel, albeit temporarily. On 15 October, the Germans threw fresh forces, the 305th Division, into the battle, making a total of six, and pressed on towards the Tractor Factory. In the isolated Spartanovka district, Gorokhov's three badly damaged brigades came under attack from the north, west and south by 16th Panzer, 60th Motorised and the left wing of 14th Panzer, respectively. The Soviet perimeter shrunk further as German units moving south from the vicinity of the Tractor Factory threatened the rear of what was left of 37th Guards and 95th Division. The

Guriev's 39th Guards beat off the attacks of 24th Panzer and 94th Division.

Chuikov's men needed reinforcement and Lyudnikovs full 138th Division came over the Volga during the night of 16 October. It deployed in support of the creaking right flank of 308th Division. Chuikov gave Lyudnikov categorical orders: 'You are personally responsible for closing the breach with 308th Rifle Division, securing its right flank, establishing close contact; under no circumstances will you permit enemy penetrations of the Barrikady Factory area and at the junction of 308th Rifle Division. You are responsible for the junction.' Chuikov sent 138th Division straight into battle. However, he then received news that Stalingrad Front's commander Colonel-General Yeremenko and his deputy Lieutenant-General Popov wished to visit his open-air headquarters, now located on the west bank of the Volga close to the Red October. Chuikov barely disguised his irritation at this untimely request, but naturally complied and moved through the city to greet Yeremenko and Popov. As he and other senior officers made their way, 'Everything round us was exploding, the noise was deafening;

Below: Soviet soldiers defending a building during fierce fighting in Stalingrad. Once again, there is an emphasis upon occupying the upper floors. The soldier in the far right corner has just been hit.

Above: A Red Army shock group in action. As members of the unit fight at street level, others scramble up the building to acquire better observation, and thus early warning of German counterattack.

German six-barrelled mortars were keeping the Volga under incessant attack. Hundreds of wounded were crawling towards the landing-stage and the ferry. We often had to step over bodies.' As Chuikov informed Yeremenko of 62nd Army's desperate need for more men and ammunition, north of the Orlovka, Colonel Gorokov's three amalgamated brigades fought a deadly game of cat-and-mouse in the smashed suburbs of Spartanovka. All day on 17 October, Gorokov's men came under continuous attack from the north by 16th Panzer, and were eventually driven south out of Rynok along the Volga, while harassed to the west by 60th Motorised. As 16th Panzer drove south, it reached the Volga knee where the river narrowed east of Spartanovka, before dividing into two channels as it moved south. Gorokov's men had nowhere to fall back to as German troops controlled the area south and west of Spartanovka.

The fighting intensified and, on 17 October, a telegram from Gorokhov to Chuikov requested permission to withdraw from the western bank of the Volga in order to continue the fight from Sporny Island in midstream. Chuikov's response was terse; he made it clear that any withdrawal would be considered an act of desertion. At the same time, the Germans persisted in their attempts to move south from the Tractor Factory towards the Barrikady and on to the Red October with its invaluable landing stage. The Luftwaffe laid down a murderous rolling barrage on 84th Tank Brigade, followed in by German assault

Above: Soldiers in the ruins of a factory in Stalingrad in late autumn. When the fighting reached its peak, buildings such as this would change hands several times a day.

groups supported by armour moving down the rail line. Chuikov recalled: 'Buildings were burning, the earth was burning and the tanks were burning.' Amid the mayhem, German troops infiltrated the defences of 84th Tank Brigade moving in behind the shattered 37th Guards and 95th Divisions. They progressed rapidly towards the north-western entrance of the Barrikady, where fierce combat erupted as Gurtiev's 308th fought for its life, literally, at the factory gates. Soviet troops prepared defences inside the nooks, crannies and workshops of the smashed buildings, ready to engage in weeks of gruesome, intimate hand-to-hand fighting. German and Soviet troops pursued each other in a deadly game of hide-and-seek often separated by no more than a wall, or a floor, in a mangled unrecognisable assembly line producing corpses, not machines. Lieutenant Wiener of 24th Panzer Division described the horrific intensity of the fighting as the battle for Stalingrad reached a ghastly crescendo. 'The front is a corridor between burnt out rooms; it is the thin ceiling between two floors. Help comes from neighbouring houses by fire escapes and chimneys. There is a ceaseless struggle from noon to night. From storey to storey, we bombard each other with grenades in the middle of explosions, clouds of dust and smoke, heaps of

Right: *A Wehrmacht veteran displays his various medals and awards.*
As well as the Iron Cross, he wears the Infantry Assault badge on his
left breast pocket, showing he has taken part in at least three attacks.

mortar, floods of blood, fragments of furniture and
human beings.'

German progress forced Chuikov and his staff to
search for a new headquarters in the middle of the
battle. The fight for the Tractor Factory was over and
giving way to the struggle for the Barrikady; with
Chuikov's command post only a few hundred yards
away, the risk of a surprise German assault or air
strike decapitating 62nd Army's chain of command
was too great. Chuikov must control the battle as
well as lead his men through it. The battle was at its
height; it was not the time for mistakes or futile hero-
ism. It was to be expected that the Germans would
renew their preliminary assaults on the Red October
with greater ferocity once Soviet troops were completely engaged within the Barrikady. Chuikov
decided to move south along the Volga during the
night of 17 October. However, in the absence of any
suitable position, he and his men had to set up the
command post in the open air, behind the Red
October, north-east of the railway line on the riverbank as it began to curve west. This area to the
south-west of the Red October was known by the
Germans as the 'tennis racket' because of the image
presented from the air by the circular railway. As

Below: Letters from home: a German soldier reads his mail whilst
sheltering in a bunker in Stalingrad. Few Germans expected the battle
for the city to have lasted into October.

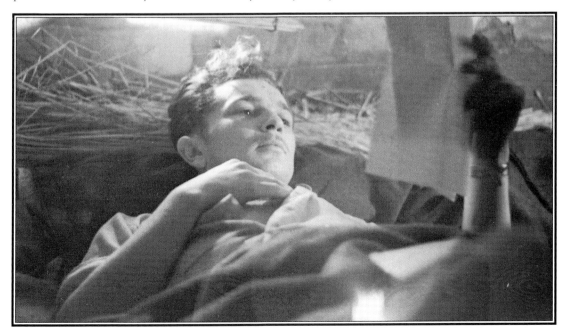

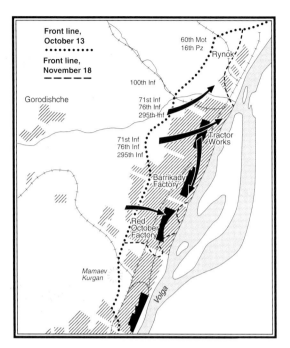

Front line,
October 13

Front line,
November 18

Gorodishche

60th Mot
16th Pz

Rynok

100th Inf

71st Inf
76th Inf
295th Inf

71st Inf
76th Inf
295th Inf

Tractor
Works

Barrikady
Factory

Red
October
Factory

Mamayev
Kurgan

Volga

Above: The third German assault on Stalingrad, showing the frontline positions on 13 October and 18 November.

Chuikov commented: 'We were barely half a mile from Mamayev Kurgan, our front line.' Chuikov's position was extremely vulnerable to an air attack, which fortunately did not come, until his engineers could dig bunkers. It was, despite its inauspicious beginnings, Chuikov's final command position, one he would not leave until 6th Army's surrender in February 1943.

On 18 October, the main German assault continued to focus upon the Barrikady and was spreading south to the Red October. Lyudnikov's 138th Siberian and Gurtiev's 308th came under attack at the gates of the Barrikady and in the Sculpture Park directly west of the factory. By the afternoon, a German regiment had broken through to the Volga, cutting off the Barrikady from the Tractor Factory, while German infantry divisions reached the rail line running the full length of the Barrikady's western walls. The Germans were moving slowly, but with a menacing intensity, across the open ground of the railway sidings, destroying pockets of Soviet resistance among the wagons and locomotives. To the immediate left of Gurtiev's men, the battle-scarred 193rd Division was under attack by Hoffman's 94th Infantry Division, trying to break into the southern end of the Barrikady.

The fighting was bitter. On 17 October, Hoffman recorded: 'Fighting has been going on continuously for four days, with unprecedented ferocity. During this time our regiment has advanced barely half a mile. The Russian firing is causing us heavy losses. Men and officers alike have become bitter and silent.' At dawn on 18 October, the recently constituted Don Front under Lieutenant-General Rokossovsky launched another diversionary attack on 6th Army's left flank. In common with its predecessors, it was a failure, but it did temporarily divert the Luftwaffe and fix German divisions in the north, away from the desperate struggle in the city, where an extra division might make all the difference between victory and defeat.

Nevertheless, the combined weight of 94th Division, 100th Jager and 389th told. At 1130 hours on 18 October, the right wing of Smekhotvorov's 193rd was swamped, leaving Gurtiev's 308th high and dry, and in chronic danger of encirclement and annihilation. Chuikov contemplated the unthinkable in a bridgehead merely 914m (1000 yds) deep: a tactical withdrawal. He could not afford the destruction of 308th Division, as that would enable a rapid capture of the Barrikady, but retreat must not turn into rout. Bold and decisive, Chuikov bit the bullet and ordered 308th Division to occupy new positions 274m (300 yds) closer to the Volga. Chuikov's reputation as a fighter permitted him to justify this decision to Yeremenko, and ultimately Stalin, but his isolation on the western bank in the middle of the battle gave him an unchallenged authority. Yet by his own admission: 'In our orders we could not and must not use such words as "withdrawal" or "retreat", so that the other commanders would not think that they could withdraw to new positions.' These comments and Chuikov's stern warnings to Gorokhov's rifle brigade commanders reveal the fragile nature of morale under the remorseless German assault. In such circumstances, a withdrawal was preferable to a clean German breakthrough and the destruction of another Soviet division. The struggle raged on as Paulus drove his men forwards towards the Volga in a desperate bid to break 62nd Army. The psychological significance of Stalingrad and the strain of battle became almost insupportable. Chuikov felt 'some inexplicable force drove the enemy to go on attacking. Fresh infantry and panzer units appeared and, regardless of losses, they rolled forwards towards the Volga. It seemed as though Hitler was prepared to destroy the whole of Germany for the sake of this one city.'

**Soviet infantryman, 62nd Army,
firing a Degtyarev DP28
light machine gun**

**Degtyarev DP28
light machine gun**

MG34 heavy machine gun

Kar 98 rifle

MP38 submachine gun

GERMAN SMALL ARMS

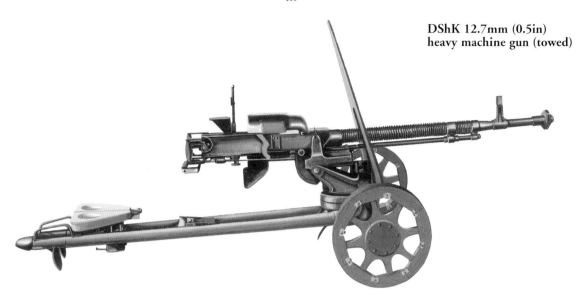

**DShK 12.7mm (0.5in)
heavy machine gun (towed)**

**Tokarev SVT-40
automatic rifle**

PPSh-41 submachine gun

SOVIET SMALL ARMS

Hungarian tank officer,
1st Armoured Division,
September 1942

Romanian infantryman,
3rd Romanian Army,
September 1942

Soviet officer, 62nd Army,
October 1942

German infantry officer,
Sixth Army,
September 1942

**PzKpfw IV Ausf E
medium tank**

**PzKpfw III Ausf E
medium tank**

**SdKfz 222
reconnaissance vehicle**

GERMAN AFVS, *FALL BLAU* SUMMER OFFENSIVE

SdKfz 250/10 halftrack mounted with 3.7cm PaK 36 gun

Sturmgeschütz III Ausf D assault gun

SdKfz 251/1 halftrack

GERMAN AFVS, WINTER CAMOUFLAGE

T-34 Model 1941
medium tank

KV-1 Model 1942
heavy tank

T-34 Model 1943
medium tank

SOVIET AFVS, OPERATION URANUS

M2 halftrack

T-70M light tank

SU-76M
self-propelled assault gun

SOVIET AFVS, OPERATION URANUS

GAZ-AAA truck

Austin K3 truck

ZiS-22(M) halftrack

SOVIET TRUCKS, WINTER CAMOUFLAGE

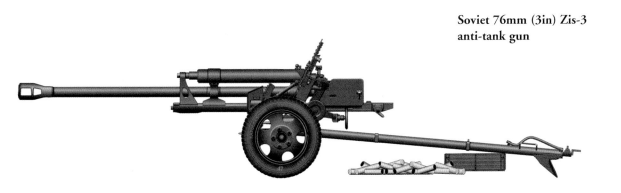

Soviet 76mm (3in) Zis-3 anti-tank gun

German 3.7cm PaK 36 anti-tank gun

German 5cm PaK 38 anti-tank gun

ANTI-TANK GUNS

Soviet ski trooper,
Don Front, November 1942

German infantry private,
Army Group Don,
November 1942

OPERATION URANUS

**German prisoner of war,
389th Infantry Division,
February 1943**

**Soviet officer,
13th Guards Rifle Division,
November 1942**

BATTLE FOR STALINGRAD

Yakovlev Yak-1
fighter

Ilyushin Il-2 *Shturmovik*
ground attack fighter

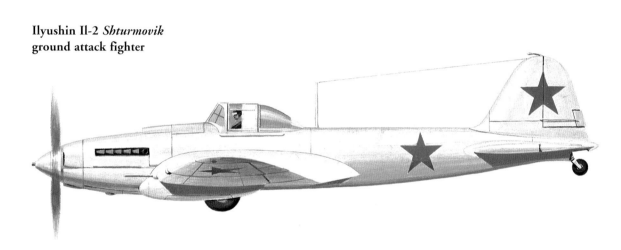

Lavochkin La-5FN fighter

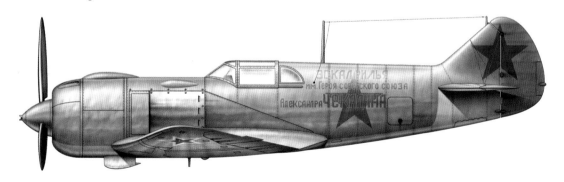

SOVIET AIRCRAFT

Messerschmitt Bf 109E fighter

Messerschmitt Bf 110C fighter-bomber

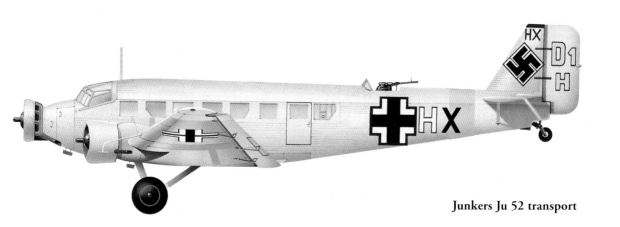

Junkers Ju 52 transport

GERMAN AIRCRAFT

**Soviet fighter pilot,
Red Army Air Force**

**German fighter pilot,
Jagdgeschwader,** *Luftwaffe*

AIRCREW

Above: A Soviet anti-tank unit in the thick of the fighting. Soviet troops manhandled these weapons around the battlefield and blunted the momentum of German attacks by inflicting heavy punishment.

Below: A Soviet anti-tank unit deployed within a building. The Red Army proved remarkably adept at such improvisation, often disguising tanks within rubble. The crew are well supplied.

By 20 October, the Germans had secured the Tractor Factory and pounded away at the Barrikady from all sides, and indeed within it, while a bitter struggle continued for Spartanovka. Soviet reconnaissance detected an ominous German build-up adjacent to the Red October, as preliminary skirmishes began in the area north of the steel plant and the Barrikady, and between Red October and the Mamayev Kurgan. The German intention was to fix Soviet units in place while reinforcing their right wing for a major assault on the southern end of the Barrikady and the Red October. Once again, Chuikov was forced to choose between defending areas virtually lost that his men had died for in their thousands, and husbanding scarce resources for the expected German onslaught. On 22 October, 94th, 305th and 100th Jager were launched against Smekhotvorov's 193rd and Gurtiev's 308th in order to pin them down as a prelude to the German assault on the Red October. The German objective was to fix the tired Soviet divisions in the centre, smash through the Red October and reach the Volga, splitting 62nd Army once again. German forces moving north up the Volga would meet German troops coming south from the Tractor Factory, before turning west, to destroy the Soviet troops trapped in the area of the Barrikady in an urban *Kesselschlacht* of annihilation. The Soviets retaliated by launching another diversionary offensive against the German flanks. This time the attack came from the south, led by Shumilov's 64th Army against 4th Panzer Army's right flank, but the change of direction did not induce a change of fortune, as Shumilov's men were

Above: Lieutentant-General Konstantin Rokossovsky at the Don Front command post on 19 November 1942. A survivor of Stalin's purge of 1937–38, he would destroy 6th Army in January 1943.

Above: A Soviet soldier enduring the winter conditions that dominated the fighting in and around Stalingrad between November 1942 and February 1943.

firmly rebuffed. Nevertheless, on 25 October, Shumilov's 64th Army sallied forth once again and hammered away at 4th Panzer for a week without conspicuous success. However, yet again, German troops were pinned on the flanks at a time when every spare man was needed in the city. On 22 October, Hoffman recorded: 'our regiment has failed to break into the factory. We have lost many men; every time you move you have to jump over bodies. You can scarcely breathe in the daytime: there is nowhere and no one to remove the bodies, so they are left there to rot.' The 193rd and 308th held on as the fighting inside the Barrikady grew more frenetic.

On 23 October, Paulus flung the 79th Infantry Division against the Red October defended by Guriev's tough Soviet paratroopers, 39th Guards. German armour and airpower supported the attack. As the German tactical *Schwerpunkt* moved south, a company – about 100-strong – of German infantry broke into the north-west corner of the Red October and engaged 39th Guards in the workshops of the plant. On 24 October, to the right, the Germans succeeded in overwhelming the central and south-western parts of the Barrikady Factory at the junction of the exhausted 193rd, whose left wing was also engaged by 79th Infantry, and Gurtiev's 308th, driving an ominous wedge between the two Soviet units. Although the fighting raged within the Barrikady and Red October, this supreme German effort was beginning to take its toll.

After 24 October, the intensity and scale of 6th Army's assaults diminished. The weather had become noticeably colder, while German night attacks, a feature of German assaults since 14 October, began to drop off, giving Chuikov's men much-needed respite. The nature of the fighting pitted German coordination by day against Soviet stealth by night, with engineers crawling forwards to throw satchels full of grenades against enemy strongpoints, quickly supported by assault parties. Hand-to-hand fighting was the rule rather than the exception, with flamethrowers, shovels and clubs the weapons of choice once the ammunition for more conventional arms ran out. Bullets and screams filled the factories as countless deadly combats took place within 457m (500 yds) of the Volga, but 3218km (2000 miles) from Berlin.

Two regiments of Colonel V. P. Sokolov's 45th Rifle Division had come across the river on the night of 26–27 October and, under the command of

Smekhotvorov's 193rd Division, had taken up positions between the Barrikady and the Red October. In a final surge of desperation, German troops drove part of Lyudnikov's 138th and Gurtiev's 308th out of the Barrikady, but still the Soviet divisions fought on. A desperate Hoffman recorded: 'our troops have captured the whole of the Barrikady factory, but we cannot break through to the Volga … we are absolutely exhausted; our regiment now has barely the strength of a company. The Russian artillery at the other side of the Volga won't let you lift your head.' Smekhotvorov's 193rd struggled to contain 79th Infantry while Guriev's men fought off German assaults inside the walls of the plant. Guriev's command post became the focal point of the conflict as 39th Guards was pressed back into the Foundry and the Calibration Shop. Chuikov rushed reinforcements into the Red October to stabilise the line. However, 79th Division's leading sections were now within 365m (400 yds) of the Volga and had the 62nd Army's landing stage under sustained fire.

Below: German soldiers in action within the city. German troops learned the black arts of city fighting quickly or perished. Both men are using captured Soviet weapons.

Yet, the 6th Army was at the end of its tether, worn down after two weeks of the most gruelling combat. The Germans held 90 per cent of the city and had the remaining sliver of Soviet territory – in places only a few hundred yards deep – under constant fire. Since 14 October, the Germans had conquered the Tractor Factory and the Barrikady, while 79th Division occupied half of the Red October. The 62nd Soviet Army had been divided, with three divisions – Zholudev's 37th Guards, Gorshny's 95th and Solugub's 112th – completely destroyed. In addition, Gurtiev's 308th and Smekhotvorov's 193rd, although still in existence, were clearly no longer fit for sustained combat, while Guriev's 39th Guards had barely clung on. Having borne the brunt of the German assault from the Tractor Factory to the northern reaches of the Barrikady, the 84th Tank Brigade no longer existed, its former presence confirmed only by scattered tanks and burnt-out shells. Colonel Gorokhov's bedraggled units had lost the unequal struggle for Spartanovka, with only a few minor units making it back across the Orlovka to Soviet lines. In total, in two weeks, 6th Army had destroyed the equivalent of seven Soviet divisions which, if not at full strength on 14 October 1942, had represented 75 per cent of

Chuikov's 62nd Army. Yet it was not enough: while, in the words of Jon Erickson, Paulus had impaled the 6th Army in his, Hitler's and Germany's manic quest for complete victory on the Eastern Front, the Luftwaffe's inability to strangle Chuikov's 62nd Army denied Paulus the triumph his men so earnestly desired.

If Chuikov's men in the heart of the city had fought magnificently, the unsung hero of this, the third battle for the city, was the massive presence of Soviet artillery on the eastern bank of the Volga. By early October 1942, despite the Luftwaffe's attentions, this Soviet artillery had become a key element in the struggle for Stalingrad. The heavy guns of Chuikov's artillery commander Major-General Pozharski – 105mm, 122mm, 155mm, 203mm, and even 280mm – had intervened decisively in support of 84th Tank Brigade on 15 October. They played havoc with the big, static target of 6th Army, as it sought to concentrate sufficient combat power to break 62nd Army. Paulus faced a dilemma borne of the Luftwaffe's inability to suppress the Soviet artillery: if German forces were not concentrated, his units would be unable to punch through the Soviet lines, but concentration in such confined surroundings made German troops vulnerable to Soviet artillery strikes. Chuikov's forward artillery observers, masterfully camouflaged in the ruined upper floors of Stalingrad's smashed buildings, became a vital part of 62nd Army's defence.

The Luftwaffe's failure stemmed from its inability to support both Army Group A in the Caucasus and Army Group B. Despite its tactical superiority, Richthofen's Air Fleet 4 did not have the means to close the Volga and isolate 62nd Army in the city. It attacked only intermittently – and never seriously disrupted – the Soviet rail network that fed men and matériel into the Stalingrad region. The Soviet distribution chain, by road and vessel across the Volga, was subjected to massive attack, but not permanently severed. Equally, although the Luftwaffe retained its tactical dominance of the Red Air Force it was, like 6th Army and Army Group Centre before Moscow, being drawn into a prolonged battle of attrition in the skies above Stalingrad. As the Soviet air force learned painful lessons, its performance improved. Colonel-General Novikov instructed his pilots to avoid dogfights and concentrate on harassing the 6th Army. A sustained night-bombing campaign against German airfields and field positions

was organised by Novikov's staff. The air offensive had several aims. First, to commit the finite and ever-decreasing resources of the Luftwaffe, both human and matériel, to an exhausting burden of round-the-clock operations for days, weeks on end. Pilots, ground crew, aircraft and airfield facilities were already on the limits of operational capabilities at Stalingrad before the 6th Army's encirclement. Secondly, as at Moscow, to deprive German soldiers and commanders of much-needed rest and sleep, of critical importance in any battle of attrition, let alone one on the scale of Stalingrad. Thirdly, by destroying German positions and sleeping quarters, to intensify the German soldiers psychological awareness and dread of the Soviet winter at a time when the weather was beginning to deteriorate. Fourthly, by forcing the Germans into a constant battle to control the skies over Stalingrad, and to defend their bases and the 6th Army, Novikov sought to distract the Luftwaffe from the Soviet lines of supply north and north-east of Stalingrad which would play a critical role in any Soviet counteroffensive. Fifthly, to improve the performance and confidence of the Red Air Force by a gradual escalation in the complexity and scale of operations, against such a feared and skilled opponent as the Luftwaffe. Finally, to support Soviet ground troops launching counterattacks north and south of Stalingrad and reduce the threat to 62nd Army's lines of supply with the period of ice floes approaching.

The Red Air Force was never the tactical equal of the Luftwaffe at Stalingrad, but, by and large, Novikov's men achieved their objectives. In the air war of attrition, Richthofen's Air Fleet 4 was never able to strike a decisive blow and, in attempting to achieve a multiplicity of objectives without the resources to achieve them, by November 1942, like 6th Army, it was but a shadow of its former self. The strain was beginning to show and, as on the ground, German strength and confidence began to wane; Soviet strength and optimism, the product of superior resources and better commanders, began to wax. The Luftwaffe's tactical approach at Stalingrad was not flawed in the same way as 6th Army's, but, like the German Army, it fell victim to the chronic lack of correlation between German ends and means, the fundamental flaw that bedevilled Germany's war in the east.

On the evening of 29 October, the fighting died down and 30 October was punctuated merely by the odd skirmish. The 62nd Army had survived the killing blow and fought the 6th Army to a shattered standstill. Chuikov quickly realised the balance of the psychological struggle was beginning to swing in their favour and planned a counterattack. The assault, undertaken by Sokolov's fresh 45th Division between the Barrikady and Red October on 31 October, gained only 137m (150 yds), but, like the Moscow counteroffensive of 5 December 1941, inflicted a savage blow to German morale. The supreme effort mounted by the 6th Army had failed and, as 1 November dawned, all German commanders knew that such an offensive could not be mounted again. The 6th Army was trapped, thousands of miles from German soil, in a seemingly unending battle of attrition against an opponent who refused to accept he was beaten. It seemed the 6th Army would be condemned to spend the winter among the shattered ruins of an unrecognisable city, a prospect to which no German officer or soldier looked forward. Yet the position of the 6th Army at the beginning of November 1942 was actually considerably worse than any of its men imagined. The Red Army was planning a counteroffensive, codenamed Operation 'Uranus' which, if successful, would not only pin the 6th Army within the confines of Stalingrad, but also destroy it.

Below: Soldiers of 8th Italian Army retreat in the face of Operation 'Small Saturn' in late 1942. The attack on Stalingrad had reached its high water mark on 29 October; months of suffering lay ahead.

CHAPTER 6

The Encirclement of 6th Army

Operation 'Uranus' 19–23 November 1942

General Paulus and German high command were aware of the vulnerability of 6th Army to a Soviet counteroffensive, particularly one from the north designed to trap it against the Volga.

As early as 12 September 1942, in conference with Hitler at Vinnitsa, in the eastern Ukraine, Paulus had expressed concern about 6th Army's exposed left flank. To the north-west of Stalingrad and directly to the south of the city, 6th Army's outer flanks were monitored by ill-equipped Romanian and Italian formations. Although the potential dangers of this situation were understood by the 6th Army and German high command, they could not be remedied unless Army Group A was withdrawn from the Caucasus. Once again, German military planning crossed swords with the plain fact that the German Army simply did not have enough men to cover the entire front.

At the tip of an enormous salient, bereft of reserves, 6th Army was trapped in an unparalleled battle of attrition. It was dependent upon a single rail line which crossed the Don at Kalach, a mere 96.5km (60 miles) from the Soviet front line. All 20 divisions of 6th Army and 4th Panzer were engaged in and around Stalingrad at the eastern extremity of the Don–Volga salient. The three panzer divisions of 6th Army – 14th, 16th and 24th – which were expected to protect 6th Army's flanks, were in no fit state to do so.

Left: As the Red Army prepared its counteroffensive, the fighting in the city between Chuikov's 62nd Army and Paulus' 6th Army continued to rage. However, the struggle was beginning to turn in favour of Chuikov's men.

Serious losses and the critical fuel situation rendered their apparent strength illusory. To the south, Hoth's 4th Panzer was a shadow of its former self. By November 1942, it did not contain a single panzer division. The 14th and 24th Panzer divisions had been given to 6th Army, while Lieutenant-General Heim's 48th Panzer Corps now acted as Army Group B's operational reserve within the Don bend. Yet the insurance offered to 6th Army was negligible. A full-strength panzer corps of approximately 60,000 was formidable, but Heim's formation consisted of 1st Romanian Armoured Division, equipped with Czech tanks of 1930s vintage, and 22nd Panzer Division, which had a reputation as the unluckiest and least effective panzer division on the Eastern Front. West of Stalingrad, 48th Panzer Corps was deployed as a 'back-stop' to 3rd Romanian Army, but Field Marshal von Weichs, Army Group B commander, needed Hitler's express permission for its use. Hitler also promised 6th Panzer Division and two infantry divisions, but, as these units were in France, December was the earliest that Army Group B could expect them to arrive.

General Dumitrescu's 3rd Romanian Army was deployed on the Don north-west of Stalingrad. On

Below: A Soviet machine-gun crew in the city. The high rate and wide arc of fire possessed by such weapons made them ideal for covering open ground with great economy of effort.

24 August 1942, Soviet counterattacks had acquired the Serafimovich bridgehead and a smaller one to the east at Kletskaya, both on the southern bank of the Don. The Romanians held a 160-km (100-mile) sector with eight infantry and two cavalry divisions, with the prospect of support from 48th Panzer Corps. In November 1942, 3rd Romanian's strength was 170,000, but each division covered 20km (12.4 miles) of the front, virtually twice the standard. The requirement to man a front bereft of substantial natural defences robbed the Romanian defences of depth and density. Equally, 3rd Romanian's anti-tank defences were dependent upon 37-mm (1.4-in) guns, regarded by German units as next to useless against modern Soviet tanks. Furthermore, the frozen Don provided little protection. During October 1942, Dumitrescu's proposal of a combined German–Romanian operation to remove the Serafimovich bridgehead was rejected because German troops could not be released from Stalingrad. It was an oversight the Germans would live to regret. To the south of Stalingrad on 4th Panzer's right wing, the German position on the Volga was held by 6th Romanian Corps, with 7th Romanian Corps further south on the Sarpa Lakes. General Constantinescu's 4th Army headquarters was to command the two Romanian corps from 21 November, but, when the Soviet offensive began, they were under Hoth's command. The five Romanian

infantry and two cavalry divisions had a combined strength of 75,380. As in the north, the Romanians were overextended and ill equipped, their defences lacking depth and density. Hoth's concerns about his right flank fell on deaf ears, because Army Group B simply did not have the means to strengthen the front as long as Army Group A remained in the Caucasus. In early October, the left wing of Stalingrad Front launched successful limited offensives in the Sarpa Lakes region. The rapid defeat of 4th Romanian revealed the exposed German position, but little was done to eliminate Soviet bridgeheads on the Volga, south of Stalingrad. A single German unit – Major-General Leyser's 29th Motorised – acted as a reserve, covering an area of 193km (120 miles). Hoth's two German infantry divisions were in Stalingrad.

The Romanian and Italian formations guarding 6th Army's flanks were not of comparable fighting quality to their German counterparts. Yet to blame them for 6th Army's encirclement and subsequent annihilation is to mistake cause and effect. The Axis formations permitted 6th Army to fight for Stalingrad, but it was Hitler who picked up the gauntlet. The Germans knew 6th Army's flanks were vulnerable, but the solution was perceived to be the capture of Stalingrad. Yet, by the end of October, it was clear a quick victory at Stalingrad was not likely. As reports of Soviet activity increased, the Germans appeared seized by an uncharacteristic lethargy, as if by ignoring the problem it might go away. A Russian counter-offensive was acknowledged as a possibility, but the

Above: Soviet troops begin Operation 'Uranus' on 19 November 1942. Operation 'Uranus' was well planned and executed; within 96 hours the Red Army had trapped 6th Army in Stalingrad.

Below: Field Marshal Erich von Manstein was given command of Army Group Don on 21 November 1942. The Wehrmacht's finest field commander, even his skills could not save 6th Army from disaster.

Above: Romanian troops man a machine gun post on the flanks of the 6th Army. The Romanians (and Italians) drew the brunt of the attack, and were poorly-equipped in comparison with their German allies.

Germans either would not – or could not – believe the Red Army capable of an operation of sufficient size and sophistication to trap 6th Army, a serious underestimation of Soviet fighting power. Thus, by November 1942, Army Group B was dispersed over a 644-km (400-mile) front with weak flanks, paltry reserves, inadequate supplies and vulnerable communications. Stalingrad consumed the German Army's attentions, but, if they were not looking elsewhere, the Soviet high command had been for some time.

The origins of the Soviet counteroffensive, Operation 'Uranus', went back to September 1942. As Zhukov returned to Moscow on 12 September to discuss the situation at Stalingrad, Stalin ordered Zhukov to keep pounding 6th Army's northern wing on the

Below: Operation 'Uranus', the ambitious (and successful) Russian offensive which cut off Paulus' 6th Army from Army Group South.

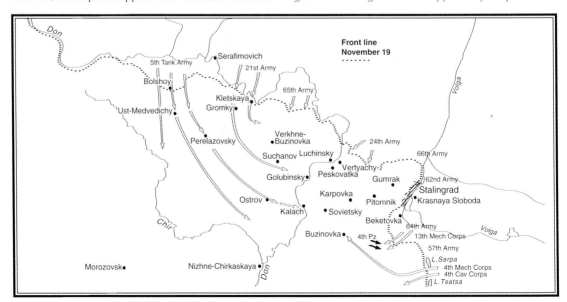

Above: German soldiers load fuel for 6th Army. The inefficient nature of the loading procedure and the grass airfield, present a powerful summary of the hopelessness of the airlift.

Don–Volga land bridge. While Stalin moved away to consult his own map showing the extent of German progress, Zhukov and Vasilevsky talked quietly about another solution. Stalin's sharp hearing provoked the inquisitive retort, 'And what does another solution mean?' Taken aback, Zhukov mumbled something about investigating other possibilities rather than limited but costly tactical assaults on 6th Army's flanks. Stalin instructed the pair to think over the situation.

At 2200 hours on 13 September, the 'solution' was revealed to Stalin. Zhukov and Vasilevsky indicated their belief that Army Group B and Army Group A were massively overextended. In their opinion, German means were insufficient to achieve the many objectives which Hitler had set them. German supply lines were stretched to the limit, and the exposed flanks of Army Group B defended by Axis formations offered the possibility of an operation to encircle 6th Army. However, it must be 'on a major scale', properly planned and equipped, unlike the chaotic improvised operations the Red Army had undertaken in the past. Stalin overlooked the oblique criticism of failed offensives he had ordered and pondered Vasilevsky and Zhukov's map. He requested an explanation of the envisaged concentration of forces at Serafimovich. Vasilevsky indicated that this was the springboard for a massive blow against the 'operational rear' of 6th Army and 4th Panzer. Stalin asked why the attack should not be made closer to

the Volga, namely further east. As Zhukov pointed out, that would enable German armour to disengage from Stalingrad and block the Soviet blow. An offensive further west would trap German armour, but give Soviet forces time to prepare a defensive front against German attacks from within and outside the Stalingrad pocket. Finally, Stalin raised the issue of whether the Red Army possessed the resources to execute such an operation. Zhukov informed an apparently satisfied Stalin that it would take approximately 45 days to deploy the necessary forces.

The 62nd Army was of critical importance. Its survival in the tactical battle of annihilation that was Stalingrad would fix 6th Army while the Red Army planned Operation 'Uranus'. It was, in effect, bait designed to create the right conditions for an operational counteroffensive. Thus, while Stalingrad was of massive political and symbolic significance to the Soviet Union, from a purely military point of view it was primarily a tactical means to an operational end. The 62nd Army was to be fed sufficient resources to hold the city, but victory at Stalingrad was never an end in itself for the Soviet high command. In contrast, Stalingrad had become the objective of the German campaign. By October 1942, oil had been forgotten:

Above: By now, the Red Army soldiers were better trained and equipped, especially for winter combat. The Wehrmacht was faced with a more formidable enemy than between June 1941 and October 1942.

all that mattered was victory on the Volga. As Stalingrad devoured German forces, 62nd Army was only given enough resources to ensure survival. This delicate calculation of resources, and the eventual destruction of the 6th Army, represents one of Soviet high command's most impressive achievements. In the words of H. P. Willmott, Stalingrad 'represented the first occasion in the Nazi-Soviet conflict when the Soviet army outfought and, crucially, out-thought the Wehrmacht, and it did so with no margin of superiority over its enemy'.

On 28 September, Yeremenko's South-Eastern Front became Stalingrad Front, the boundary of which ran from the northern suburb of Rynok, through the city and south along the Volga past the Sarpa Lakes. Lieutenant-General Gordov's Stalingrad Front was replaced by Rokossovsky's Don Front. On the middle Don, incorporating the Serafimovich bridgehead, a newly reconstituted South-Western Front under Lieutenant-General Vatutin was deployed against 3rd Romanian. Its existence remained a closely guarded secret. In early October, Vatutin, Rokossovsky and Yeremenko were informed of Stavka's intentions and, between 6 and 9 October, the basic framework of Operation 'Uranus' was laid down. The plan envisaged

the encirclement and annihilation of German forces in the Stalingrad region. Two armoured thrusts – one from the north moving south-east and one from south of Stalingrad moving north-west – would meet at Kalach on the Don, trapping the Germans against the Volga. The breakthrough operations would target 3rd and 4th Romanian Armies, north-west and south of Stalingrad, while Don Front would fix and engage 6th Army's left flank east of Kletskaya. The main blow in the north was to be delivered by Vatutin's South-Western Front, consisting of Lelyushenko's 1st Guards, Romanenko's 5th Tank Army and Chrisyakov's 21st Army, with a strength of 338,631. South-Western Front planned to attack as follows: the right wing of 1st Guards would prevent 8th Italian from interfering with South-Western Front's right flank as it moved south. On the left flank, 21st Army would assault 3rd Romanian's right flank with the help of Don Front's 65th Army. In the centre, 5th Tank Army was to transform tactical victory into operational success by penetrating deep behind Romanian lines into 6th Army's rear, where it would meet Soviet forces coming north from south of Stalingrad. It contained powerful exploitation forces: Major-General Butkov's 1st Tank Corps and Major-General Rodin's 26th Tank Corps, supported by six rifle divisions and the 8th Cavalry Corps. The 21st Army's 4th Tank Corps under Major-General Kravchenko was to cooperate with 5th Tank Army forces to ensure the destruction of Romanian forces. The deep operation had absolute priority; tank corps were to avoid tactical skirmishes. To secure the outer ring of encirclement, the right wing of South-Western Front was to establish a defence line on the Chir. Major-General Stepanov's 17th Air Army would cover South-Western Front from the air.

On South-Western Front's left, Rokossovsky's Don Front prepared to attack from Kletskaya and on the Don–Volga land bridge. On the right, Major-General Batov's 65th Army was to cooperate with Christyakov's 21st Army to sever 3rd Romanian's junction with 11th German Corps. Once through, 65th Army's left flank was to meet Major-General Galinin's 24th Army at Vertyachy, encircling 11th German Corps. The destruction of 11th Corps was not, however, the primary aim of Don Front's attack. It had insufficient forces to achieve this and, given the Soviet inability to break the German line north of Stalingrad during September and October 1942, was under no illusions. The main aim of Don Front's 65th, 24th and 66th Armies was to prevent German forces

Right: The strain and anger on the face of this sorely pressed German soldier still fighting in the city of Stalingrad are very clear. The hunter had now become the hunted.

interfering with South-Western Front. Anything else would be a bonus. Air support would be provided by Major-General Rudenko's 16th Air Army. The Stalingrad Front's southern thrust was to be undertaken by Major-General Shumilov's 64th Army, Major-General Tolbukhin's 57th Army and Major-General Trufanov's 51st Army. Shumilov's 64th Army, closest to the city, would fix 4th German Corps in Stalingrad. On its left, Tolbukhin's 57th and, further south, Trufanov's 51st Army would break into 6th Romanian Corps. Once the breach was complete, 57th Army's 13th Tank Corps would strike north-west in conjunction with 51st Army's exploitation group – 4th Mechanised Corps – towards Kalach. The 4th Cossack Cavalry Corps of 51st Army, together with three infantry divisions – 126th, 302nd and 91st – would move south-west on Kotelnikovo to form an outer ring of defence. The dates of the attack were tentatively set as 9 and 10 November for the north and south, respectively, the time difference being related to the relative distances to be travelled by South-Western Front and Stalingrad Front, roughly 128km and 97km (80 miles and 60 miles), respectively.

The Germans were not completely surprised by Operation 'Uranus', but were shocked by its scale and ambition. There are several explanations for the Germans' lack of preparation, one of which was Soviet *maskirovka. Maskirovka* was a process of camouflage,

Below: Soviet field commanders consult maps; orientation on the featureless snow-covered steppe was a significant problem and had to be checked regularly.

Above: A powerful image indicating the difficulty and futility of the Luftwaffe's airlift. The soldiers are fixed on the aircraft. It is almost as though they are expecting something disastrous to happen.

disinformation and deception designed to disguise the scale, timing and direction of Soviet attacks. Stavka understood the impossibility of entirely disguising their intention to attack, but the success of *maskirovka* is borne out by Chief of the German General Staff, Colonel-General Zeitzler. On 28 November 1942, he commented that 'among the distinctive characteristics of Russian preparations for the offensive one must include excellent concealment of all units participating in the attack especially the tank formations'. A staggering effort was required to prepare 1,050,000 men, 13,540 guns and 894 tanks, in two months, whilst hiding Soviet intentions. Numerous bridges had to be built across the Volga, while human signallers with lanterns directed one-way rail traffic at night, with trains passing every 12 minutes. Novikov's air armies prevented sustained Luftwaffe reconnaissance or systematic interdiction of Soviet rail traffic. Soviet formations were moved at night and camouflaged by day under strict radio silence, while false radio nets were created to mislead and reassure the Germans. Soviet army commanders were kept in the dark until early November, and the troops did not receive orders until the night before the offensive. Security was reinforced by the absence of written orders; wherever possible instructions were passed by oral briefings and map exercises. The Red Army was broadly successful in its *maskirovka* campaign, but the Germans had several warnings that a Soviet offensive was imminent.

Foreign Armies East, the German Army's intelligence unit, headed by Colonel Reinhard Gehlen, was aware of Soviet movement, but failed to decipher the scale and significance of Operation 'Uranus'. On 12 November, Gehlen informed Army Group B that 'an attack in the near future against Rumanian Third Army with the objective of cutting the railroad to Stalingrad and thereby threatening the German forces further east and compelling a withdrawal from Stalingrad must be taken into account'. Yet Gehlen failed to appreciate that Soviet intentions amounted to more than cutting 6th Army's supply lines and forcing a withdrawal. Nor did Gehlen appreciate the scale of Soviet preparations south of Stalingrad. If the Germans had chosen to look, there was evidence of the ambition and imminence of the Soviet offensive. However, German strategic intelligence did not believe that the Soviets had the capacity to launch such an operation, while it was assumed Stalingrad's capture would redeem the difficulties of the German situation. Equally, Gehlen's sources informed him of Soviet preparations for a massive counteroffensive west of Moscow.

The Germans fell victim to their understanding of the value that the Soviets, especially Stalin, placed on Moscow. In September 1942, Zhukov believed that the Red Army's strategic reserves would enable it to launch two counteroffensives: Operation 'Uranus' around Stalingrad, and Operation 'Mars' west of Moscow. As David M. Glantz recounts in his book, *Zhukov's Greatest Defeat*, on 26 September Stalin announced: 'You may continue to plan your offensive. Conduct two efforts. Zhukov will control the Rzhev operation and Vasilevsky the operation at Stalingrad.' The objective of 'Mars' was to annihilate 9th German Army in the Rzhev salient. If successful, Zhukov planned to transform operational into strategic victory by launching Operation 'Jupiter'. The aim of 'Jupiter' was to destroy Army Group Centre, while 'Uranus' was to be followed by Operation 'Saturn' which, by reaching Rostov, would destroy the rest of Army Group B and trap Army Group A in the Caucasus.

The scale of the Red Army's 'cosmic' strategic design was breathtaking. German intelligence never considered a strategic conception of this size and assumed two simultaneous counteroffensives, such as 'Mars' and 'Uranus', were beyond the Red Army. This induced the Germans to downgrade Operation 'Uranus' in comparison with 'Mars'. As Glantz demonstrates, on 6 November 1942, Gehlen nailed his colours to the mast. His report stated that 'the point of main effort of the coming operations looms with increasing distinctness in the area of Army Group Centre'. He concluded: 'The enemy's attack preparations in the south are not so far advanced that one must reckon with a major operation here in the future simultaneously with the expected offensive against Army Group Centre.' On 17 November, Stalin confirmed that 'Uranus' would commence on 19 November, while 'Mars' would begin on 25 November 1942. The two Soviet offensives, although part of a very ambitious strategic design, were not deliberately formulated to act as a foil for each other; German underestimation of Soviet means and capability, as well as their own inability to cover the front, ensured this happened. In being forced to choose, Gehlen's judgment was that

Above: A 'hiwi': some captured Russian soldiers or deserters agreed to do menial service for the Germans, in return for bare survival rations or pay. The fate of such men was a tragic one.

any Soviet offensive in the south would be of secondary importance to the attack on Army Group Centre. The German preoccupation with Operation 'Mars' indirectly facilitated Soviet success in the south, but the heart of the problem was the lack of correlation between German ends and means. As 'Uranus' and 'Mars' exploded upon Army Group B and Army Group Centre, respectively, the 450,000 men of Army Group A were stranded in the Caucasus.

Gehlen's warning to Army Group Centre ensured that Operation 'Mars', in sharp contrast to 'Uranus', was a disaster. Between 25 November and 23 December, General Konev's Western Front and General Purkhaev's Kalinin Front suffered 100,000 killed and more than 235,000 wounded. General Model's 9th Army won one of the great German defensive victories of the war. It was later claimed that 'Mars' was merely a diversionary operation, designed to lure German strategic reserves from Operation 'Uranus'. The historical record revealed by David M. Glantz does not support this conclusion. Operation 'Mars' was a massively significant operation in its own right, in which 668,000 men and 2000 tanks were committed, with 415,000 men and 1265 tanks

Above: German soldiers stand in line to unload small boxes of supplies brought in by the Luftwaffe. How Hitler and Göring planned to supply 250,000 men for several months was a question never answered.

Above: A German soldier with a container of supplies that is either about to be loaded into the air-drop canister behind him or has been received.

ready to be used in 'Jupiter'. In Operation 'Uranus', Vasilevsky committed 700,000 men and 1400 tanks, with a further 400,000 men and 1200 tanks in what became Operation 'Little Saturn' in December 1942. Operation 'Mars' diverted German attention and resources from 'Uranus' more by accident than design. Nevertheless, the disaster of 'Mars' at the hands of Zhukov – one of the most talented commanders – could not hide the fact that a new Red Army was evolving in the autumn of 1942.

Zhukov and Vasilevsky were at the forefront of these developments. Stalin now permitted Stavka representatives, usually Zhukov and Vasilevsky, to go out into the field to ensure Stavka's strategic conception was translated into action on the ground. They reported to Stalin every evening and were disliked – especially the bullying Zhukov – by Front commanders as interfering and unreasonably demanding. Nevertheless, the system was considerably better than the distant command practised by Stalin in 1941 and 1942. Equally, by October 1942, incompetent Stalinist cronies such as Budenny, Voroshilov and Kozlov had been removed. They were replaced by younger, more competent generals such as Zhukov, Vasilevsky, Vatutin, Rokossovsky, Yeremenko, Petrov, Konev and Malinovsky, who would lead the Red Army to Berlin. They received support from a new generation of army commanders who rose out of the ashes of disaster. Yet it would have counted for nothing had Stalin denied his commanders sufficient freedom to exercise their talents. As Hitler began to interfere in the smallest tactical detail, Stalin began to listen to his generals. On 9 October 1942, Stalin made the military commander master in his own house, relegating political commissars to a level of definite subservience. The psychological significance of this recognition by Stalin of the professional worth and importance of the Red Army's officer corps cannot be overestimated. It is no coincidence that within weeks of Stalin's decision during 'Uranus', if not within 'Mars', senior Soviet commanders began to display a new level of initiative and flexibility.

As Stalin rehabilitated the Soviet officer corps, he tolerated an unofficial renaissance in the Soviet military ideas of deep battle and deep operations developed in the 1920s and 1930s. Soviet manoeuvre warfare was not a pale imitation of German methods. In the aftermath of World War I, Soviet military theorists concluded strategic victory could only be achieved through successive operations over a number

Above: The power of the Russian winter. The desolate wasteland is the mighty Volga, a mile wide. The decline of the Luftwaffe made supplying 62nd Army relatively straightforward by December 1942.

of months, or years. In the early 1920s, the theory of successive operations became a formal part of Soviet military doctrine. In Soviet eyes, the scale and duration of the fighting in World War I confirmed their suspicions following the Russo-Japanese War of 1905 that the word 'tactics', originally coined to describe the fighting of small pitched battles, was inadequate to describe the modern scale of fighting. In January 1905 at the battle of Mukden, three Russian armies numbering 300,000 troops opposed six Japanese armies of 270,000. The fighting lasted six days, covering a front of 160km (100 miles). In 1907, Major (later General) Alexsandr Svechin historically described this scale of fighting as the operational level of war, occupying an intermediate position between strategy and tactics. As such, Soviet doctrine was at odds with the strategic concept of the *Vernichtungschlacht*, and the German belief that strategic victory could be achieved purely through tactical excellence in battle. Therefore, by the early 1920s, the Soviets believed strategic victory was the result of operational victory which, in turn, was the product of tactical victories in battle. In contrast to the Wehrmacht, Soviet military doctrine explicitly acknowledged the operational level of war, but, if strategic victory was the product of successive operations, the key was to ensure they were successful. In 1923, Svechin labelled the art of planning the sequence of battles that would achieve operational objectives 'the operating art', known in English as Soviet Operational Art. Svechin argued that tactics makes the steps from which operational leaps are assembled. Strategy points out the path.

In 1926, Marshal Tukhachevsky confirmed the inherent connection between successive and deep

operations. He believed that 'modern operations involve the concentration of forces necessary to strike a blow and the infliction of continual and uninterrupted blows throughout an extremely deep area. The nature of modern weapons and battle is such that it is an impossible matter to destroy the enemy's manpower in one blow in a single day. Battle in modern operations stretches out into a series of battles not only along the front but also in the depth.' Tukhachevky's contribution was followed in 1929 by that of General Triandafillov. In *The Nature of the Operations of Modern Armies*, he laid the foundations of deep battle and deep operations. He believed that the tactical strength of frontline defences encountered in World War I sprang fundamentally from their operational rear, that is the network of roads, rail, supplies, communication, organisation and command that gave life and direction to the fighting troops. Fighting spirit and tactical ability were vital, but, without the systemic support provided by the operational rear, victory could not be achieved in a prolonged war. In Triandafillov's eyes, the key to military victory was to break the enemy's line and strike deep into the operational rear. At the heart of his theories was the tactical idea of deep battle, the first step towards an operational leap. Once the strategic commander had determined why, where and when an operation should take place, Soviet front commanders would deliberately deploy on a broad front. This was designed to force the enemy to defend his entire frontage, diluting the depth and density of his defences and increasing the chances of breakthrough in the deep battle. As the enemy commander dispersed his forces, *maskirovka* would leave him uncertain of the Soviet main effort and unable to concentrate his reserves. As Soviet commanders secretly concentrated overwhelming forces on designated breakthrough sectors, a general assault across the front would fix the enemy formations. Simultaneously, artillery, air-power and airborne troops would strike and land deep in the enemy's tactical position to ensure localised tactical annihilation in the breakthrough sectors. These shock forces, in conjunction with massive concentrations of armour and infantry, would smash through and dislocate enemy commanders from their men, inducing the enemy's tactical defences to collapse.

The purpose of deep battle was to create optimum conditions for the deep operation. Deep battle emphasised tactical annihilation, whereas the deep operation concentrated on operational manoeuvre executed by Soviet mobile forces moving through the breach. In Triandafillov's words, the deep operation was to be 'a series of consecutive or simultaneous blows that would fall upon the whole enemy force, disrupt his organisation, command and control, reserves, movement and thereby deprive him of the possibility of

Below: Soviet troops fighting in the workshops of the Red October in December 1942. As 6th Army's strength faded, Chuikov's 62nd Army began to claw back territory lost during the early weeks of the battle.

further serious opposition'. Tempo and manoeuvre were to inflict 'systemic paralysis'. If the strategy were successful, the enemy would be levered out of the area in dispute before he was annihilated, turning tactical victory into operational victory for the Red Army. Therefore, Soviet manoeuvre war was different in conception and execution from German Blitzkrieg. The German Army engaged in tactical manoeuvre to encircle and physically annihilate the enemy in a cauldron battle. In contrast, Soviet theory proposed tactical annihilation as a means to operational manoeuvre. In 1937, Tukhachevksky and others associated with these doctrinal developments perished in Stalin's purge. As Stalin's reactionary cronies imposed outdated methods upon the army, the concepts of deep battle and deep operations gathered dust while war approached. In 1941, as the Red Army reeled under the German onslaught, it did what it could to survive. Most Soviet commanders and units did not possess the skill, equipment or opportunity to conduct offensive operations as envisaged by Triandafillov and Tukhachevsky.

Ironically, the operational encirclement and subsequent annihilation of Axis troops at Stalingrad was not typical of Soviet manoeuvre warfare: indeed, in some respects, it had more in common with German methods. It was a piece of creative military art provoked by the ability of new commanders such as Zhukov and Vasilevsky, as well as the German preoccupation with Stalingrad. Nevertheless, the methods

by which the Red Army created and defended the Stalingrad cauldron, as well as its subsequent destruction, make this a distinctly Soviet operation. Stalin never acknowledged the debt which Soviet victory owed to the past, but there is little doubt the new generation of Soviet commanders drew inspiration from interwar Soviet military thought.

On 11 November, Zhukov and Vasilevsky informed Stalin of their shared belief that 'there is now every reason for the offensive to be opened by the troops of South-Western and Don Fronts on the nineteenth, and by the troops of the Stalingrad Front on the twentieth'. Meanwhile, on 8 November, in a speech to old party comrades at the Munich Beer Hall, Hitler belittled Soviet resistance in Stalingrad and claimed victory was near. At 0630 hours on 11 November, 6th Army attacked 62nd Army once again. The attack coincided with the appearance of ice floes on the Volga. The remaining strength of 6th Army was hurled into battle: five infantry divisions – 389th, 305th, 79th, 100th Jager and 44th – plus 14th and 24th Panzer assaulted the Russian line. The Germans reached the Volga between the Red October and the Barrikady, splitting the 62nd Army for the third time. On the Volga, behind the Barrikady, Lyudnikov's 138th Siberian Division was cut off from the rest of 62nd Army. The Germans renewed the offensive on 12 November, but, after making little progress, 6th Army's attack declined. As skirmishing continued, 62nd Army held its ground. Few in the city had any inkling of the dramatic turn of events that awaited them.

On 17 November, Zhukov left Stalingrad to command the ill-fated Operation 'Mars'. Vasilevsky was immediately faced with a bizarre crisis. Stalin had received a letter from Major-General Volsky pleading with him to cancel 'Uranus' because it was doomed to failure. Volsky was no ordinary corps commander: he commanded 4th Mechanised Corps which had been assigned a key role in the offensive. Volsky was a protégé of Vasilevsky and, when questioned by Stalin, Vasilevsky could only say he regarded Volsky as a capable officer whose corps was in excellent trim, but that he was at a loss to explain his actions. In Vasilevsky's presence, Stalin telephoned Volsky and, to Vasilevsky's utter astonishment, was not unduly harsh with Volsky. Stalin, the torturer of generals, declared Volsky had given his word he would fulfil his mission. Vasilevsky was to execute Operation 'Uranus' as planned, but keep an eye on Volsky. Stalin's tolerance of Volsky's amazing antics

Above: Paulus returns to the pocket on 21 November 1942. At this early stage, he hoped Hitler would permit him the freedom to break out, but when the Führer refused, Paulus could not disobey.

and Vasilevsky's faith in his abilities were eventually endorsed as Volsky carried out his mission in 'Uranus'.

As the South-Western, Don and Stalingrad Fronts prepared themselves for the operation that would transform the course of the war, at midnight on 18 November, Chuikov was told of the coming offensive and told to stand by. At 0720 hours on the morning of 19 November 1942, the South-Western and Don Fronts issued the code word 'Siren'. Thousands of Soviet artillery men loaded their weapons. At 0730 hours, the guns opened a massive 80-minute bombardment. As it continued, Soviet armour and infantry moved up into the line. At 0848 hours, the guns launched their last salvo; at 0850 hours, South-Western and Don Fronts attacked on a 320-km (200-mile) front. However, the three designated breakthrough sectors totalled only 23km (14 miles). On the right, Lelyushenko's 1st Guards pinned 8th Italian Army as Romanenko's 5th Tank Army bore down on 3rd Romanian's left wing from Serafimovich bridgehead. At Kletskaya, Christyakov's 21st Army and Batov's 65th Army, from the Don Front, attacked the right wing of 3rd Romanian, while Galinin's 24th and Zhadov's 66th attacked on the Don–Volga land bridge.

By noon, Soviet shock forces had broken through General Dumitrescu's 3rd Romanian Army, but Don Front encountered stiff German resistance. Army Group B initially assumed Don Front was conducting the main assault and deployed 16th Panzer against it, rather than 21st Army bursting out of the Kletskaya bridgehead further west. At noon, Christyakov committed Kravchenko's 4th Tank Corps and Pliev's 3rd Cavalry Corps. As Batov's 65th Army battled with the right wing of 3rd Romanian Army, 4th Tank Corps and 3rd Cavalry Corps drove through the Romanians. On the left, 3rd Romanian put up fierce resistance against the 5th Tank Army's right wing, but at 1230 hours Romanenko ordered his mobile groups to attack. On the right, Major-General Butkov's 1st Tank Corps finally overwhelmed 47th Romanian Division, while on its left Major-General Rodin's 26th Tank Corps broke through, followed by the 8th Cavalry Corps. The line had been breached and, although several Romanian units continued to fight bravely for several days, the die was cast. Obeying their instructions to avoid tactical encounters and strike for Kalach with all speed, South-Western Front's operational groups charged on.

Hitler gave permission for Heim's 48th Panzer Corps to engage, but it was directed against Don Front before it was realised that South-Western Front was the main Soviet effort. The trials and tribulations of 22nd Panzer continued; to ensure a quick engine start, many crews had dug pits lined and covered with straw to insulate armour against the cold. Yet when the call to action came, more than half 22nd Panzer's 100 tanks would not start because field mice in the warm straw had chewed up the tanks' electrical wiring. As 48th Panzer Corps moved west through the night, it lost contact with 1st Romanian Armoured. Therefore, instead of being confronted with a powerful armoured fist, South-Western Front's mobile groups were engaged in a piecemeal and confused fashion. In the early hours of 20 November, Rodin's 26th Tank ambushed 1st Romanian and, having shot up the unfortunate Romanians, crashed on towards Kalach. The rest of 48th Panzer Corps ran into Butkov's 1st Tank Corps and, after a messy scrap, was forced back. As Soviet armour advanced, 48th Panzer retired on a parallel course until Hitler ordered it north-west to rescue General Lascar's encircled Romanians. Army Group B ordered Paulus to halt operations in Stalingrad and deploy his panzer divisions west. As the Germans took defensive precautions to protect their northern flank and western lines of supply and communication, they had little inclination of the southern blow Vasilevky was about to inflict on them.

At dawn on 20 November, south of Stalingrad, 64th, 57th and 51st Armies deployed on a 201-km (125-mile) front. However, poor visibility delayed the

Above: A face of bitter resignation. As Stalingrad burns around him, this German soldier endures the struggle. He seems adequately supplied, but soon 6th Army would suffer serious malnourishment.

assault. In Moscow, a tense Stavka ordered Yeremenko to get on with it, but he replied that he was on the spot and it was his decision. At 0920 hours the fog lifted and, at 1000 hours, the Soviet guns opened up. The 6th Romanian Corps crumbled and, by noon, Tolbukhin's 57th Army committed 13th Tank Corps, while on the left Trufanov's 51st Army deployed Volsky's 4th Mechanised Corps. As both moved northwest, 4th Cossack Cavalry Corps moved south-west towards the Aksai river. The advance of 13th Tank Corps was abruptly interrupted by a painful collision with Major-General Leyser's 29th Motorised Division. Colonel Tanaschishin's armour was only able to renew its advance when Leyser was ordered to withdraw west to the Chir to protect Army Group B's rear. The 4th Mechanised Corps faced little concerted resistance, but made slow, cautious progress as Volsky probed north in fierce blizzards. As Volsky fretted about his flanks, Hoth's 4th Panzer headquarters, threatened by 57th Army, withdrew west, handing a distinctly poisoned chalice to 4th Romanian Army.

Rodin's 26th Tank Corps continued its south-eastern progress. As 21st Army dealt with bypassed Romanians, Kravchenko's 4th Tank Corps forged on.

Above: A member of Chuikov's 62nd Army has a cigarette in the ruins of Stalingrad. The troops used by the Red Army were drawn from all over the Soviet Union, and many did not speak Russian well or at all.

Meanwhile, Don Front's 65th Army slowly forced German troops towards Stalingrad. During the night of 20–21 November, 4th Mechanised refuelled, but, as Volsky tarried with a yawning gap in front of him, Yeremenko gave him a categorical warning to speed up his advance or forfeit his command. The German situation was deteriorating rapidly. On 21 November, Paulus was chased out of his headquarters west of Stalingrad at Golubinskaya by forward detachments of Rodin's 26th Tank Corps. By the evening of the 21st, South-Western Front had advanced 97km (60 miles) into the German operational rear, while 4th Mechanised had progressed 48km (30 miles).

In the early hours of 22 November, 26th Tank Corps struck a key blow by capturing the bridge over the Don at Kalach with an inspired piece of trickery. Rodin ordered Lieutenant-Colonel Fillipov to reconnoitre the bridge. Fillipov's group advanced, headlights blazing, speed regarded as more vital than stealth. German sentries assumed captured Russian armour was being driven to the nearby tank gunnery range as targets. To Fillipov's amazement, he was unmolested, and he formulated an audacious scheme to capture the bridge. The detachment formed up and marched towards and across the bridge. Two Soviet tanks got over the Don before the Germans realised their awful mistake, but Fillipov's group overwhelmed them and took the bridge at 0600 hours. In expectation of a furious German reaction, an ecstatic Fillipov radioed Rodin to appraise him of the situation and to request help. As German units whirled about, unsure of whether to attack or retreat, Rodin's 26th Tank Corps won the race to Kalach and secured the bridge.

After securing Kalach, 26th Tank Corps resumed its advance while Butkov's 1st Tank Corps wheeled south-west to secure the Soviet line on the Chir. On their left, Kravchenko's 4th Tank Corps was closing on the Don at top speed. Meanwhile, following Yeremenko's warning, Volsky had pressed on. The 4th Mechanised Corps brushed past isolated pockets of resistance and did not pause until the morning of the 23rd November when Volsky's advanced guard reported a concentration of armour in Kalach. Volsky ordered one of his brigade commanders to scout the area and look for an open flank. At 1400 hours on 23 November, 4th Mechanised Corps stumbled upon the forward elements of Kravchenko's 4th Tank Corps east of Kalach at Sovetsky. In just hours, 4th Tank and 26th Tank had closed up and met 4th Mechanised, with 13th Tank Corps close behind.

As both sides raced west for the confluence of the Don and Chir, the Soviets in good order and Axis formations in frantic haste, Soviet command estimated it had encircled between 85,000 and 90,000 troops. In fact, more than 250,000 men were trapped in a pocket 56km by 32km (35 by 20 miles). It contained 14 infantry, three panzer and three motorised German divisions, two Romanian divisions, and a single Croatian regiment, plus various specialist signaller and engineer units. It also contained thousands of Russians, known as 'hiwis', who scraped a meagre existence doing menial tasks for German units. As early as 1900 hours on 22 November, 6th Army signalled to Army Group B 'the Army is encircled ... South front is still open east of the Don. Don is frozen over and crossable ... there is little fuel left; once that is used up, tanks and heavy weapons will be immobile. Ammunition is short, provisions will last for six more days ... request freedom of action ... situation might compel abandonment of Stalingrad and northern front.' It was Hitler's decision. If 6th Army was to hold, it needed help. However, to the south, the most immediate source of support, the 450,000 men of Army Group A, had problems of their own.

CHAPTER 7

The Caucasus Campaign and Army Group A

25 July to 12 November 1942

Hitler's Directive 45 of 23 July 1942 instructed Field Marshal List's Army Group A to cross the Don and head south into the Caucasus.

Army Group A's objectives were to capture the Soviet oilfields north of the Caucasus mountains at Maikop and Grozny, before moving on to capture Baku in Azerbaijan, which produced 80 per cent of Soviet oil. Army Group A was thus expected to defeat the Soviet forces in the Caucasus and conquer vast tracts of land before exploiting the rich oilfields. These initial objectives were in line with those outlined in Operation 'Blau'. However, in a gross overestimation of German capabilities, Hitler demanded Army Group A capture the Black Sea coast and its ports. It was over 483km (300 miles) from Rostov to Grozny and a further 322km (200 miles) from Grozny to Baku. Hitler envisaged the conquest of this enormous area with 21 divisions in a region bereft of infrastructural support. Army Group A would be virtually dependent on a single rail supply line and fuel drops from Lieutenant-General Pflugbeil's 4th Air Corps, part of Richthofen's overstretched Air Fleet 4. In common with previous campaigns, the German expedition into the Caucasus took little account of the realities of geography, distance and time, and seriously underestimated the fighting potential of the Red Army. As with operations

Left: An abandoned German Mark IV tank with its turret blown off. A suitable metaphor for the Caucasus, which promised much, achieved little and was eventually abandoned.

'Barbarossa' and 'Blau', and Army Group B's initial advance east into the Don bend, Army Group A's campaign got off to a flying start. By 9 August, 17th Army had taken Krasnodar on the river Kuban while 1st Panzer took Maikop. Yet as the Soviets retreated, they completely destroyed Maikop's oil facilities and more significantly, avoided encirclement by adopting a strategy of trading space for time. However, in mid-August 1942, as Army Group A prepared the second stage of its offensive, most German commanders were convinced that Soviet resistance in the Caucasus would be broken within a few weeks.

As Field Marshal List reshuffled his forces, the Red Army regrouped to face the new German onslaught. The defence of the Caucasus was under the protection of Marshal Budenny's Northern Caucasus Front. Budenny was a military anachronism with an impressive moustache and a less than impressive brain. A crony of Stalin's, his career had risen in conjunction with that of his mentor. A cavalry man of the old school, Budenny struggled with the combined speed and power of mechanised warfare. During July and early August, his North Caucasus Front had failed to contain Army Group A. It seemed that Budenny was living out his last days as an active

Below: Soviet troops dig in on the Kuban Steppe in the North Caucasus to protect the Red Army's fighting withdrawal towards the Caucasus mountains.

Front commander before assuming less onerous duties as the commander-in-chief of the Soviet cavalry. In August 1942 Budenny assigned the defence of the Black Sea coast to the Black Sea Group under Lt-General Cherevichenko, whose forces included Major-General Kotov's 47th Army, charged with defending the northern port of Novorossiisk. On 47th Army's right flank, Major-General Ryazhov's 56th and Major-General Grechko's 12th Army were charged with defending the vital port of Tuapse. To the south of Maikop, guarding 12th Army's right flank and the northern approaches to the port of Sukhumi, was Major-General Kamkov's 18th Army. On the Soviet right, deployed on the River Kuma, 160km (100 miles) north of Mozdok, was the Northern Group commanded by Lt-General Maslennikov, part of Lt-General Tyulenev's Trans-Caucasus Front. Tyulenev's 46th Army guarded the passes of the Caucasus mountains with 37th Army, 9th Army and 44th Army dug in on the River Terek.

On 19 August List's Army Group A renewed its offensive on a 483-km (300-mile) front. On the German right was Group Ruoff. General Richard Ruoff's group contained his own 17th Army, General Dumitrescu's 3rd Romanian Army and the 5th Romanian Cavalry Corps. List sent Ruoff 57th Panzer Corps from 1st Panzer to add power and mobility to the advance. Group Ruoff advanced in three separate columns, each of which had its own tactical objective.

Above: German armour, artillery and infantry in action during late July 1942 in the Northern Caucasus, south-east of Rostov. The flat, open terrain was ideal for rapid mechanised advances.

On the right flank, General Wetzel's 5th Army Corps marched on Novorossiisk, while 57th Panzer Corps approached Tuapse from Maikop. To its left, two German mountain divisions began a long march which envisaged them capturing the Caucasus mountain passes before descending out of the southern foothills upon the naval base of Sukhumi, some 402km (250 miles) south-east along the coast from Tuapse. The task of 3rd Romanian Army would be to concentrate on reducing Soviet resistance north of Novorossiisk in the Taman Peninsula. The aim was to secure a seaborne line of communications and supply from the Kerch Peninsula in the Crimea.

As Group Ruoff moved west and south-west on the Black Sea coast, on its left Field Marshal von Kleist's 1st Panzer Army headed south-east, led by Mackensen's 3rd Panzer Corps and von Schweppenburg's 40th Panzer Corps. 1st Panzer Army was to cross the 274m (300-yd) barrier of the River Terek (upon which the Trans-Caucasus Front was planning to make its stand), capture Grozny, and then advance another 322km (200 miles) south to Baku. All this was to be achieved before winter, which would break up the roads upon which Army Group A was virtually dependent upon for supply, as the lure of Stalingrad drew off more and more of 4th Air Corp's resources. Pflugbeil's air corps had played a key role in Army Group A's rapid advance across the Don through the Kuban steppe to Krasnodar and Maikop. In early August General Halder had expressed concern about the fuel situation, although he remained optimistic. In his account of the German 1942 campaign *Stopped at Stalingrad*, Dr

Joel Hayward quotes List on 4 August as believing 'a fast thrust to the southwest with sufficient mobile forces will not encounter serious enemy resistance anywhere forward of Baku'. Nevertheless, as Army Group A's advance diverged from Army Group B, so Group Ruoff and 1st Panzer were increasingly isolated from each other, and the further they went in pursuit of objectives that were probably beyond their collective means. Indeed, as the forces of Army Group A moved off, their ability to achieve their ambitious objectives was further undermined by Hitler's prioritisation of Stalingrad after the disappointing capture of the wrecked Maikop.

On 19 August Richthofen diverted the majority of Pflugbeil's 4th Air Corps to support Lt-General Fiebig's 8th Air Corps over Stalingrad. Richthofen explained to List that, since the orders came from Hitler, he had no choice. As Admiral Oktyabrskii's Black Sea Fleet remained more or less unchallenged – except from the very airpower that was now being removed – even if Group Ruoff captured the Black Sea ports, it was difficult to see how the small German naval assets in the Black Sea could be used to sustain the advance. This left Army Group A dependent on road and horsedrawn supply. If Soviet resistance was not broken quickly, Army Group A would find itself in a situation that had plagued the entire German war in the east, namely insufficient means to achieve unreasonably ambitious aims. The

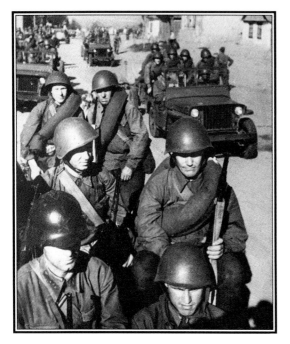

Left: The Red Army's resistance, especially on the Black Sea coast, had stiffened considerably by late August 1942. Army Group A continued to make progress but by then it had slowed to a snail's pace.

leaving it reliant upon extended motorised supply lines of between 322km and 483km (200 miles and 300 miles). As wear and tear diminished the number of trucks available, Army Group A increasingly used pack mules to support 1st Panzer's advance. To Hitler's intense irritation, towards the end of August, at the height of the campaigning season, the same List who had been so optimistic a month earlier began to suggest that 1st Panzer should halt operations and take up winter positions. Nevertheless, 1st Panzer ground its way forward, aided by the incompetence and confusion among the commanders of the Trans-Caucasus Front. On 18 August the defences of Maslennikov's Northern Group on the River Kuma were broken. As Maslennikov's forces fell back to avoid encirclement, 1st Panzer's 40th Panzer Corps slowly moved on the river Terek.

Kleist's armour was to capture Mozdok, cross the Terek and take Grozny before advancing on Baku. As the 9th and 44th Soviet Armies dug themselves in on the southern bank of the Terek, Richthofen permitted Pflugbeil to dispatch a group of German fighters to support von Scweppenburg's 40th Panzer Corps. The absence of the Luftwaffe enabled the Soviet air force to begin playing an increasingly influential role in the campaign and it now con-

withdrawal of 4th Air Corps to Stalingrad took from Army Group A a vital element of German manoeuvre warfare, one which, in common with the panzers, possessed the speed, mobility and firepower necessary to achieve a quick victory. In the words of Hayward, 4th Air Corps 'no longer possessed the ability to affect decisively the outcome of battles in the Caucasus or even to conduct systematic interdiction in the enemy's rear areas'. The simple truth was that, as in Operation 'Barbarossa', Germany lacked the means for Army Group B and Army Group A to simultaneously achieve their objectives. Once the capture of Maikop flattered to deceive, Hitler seemed to lose interest in the Caucasus campaign. As Hitler robbed Peter to pay Paul, Army Group A was denied the resources to subdue Soviet resistance in the Caucasus.

By the final days of August, instead of the rapid advance pictured by List, Army Group A's advance slowed dramatically to an average of 3–4km (1.9–2.5 miles) a day. Army Group A's rail supply line ended in the eastern Ukraine, with the remaining distance covered by trucks and aircraft. Hitler's decision to divert the majority of 4th Air Corps to Stalingrad critically undermined Army Group A's combat power,

Right: Italian troops attack a Soviet position in high summer. During July 1942 Italian troops had played an active role in Army Group A's advance on Rostov.

Above: If used properly cavalry were an invaluable asset in terms of mobility, given the huge expanses of southern Russia. Soviet troops in the Caucasus and elsewhere made extensive use of the horse.

trolled the tactical initiative. However, Soviet air-power did not prevent the capture of Mozdok on the northern bank of the Terek on 25 August. The Terek was a major obstacle, being 274m (300yds) wide and fast flowing, with a southern bank that was considerably higher than the northern shore. Yet all was not well within the Soviet Trans-Caucasus Front. As the North Caucasus Front was disbanded, Budenny's incompetent influence on the Caucasus campaign was replaced by the more malevolent and insidious contribution of Stalin's henchman, Lavrentia Beria.

A member of the State Defence Committee, Beria was sent by Stalin to Lieutenant-General Tyulenev's Trans-Caucasus Front as the Stavka representative. This would tend to confirm the suspicion that Stalin gave military professionalism its head on critical sectors of the front but maintained a ruthless political grip in what he considered less significant theatres, even in this war for the highest of stakes. Beria had a murderous reputation as a sadistic and power-hungry operator. A Georgian by birth – like Stalin – Beria had cut his teeth in the mid 1920s with his ruthless suppression of nationalist sentiment in the Caucasus. As a reward, Stalin made Beria a member of the Central Committee in 1934 and head of the NKVD in December 1938. It is no exaggeration to say that the majority of Soviet generals lived in fear of and hated Beria.

Beria's military contribution to the defence of the Caucasus was disastrous, and more than compensated for the supply difficulties which 1st Panzer was experiencing. Beria clashed with several army commanders and, instead of summoning the military reserves Tyulenev requested, deployed more NKVD troops who were answerable only to himself. On 23 August

he ordered the creation of a Caucasian Range Operational Group. The grand name betrayed a lack of substance as his cronies more or less hijacked command of 46th Soviet Army which, at the time, was defending the passes of the Caucasus mountains. As German troops advanced steadily through the mountains and planted the German flag on the 5633m (18480ft) summit of Mt Elbrus, Stalin sent stern orders that a new operational plan should be devised by Lt-General Tyulenev's staff. If Stalin's intervention curtailed Beria's direct influence upon the conduct of military operations, Stalin gave him full reign to wage virtual civil war upon the peoples of the Caucasus whose loyalties he suspected. Beria's private NKVD army inflicted terrible vengeance on the Kalmyks, Ingush, and the Chechens. In a campaign of mass murder and deportations, his cruel talents were exercised to the full in the execution of his vengeful master's wishes.

Maslennikov's Northern Group, consisting of 37th, 9th and 44th Army – the latter commanded by Lieutenant-General Petrov, the defender of Sevastopol – prepared its defence on the Terek. However, Maslennikov ignored Tyulenev's advice that the Germans would not only attempt to cross the Terek at Mozdok. On 30 August a small group of German troops crossed the Terek west of Mozdok and established a small bridgehead. Caught on the hop, Maslennikov failed to react with sufficient speed and although the German bridgehead came under air attack by 2 September, von Schweppenburg's 40th

Above: Captured Romanian and Italian troops move off into captivity. Internment in Russia, especially during the winter months with inadequate food rations and clothing, tested the endurance of such men.

Panzer Corps reinforced the troops on the southern bank of the river, securing a major tactical triumph. However, the Soviet defences did not crack and in the first half of September 1942, 1st Panzer battled its way mile by mile under heavy air attack towards Grozny, east of Mozdok. The defence of Grozny was increasingly controlled by Petrov. In conjunction with the rare luxury of localised air support, while German forces struggled to sustain their mobility through a lack of fuel, Petrov's forces constantly harassed 1st Panzer, alternating between tactical defence and attack. The official objective of 1st Panzer remained Baku; as most of its soldiers now realised they would be lucky to reach Grozny before the weather began to deteriorate.

However, at the end of August, German troops belonging to the 1st and 4th Mountain Divisions on the right of 1st Panzer appeared to be making steady progress. Their objective was the southern Black Sea port of Tuapse. However, after reaching the summit of Mt Elbrus, the advance began to peter out. To climb the Caucasian range was one thing; to descend the southern valleys in strength into the foothills and defeat the Soviet forces in Sukhumi was quite another. Hitler raged at the mountain troops for wasting time in the pointless, vainglorious ascent of Mt Elbrus and urged on them towards Sukhumi. He insisted that the capture of Sukhumi in conjunction with what he believed to be the imminent fall of the northern ports of Tuapse and Novorossiisk would cripple the Soviet Black Sea Fleet, releasing German naval assets to breathe new life into the Caucasus campaign. As the

malign influence of Beria declined, Soviets troops abandoned Beria's idea of fighting the Germans in the mountains and instead defended the southern exits of the Caucasus passes. Naturally, the German troops lacked the heavy weapons to blast their way through and struggled against fierce resistance. The mountain troops had been dependent on being provisioned by Pflugbeil's 4th Air Corps as they descended the southern foothills, but in the absence of re-supply, their advance halted 24km (15 miles) short of Sukhumi.

During September 1942, as two of the three German thrusts ground to a halt in the face of logistical collapse and stiff Russian resistance, German hopes increasingly lay with 3rd Romanian Army and Group Ruoff. In the early days of the second phase of the German Caucasus offensive, it was General Dumitrescu's 3rd Romanian that set the pace, to the embarrassment of their German colleagues. As 17th German Army moved south from Krasnodar across the far northwestern foothills of the Caucasus ranges towards Novorossiisk and Tuapse, 3rd Romanian progressed along the eastern shore of the Sea of Azov. Budenny was determined to defend the Taman Peninsula and Novorossiisk and on 17 August, he set up the Novorossiisk Defence Region. It was made up of Major-General Kotov's 47th Army, Rear Admiral Gorshkov's Azov Flotilla, and a mixed Soviet air

Above: A German infantryman glares at the camera with barely controlled anger. By September 1942 Army Group A's triumphal progress through the Caucasus had been replaced by bitter fighting.

Below: Soviet troops relax in a break from the fighting. It is clear they do not expect an imminent attack but such men lived a day-to-day existence as the Wehrmacht continued to pound the Red Army.

presence. The Romanians moved into the Taman region, crossed the Kuban, and took the ports of Temryuk and Anapa on 31 August. This was achieved without substantial air support and induced the Soviets to abandon the last outpost of Soviet resistance on the Taman Peninsula. The benefits of the Romanians' prodigious efforts were that immediate. German naval forces in the Black Sea under Admiral Schwarz undertook Operation 'Blucher', the transportation of the 3rd Romanian Mountain Corps and 46th German Infantry Division. The divisions were moved across the Kerch Straits on 1 and 2 September along with fuel, ammunition, vehicles and horses. This was a considerable boost to the German advance into the Caucasus. In the first two weeks of September, Admiral Schwarz's group transported 30,605 men, 13,254 horses and 6265 vehicles to the region.

Group Ruoff prepared to move on Novorossiisk with the intention of advancing down the Black Sea coast towards Tuapse and Sukhumi. However, the right wing of 47th Army proved a tougher nut than its left wing in the Taman Penisula. Equally, within days, the diversion of the Luftwaffe provoked the return of Soviet airpower to the region. As the remaining strength of Pflugbeil's 4th Air Corps was dispersed throughout the Caucasus in support of Army Group A, those dedicated to 17th Army struggled to dominate the air over the battle of Novorossiisk. The 47th Army forced 17th Army to fight for every yard as it withdrew to the outskirts of the city. Soviet defences were boosted by the arrival of reinforcements, tough naval marines evacuated from

the Taman Peninsula by Rear Admiral Gorshkov's Azov Flotilla. The Luftwaffe's reconnaissance planes spotted the marines' withdrawal but 4th Air Corps could no longer undertake simultaneous close air support and attack them. The marines were deployed in the hills immediately to the south as Budenny sought to ensure that if Novorossiisk fell, Group Ruoff would have to fight its way down the coastal road. In the early days of September, Wetzel's 5th Infantry Corps became involved in days of fierce hand-to-hand fighting on the outskirts of Novorossiisk and by the 6 September, had battled its way into the port. However, it took four days to subdue the city and General Wetzel finally announced the city's capture on 10 September. Once again, a German advance that was supposed to be characterised by rapid and decisive movement had become trapped in bitter attritional fighting.

Yet it was only a partial victory; 5th Army Corps did not control the high ground south of the city and it was this which controlled access to the coastal road and would be vital to a rapid advance. Wentzel's troops suffered heavy casualties in repeated attempts to break out south of Novorossiisk. Indeed, Soviet resistance increased, to the extent that 3rd Romanian Mountain Division incurred serious casualties in holding heavy Soviet counter-attacks on 25 and 26 September. The pyrrhic victory at Tuapse was the last tactical victory achieved by Army Group A under Field Marshal List's command. An expert on

Above: As Army Group A advanced on the Terek river barrier north-west of Grozny, Soviet resistance increased. A Soviet T-34 moves up to the frontline; 1st Panzer Army would be bogged down on the Terek.

the peculiar difficulties of mountain warfare, List advised Hitler to withdraw the German troops to the northern foothills of the Caucasus. The rest of these high-quality troops were to be committed to breaking the Soviet stranglehold on the Tuapse coastal road. However, Hitler refused to accept that the offensive had to be terminated. After a meeting with List at Stalino in the eastern Ukraine, the Operations Chief of the German armed forces high command, General Jodl, relayed List's concerns to Hitler. Soviet troops continued to defy 57th Panzer Corps and the 44th Jager Corps north-east of Tuapse, but Hitler raged at what he perceived to be the disloyalty of Jodl and List's lack of commitment to the fight. He sacked List and took upon himself the command of Army Group A from a distance of 3218km (2000 miles).

In Dr Joel Hayward's words, 'as autumn wind and rain replaced summer sun, the Caucasus campaign steadily petered out, with only very minor changes in the line occurring after the middle of September'. 1st Panzer struggled to take advantage of its bridgehead on the southern bank of the Terek river. As it rumbled its way towards Grozny, it faced bitter Soviet resistance on the ground as well as in the air, where Soviet airpower capitalised upon the weak-

Right: Major-General Rodin (seated) the commander of 26th Tank Corps, discusses his plan for Operation 'Uranus' with his senior officers. Some of his men successfully captured the bridge at Kalach intact.

ness of the Luftwaffe. By October 1942, with their supply lines threatened by autumn rains and snows, German mountain troops abandoned their advance on Sukhumi. The 17th Army struggled to free itself from the dual snare of Novorossiisk and Tuapse and came to a halt. In October 1942, Army Group A made one last effort to break Soviet resistance and advance on Baku. On 18 October, 1st Panzer's 52nd Infantry Corps found a weakness in the defences of 37th Soviet Army positioned at the western edge of the Terek bend. Field Marshal von Kleist decided upon a full-scale assault and Richthofen released Pflugbeil's 4th Air Corps from Stalingrad.

The assault began on 25 October, led by General von Mackensen's 3rd Panzer Corps. The objective was the city of Ordzhonikidze,which held the key to the excellent military road running south through the Caucasus mountains into Georgia, giving access to the western Black Sea port of Batumi and Baku in the east. Rested and refuelled, 3rd Panzer Corps burst through the Soviet 37th Army. On 28 October, 13th Panzer and 2nd Romanian Mountain Division took Nalchik 97km (60 miles) north-west of Ordzhonikidze. 3rd Panzer Corps continued its offensive on the town of Alagir, 32km (20 miles) west of Ordzhonikidze, in the Caucasus foothills. As

13th Panzer advanced on Ordzhonikidze, 23rd Panzer captured Alagir on 1 November and swung east. However, as 3rd Panzer Corps moved on Ordzhonikidze, Soviet resistance stiffened considerably: the Trans-Caucasian Front was feeding reserves in to support 37th Army. On 3 November, in shocking weather, 3rd Panzer Corps – only 3.2km (2 miles) west of Ordzhonikidze – suffered serious casualties, gaining a few hundred yards. As 1st Panzer inched forward on 6 November, the Luftwaffe conducted three raids on the coveted city under the personal command of Richthofen, and was dismayed at 3rd Panzer Corps' failure to follow up. In a matter of hours the reason became clear; instead of fighting its way into the city, Mackensen's corps was fighting for its life. As 3rd Panzer Corps struggled west of Ordzhonikidze, a brilliantly timed Soviet counter-attack to the city's north had cut 13th Panzer Division's supply lines. In desperate fighting, all thoughts of capturing Ordzhonikidze disappeared. On 9 November Mackensen sent the SS Wiking Division and 23rd Panzer forward to break the Soviet stranglehold. On the night of 11/12 November, days before the crushing blow of Operation 'Uranus', 13th Panzer limped north to safety. Army Group A's advance came to a halt with no thoughts of resumption. In a matter of weeks, 3rd Panzer Corps had suffered 1275 dead, 273 missing and 5008 wounded. In June 1942 Hitler had declared Germany's entire war

Left: Operation 'Blau' and the subsequent advance of Army Group A into the Caucasus, attempting to reach the oilfields of Baku.

Above: As Army Group A advanced on Ordzhonikidze during early November 1942, the Soviet winter closed in. Russian armoured vehicles coped far better with such conditions than the German tanks.

effort was dependent upon the capture of Soviet oil resources but by November, Army Group A had failed to achieve any of its objectives, apart from the flawed victories of Novorossiisk and Maikop. The offensive had faltered on the outskirts of Grozny, and Baku remained a distant mirage. Yet Army Group A's failure was significant in its own right, despite giving the appearance of a sideshow after Maikop.

The rupture between Hitler and his generals which had been simmering beneath the surface since December 1941 now burst into the open. This had serious implications for the ability of the German Army to conduct rational military operations on the Eastern Front. As Army Group A stalled in the Caucasus and 6th Army became mired in Stalingrad, Hitler withdrew from contact with his generals, plagued by a paranoid distrust of their commitment to the struggle. He ate alone and insisted the minutes of all discussions were recorded. Halder, the Chief of the General Staff, took the brunt of Hitler's displeasure, forfeiting his position on 24 September. Zeitzler, a resilient figure, had to fight a constant battle with Hitler for the rest of the Stalingrad campaign. As Hitler subconsciously – although never openly – admitted the Soviet oilfields of Baku were out of German reach, he became obsessed with Stalingrad.

He involved himself in the smallest tactical detail while ignoring the painful reality that his objectives were beyond German means. Yet he refused to give up the ground the Germans had taken in the Caucasus, ostensibly to prevent the release of Soviet forces to Stalingrad, but in reality because Hitler found the concession of ground almost too painful to contemplate. Despite all this, National Socialist ideological fervour and the will to fight could not alter the plain fact that Army Group A and Army Group B simply lacked the manpower, the supplies, the armour and the airpower to achieve the goals that Hitler had set for them. Ironically, perhaps, the abiding characteristic of the German armies and their soldiers was their will to fight. The soldiers of Army Group A and Army Group B, many convinced Nazis in awe of the Führer, many simply clinging to the basic instinct for survival, fought on to the end. The 6th Army's bitter resistance in the last days of January 1943 amazed Soviet commanders.

However, as German commanders and soldiers recognised in the autumn of 1942, the Red Army, epitomised by Chuikov's 62nd Army in Stalingrad, found an equal will to fight. Soviet soldiers, some convinced Communists, others patriots of whatever nation – predominantly Russian – they belonged to, others through desire to revenge German atrocities, began to fight with a determined tenacity. In the hands of better commanders, the Soviet soldier of late 1942 and early 1943 was a tougher proposition than the

Right: Soviet officers in the Caucasus during the winter of 1942–43.
The enormous Soviet casualties of 1941 ensured the Red Army's junior
officers were often very young and inexperienced.

hapless victim of June 1941. Bolstered by the surging
Soviet war economy and supplies from Britain and
America, Soviet armies prepared to take the fight to the
Wehrmacht. As the struggle intensified, few Red Army
units could match the tactical prowess of the best
German units, but the gap was closing. At the operational level, the Stalingrad campaign would demonstrate that the Soviet high command, led by Vasilevsky,
contained commanders who were a match for their
famed German counterparts. Soviet military strategy,
although unduly ambitious, was now directed by Stalin
with his generals, and not at their expense. German
strategy fell into a malaise dominated by Hitler's inflex-
ible determination to conquer Stalingrad. As Halder
fell, despite Zeitzler's best efforts, the general staff lost
its strategic input. In the coming months, it was
reduced to the executor of Hitler's wishes.

Hitler refused to accept the limits of German
national power had been reached. The monstrous

Below: By December 1942 the Luftwaffe was using all manner of
aircraft, even such obsolescent types as the Henschel Hs 123 shown, in
an attempt to fulfil its commitments.

gamble of June 1941 and June 1942 had failed. As the
Anglo-American alliance marshalled its latent military
power for an assault on the Third Reich, in November
1942 Hitler's grand project began to crumble.
Montgomery's 8th Army was chasing Rommel west
across North Africa after its triumph at El Alamein. On
8 November, as part of Operation 'Torch', British and
American troops landed in Morocco and Algeria and
began moving east. Army Group A had faltered and
Hitler's refusal to compromise with reality at Stalingrad
was about to condemn the 6th Army to disaster.

CHAPTER 8

The Destiny of 6th Army

Survival or Disaster
2–28 December 1942

In the words of Professor John Erickson, between 19 and 23 November 1942, 'the impossible, the unthinkable and the unimaginable happened on the Eastern Front'.

The Stalingrad cauldron contained 250,000 troops made up of five German corps: Janicke's 4th, Heitz's 8th, Strecker's 11th, Seydlitz's 51st and Hube's 14th Panzer. As Hitler travelled from his mountain retreat in Bavaria to take a 'closer' hand in developments from eastern Prussia, he faced arguably his biggest decision since the outbreak of war in September 1939. Should he order 6th Army to stand and fight, or should he permit a breakout? A withdrawal to the Chir would guarantee 6th Army's survival as a viable, if battered, force and stabilise the German military position in the southern Soviet Union. However, it would also confirm to the world the complete failure of the German 1942 offensive and defeat at Stalingrad.

As Stalingrad Front smashed through 6th Romanian Corps on 20 November, the significance of Operation 'Uranus' began to dawn on the Führer. Hitler summoned Field Marshal von Manstein from 11th Army at Vitebsk and ordered him to form Army Group Don. It was to contain the Red Army on the Chir, maintain the German position in southern Russia, and prepare a rescue plan for 6th Army. It is customary to blame *Reichmarshal* Göring for making Hitler to believe an airlift possible. However, Dr Joel Hayward has convincingly demonstrated that Hitler

Left: The smashed wreckage of the city of Stalingrad. In the last days of November 1942 Paulus' 6th Army suspended active offensive operations. The attention focussed on maintaining the defence of 6th Army's perimeter.

Above: Soviet troops in Stalingrad suitably clad for the winter months. On the left is Vasily Zaitsev, a celebrated Soviet sniper at Stalingrad. The Soviet authorities deliberately orchestrated a 'cult of the sniper'.

received other, expert advice about an airlift, even before he spoke to Göring. On 20 November Hitler called Lieutentant-General Hans Jeschonnek, the Chief of the Luftwaffe General Staff, to the Berghof. Hayward believes Hitler informed Jeschonnek that he had set up Army Group Don and was organising a relief force to alleviate 6th Army's temporary encirclement. On the critical assumption of it being a temporary encirclement, Jeschonnek argued that if sufficient transport aircraft, bombers and airfields were available, an airlift was possible. Significantly, he alluded to the 100,000 German soldiers supplied by the Luftwaffe in the Demyansk pocket north of Moscow during the spring of 1942. It was a seductive comparison that Hitler seized upon to justify his decision to forbid 6th Army's escape. Yet the Demyansk operation involved the supply of 100,000 men, not 250,000, in spring, not winter, against negligible, and not increasing, Soviet airpower. The Demyansk pocket needed a daily minimum of 300 tons of supplies. To guarantee the daily arrival of a minimum of 150 aircraft necessary to meet this target, the Luftwaffe committed 500 Ju-52s. The 6th Army calculated that the 250,000 men in the Stalingrad pocket would require 750 tons (later stripped down to a bare minimum of 500 tons). The Demyansk comparison was misleading: the Luftwaffe did not possess sufficient aircraft to sustain such a colossal airlift, particularly as Hitler had just committed more Ju-52s to Rommel's lost cause in North Africa.

At 1525 hours on 21 November 1942 Hitler instructed von Weichs to inform Paulus that 'Sixth Army will hold positions despite the threat of temporary encirclement ... keep railroad line open as long as possible. Special orders regarding air supply will follow!' At Nizhne Chirskaya, where Paulus made his temporary HQ outside the pocket, General Hoth and commander of 9th Luftwaffe Field Division, Major-General Pickert, were incredulous at the idea of an airlift. Field Marshal von Weichs, Paulus and his five corps commanders were unanimous in their opinion that 6th Army must break out before the Red Army consolidated its position west of Stalingrad; if not, it would be trapped for weeks, not days. Richtfhofen, the commander of Air Fleet 4, and Lt-General Fiebig, commanding 8th Air Corps, both confirmed to 6th Army's Chief of Staff, Major-General Schmidt, that a sustained airlift in the middle of winter was out of the question. However, Paulus, whatever his personal beliefs, was not a man to disobey the Führer. As Pickert urged a breakout, Schmidt informed him that Hitler had expressly ordered 6th Army to remain in position. Schmidt also suggested, in an exchange replete with tragic irony, that a breakout west with little fuel over difficult terrain against strong

Soviet forces ran the risk of catastrophe. At 1400 hours on 22 November, Paulus flew back into the cauldron and set up a new headquarters at Gumrak. Having made Weichs aware that 6th Army had sufficient supplies to last six days, he began to deploy 6th Army for a rapid breakout, should Hitler order it. Hitler had shown a marked disinclination towards withdrawal long before Stalingrad, most notably at Moscow. He was inclined to assume that withdrawal always escalated into uncontrollable rout and collapse of the will to fight. In fact, his belief in the power (and fragility) of will played a key role in his decision to deny 6th Army the chance to escape. His apparent success in halting the Moscow counter-offensive made him scornful and suspicious of his generals, especially their inclination to withdraw rather than fight. Hitler had come to regard Stalingrad as a battle of wills between himself and the German peoples against Stalin and the Soviet peoples. It was unthinkable that the inferior Slavs should chase the Wehrmacht out of Stalingrad.

Below: Troops of 8th Italian Army on the middle Don during early December 1942. On 16 December 1942 a massive Soviet offensive, Operation 'Small Saturn', descended on the Italians and crushed them.

The Führer found little objective counsel from Göring. Göring's star had waned since his failure to win the Battle of Britain, and he saw the airlift as a good opportunity to redeem himself. On 21 November he pompously assured Hitler that the Luftwaffe was at his service. As the sychophantic Göring ingratiated himself, Zeitzler fought an unequal struggle to dissuade Hitler from authorising an airlift. Hitler did not speak to Weichs, Richthofen, Fiebig or Paulus between 22 and 24 November. Hitler should have received – but thanks to Göring, did not – objective advice from a chastened Jeschonnek. In discussion with Richthofen and, following a closer analysis of the Luftwaffe's capabilities, Jeschonnek concluded that even in perfect conditions, the Luftwaffe could not sustain 6th Army. However, Hitler ignored his objections in the face of Göring's smooth personal assurances to the contrary. Indeed, Göring went so far to order Jeschonnek not to inform the Führer about his information which clearly indicated that it was impossible for the Luftwaffe to carry the required weight of supplies. Hitler arrived in East Prussia on the night of 23 November, and in Hitler's presence, Zeitzler confronted Göring with the impossibility of the

Left: Lieutenant-General Shumilov, commander of 64th Army. Shumilov's men were heavily involved in the initial battles for Stalingrad and in the execution of Operation 'Uranus'.

gation of Lieutenant-General von Seydlitz-Kurbach, all five corps commanders had agreed to recommend a breakout to Paulus. A direct descendant of Frederick the Great's dashing cavalry commander, Seydlitz had led the German relief force which had broken the Soviet ring at Demyansk in spring 1942. However, within hours of the Soviet offensive, Seydlitz concluded that 6th Army must break out if it was to survive. In September 1942 Seydlitz had been earmarked to succeed Paulus should 6th Army emerge victorious at Stalingrad. Now, in unimaginably different circumstances, he urged the more cautious Paulus to break the encirclement. At 2130 hours an anxious Paulus cabled Hitler to request 'withdrawal of all the divisions from Stalingrad itself and further considerable forces from the northern perimeter ... in view of the situation, I request you to grant me complete freedom of action.'

As Paulus waited, Seydlitz attempted to force the issue by ordering 94th Division in the north-eastern corner of the pocket to withdraw. There seems little doubt it was Seydlitz's intention to force the hand of Paulus, inducing him to confer retrospective authority on a mutinous act. He did not. As 94th Division abandoned its positions, it suffered a vicious counter-attack from Chuikov's 62nd Army. German soldiers loitered with stressful intent throughout the night of 23 November, but on 24 November at 0838 hours, Hitler definitively committed 6th Army to the Volga. Hitler

Luftwaffe's task. However, Hitler's mind was made up. On the night of 23 November, Hitler declared Stalingrad a *Festung* (fortress) to be defended to the last. In the face of Zeitzler's objections, Hitler replied, 'It is the garrison of a fortress, and the duty of fortress troops is to withstand sieges. If necessary they will hold out all winter, and I shall relieve them by a spring offensive.' The 6th Army was now trapped and fighting for its life. In Hayward's opinion, 'responsibility for the decision to supply Sixth Army – one of the most fateful decisions of the war – rests with three individuals: Jeschonnek, Hitler and Göring'. Hitler listened to what he wanted to hear, while Göring was prepared to say what the Führer wanted to hear.. The unfortunate Jeschonnek was both too early and too late with his advice.

Although von Weichs was informed, as Paulus returned to the pocket he remained unaware of discussions between his corps commanders. At the insti-

Below: Soviet cavalry charging German positions. These men are Cossacks and fierce, unforgiving opponents. This photograph looks suspiciously like a re-enactment.

Above: Katyusha rockets known laconically as 'Stalin's Organs'. While not particularly accurate, as an area weapon fired en masse, they had an awesome reputation and significant psychological value.

formally declared that 'Sixth Army will adopt hedgehog defence ... present Volga front and northern front to be held at all costs ... supplies coming by air'. The die was cast. As the airlift began, a bizarre postscript developed. A furious Hitler learned of the 94th Division's withdrawal and the unofficial preparations of 6th Army to break out. Suspecting Paulus to be responsible, he ordered him to place the northern area of Stalingrad under the special command of Seydlitz. The irony of Hitler's statement that 'this commander will be responsible to the Führer that this fortified area is held at any price' cannot have been lost on Paulus.

As the breakout failed to materialise, 6th Army dispersed to resume its defence of the pocket. Paulus made his headquarters at Gumrak, 16km (10 miles) west of Stalingrad. The battered 94th Infantry Division held the north-eastern area of the pocket. On its right was 389th Division on the Orlovka river, with the 305th Division directly west of the Tractor Factory. The 79th and 100th Jager divisions resumed their positions west of the Barrikady and the Red October, while 295th Division continued its contest with Batyuk's 284th Siberian for the Mamayev Kurgan. In the Minina suburb, south of the Tsaritsa, 71st Division held the Volga. The Germans conserved their strength, and 62nd Army recuperated and waited for the Volga to freeze. To the west of 71st Division, 371st Division, 20th Romanian and, further west, 297th Division defended the southern edge of the pocket. On the Volga, Shumilov's 64th Army guarded the perimeter with Tolbukhin's 57th Army on the Kalmyk steppe to its left. The Germans' western defences were manned

by 29th Motorised, 14th Panzer and 3rd Motorised Divisions contained by Christyakov's 21st Army transferred to the Don Front from South-Western Front. In the north-west, Batov's 65th Soviet Army faced 376th, 44th, 384th and 76th divisions. The northern side of the pocket was held, from west to east respectively, by 113th, 60th Motorised and 16th Panzer, with 24th Panzer Division linking up with 94th Division. Galinin's 24th Army held a close watching brief, with Zhadov's 66th Army deployed on the Volga, north of Rynok.

The cauldron was 56km by 40km (35 by 25 miles) with a perimeter of approximately 129km (80 miles) containing 20 German divisions of the highest quality and experience. The combined armies of the Don and Stalingrad Fronts – seven in total, including Chuikov's shattered 62nd Army – maintained the isolation of 6th Army. The outer Soviet perimeter along the Don, Chir and Aksai river to south-west of Stalingrad was over 322km (200 miles) in length. The distance between the inner and outer lines of encirclement was only 32–48km (20–30 miles) and west of the cauldron, where German troops retained bridgeheads over the Chir, was only 16km (10 miles). The morale of 6th Army was incredibly high and remained so until after Christmas 1942. German soldiers carried a remarkable faith in their Führer, a man who, in their eyes, had resurrected Germany and led the Wehrmacht to a string of famous victories. The average

German soldier, although he had acquired a new respect for the Soviet soldier in Stalingrad, retained his belief in the superiority of German arms. With access to information about the paucity of German reserves and the speed of the Soviet build-up around Stalingrad, the senior German officers of the 6th Army took a less sanguine view of their army's fate.

As Stalin and Vasilevsky laid their plans, they worked on the assumption that Operation 'Uranus' had encircled between 85,000–90,000 German troops. Stalin insisted 6th Army's annihilation was the Red Army's priority, but Stavka had no idea that the true figure was closer to 250,000 German troops. There is little doubt that the Red Army would have struggled to contain an early breakout by 6th Army. Soviet planning in the immediate aftermath of Operation 'Uranus' was based upon this completely false estimate of the forces at Stalingrad, and it was not until late December 1942 that the Red Army began to revise its intelligence picture. On 24 November Vasilevsky ordered the pocket's destruction by Rokossovsky's Don Front and Yeremenko's Stalingrad Front. He sought to ensure that the cauldron's annihilation was compatible with the ambitious Operation 'Saturn', the aim of which was to transform tactical and operational victory at Stalingrad into strategic victory over the Wehrmacht in southern Russia. Soviet forces directly north of Rostov would annihilate 8th Italian Army guarding Army Group B's left flank on the Don. Simultaneously, powerful Soviet armies would attack Manstein's Army Group

Don on the Don-Chir line west of the Stalingrad pocket. The second phase of 'Saturn' envisaged a classic deep operation aimed at Morozovsk and Tatinskaya, specific operational objectives which underpinned Army Group Don's entire supply and communications network. The paralysis of the German operational rear would induce the withdrawal or destruction of Manstein's Army Group Don, thus completing the isolation of 6th Army. The strategic objective was Rostov, the gateway to – or exit from – the Caucasus, at the mouth of the Don. By reaching Rostov, Stavka sought to trap Army Group A in the Caucasus. The potential destruction of the remaining strength of Army Group B, the defeat of Army Group Don, and the loss of Army Group A, all represented a strategic threat of catastrophic proportions to the Wehrmacht. In summary, as German forces moved west to secure the Wehrmacht's operational and strategic position, the successful execution of Operation 'Saturn' would render incompatible 6th Army's survival with German strategic interests. In an outstanding display of 'the operating art', Vasilevsky, with Zhukov, had identified that the key to tactical survival and success at Stalingrad lay in the Volga lifeline and the operational rear of 6th Army. Now, adding to a campaign that incorporated the Red Army's doctrinal ideas of successive and deep

Below: The 6th Army was beleaguered on all sides. Soviet armies kept up the pressure on the cauldron's perimeter while Chuikov's 62nd Army launched periodic assaults within the city.

Above: A tired looking Paulus discusses his options with one of his senior commanders. Hitler's insistence on 6th Army remaining on the Volga left Paulus with very few options.

Below: Soviet armour advances on Kalach west of Stalingrad. The securing of Kalach and its bridge over the Don by Rodin's 26th Tank Corps played a key role in the encirclement of 6th Army.

operations, Vasilevsky discerned that the route to 6th Army's destruction lay not in Stalingrad, but in Army Group Don's operational rear west of the Don-Chir line, and the German strategic centre of gravity as Rostov. However, if Hitler had allowed 6th Army to break out in the early days of the encirclement, Vasilevksy's brilliant campaign plan would have counted for nought. A humiliating withdrawal from Stalingrad by a bloodied 6th Army would still have represented a major defeat, but would not have been on the scale of its annihilation in January 1943.

As Army Group Don commander, Field Marshal von Manstein's mission was to rescue 6th Army and stabilise the German position in the great Don bend, as well as in southern Russia as a whole. Army Group Don was a mixture of German and Romanian troops. The 6th Army was technically part of Manstein's command but had little to offer, even though its encirclement dominated Army Group Don's operations. Dumitrescu's 3rd Romanian Army had been incorporated into an *ad hoc* grouping of German and Romanian forces under Major-General Karl Hollidt. Hollidt's forces had performed wonders to hold the Chir, even retaining bridgeheads on the eastern bank. On Hollidt's right was Hoth's 4th Panzer, bereft of its German armoured forces, while 16th

Motorised Division was 241km (150 miles) away on the Kalmyk Steppe, holding a tenous link between Army Group Don and Army Group A. Army Group Don was reinforced by 336th German Infantry, 7th and 15th Luftwaffe Field divisions, plus 11th Panzer Division. In December 1942, Army Group Don also received the 6th and 23rd Panzer divisions. Nevertheless, the stabilisation of the Chir also immobilised German units. While they had no reserves to confer operational flexibility upon Army Group Don, Soviet armoured reserves flooded into the area.

Unknown to Manstein, Vasilevsky was putting the final touches to Operation 'Saturn' on 25 November, while Manstein fully understood the implications of any Soviet thrust towards Rostov. The only viable operational, not tactical, solution was to extend 6th Army's temporary encirclement, creating time to consolidate the German position in the Don bend. Subsequently, a corridor cut through to 6th Army would enable it to break out while it retained the strength, followed by the creation of a new German front on the Don-Chir line. This would shorten the line, permitting a greater concentration of force and density in German defences which would also benefit from shorter supply lines. In such circumstances, given the depth of the German defences and the availability of armoured reserves, a Rostov operation would have posed a serious challenge to the Red Army, despite the number of Soviet armies released from Stalingrad. It would also create time and space

Above: Soviet troops maintained a close watch on the pocket while their commanders planned future operations. Here field officers of the South-Western Front discuss the proposed Operation 'Saturn'.

Below: Soviet troops were adequately clothed for the Russian winter but living in the field between October 1942 and February 1943 was far from easy even for an army familiar with the conditions.

for Army Group A's withdrawal from the Caucasus. Hitler's refusal to consider 6th Army's withdrawal from the Volga entirely undermined Army Group Don's mission. The only rescue operation Hitler would contemplate was a German force cutting through and sustaining a corridor of supply to 6th Army's fortress. Army Group Don did not possess the means to stabilise the German front and fashion a permanent link with the beleaguered army simultaneously. Furthermore, Hitler's insistent refusal to release 6th Army from its tactical captivity on the Volga imposed an operational straitjacket upon Army Group Don that the Red Army was not slow to exploit.

Manstein set about turning Army Group Don into a viable fighting force, as Vasilevsky supervised the Don and Stalingrad Front's preparations to destroy 6th Army. On 30 November, still believing that the Red Army had encircled between 85,000 and 90,000 men, Vasilevsky issued final instructions for the assault. Yeremenko's Stalingrad Front was to attack north with Tolbukhin's 57th and Shumilov's 64th Armies. To the east, Chuikov's 62nd Army was to prevent the redeployment of German troops west of the city. The Don Front would attack from the west, north and northeast of the pocket. Christyakov's 21st and Batov's 65th Army would conduct the main assault from the west. In the north, Galinin's 24th Army would attack south towards Gorodische, while on the Don-Volga landbridge, Zhadov's 66th Army would fix German units in place and make contact with 62nd Army's right wing. The aim was to isolate and splinter the western edge of the pocket before Don Front and Stalingrad Front forces made contact at Gumrak.

On 2 December Stalingrad Front attacked, followed by Don Front on 4 December. After four days of fierce fighting, both Soviet fronts had made relatively little progress and suffered heavy casualties for their small gains. The 6th Army – ironically occupying Soviet defensive positions which were originally built to fend off 6th Army in early September 1942 – had been hard pressed but the pocket showed no sign of collapse. Operating on interior lines over the short distances within the pocket, German tactical reserves fought with a tenacity and effectiveness that stunned Soviet commanders. On 4 December Vasilevsky terminated the assault and informed Stalin that a considerable reinforcement of Soviet forces was essential. Stalin agreed to send further troops and signalled his iron determination to annihilate 6th Army by sending the elite 2nd Guards Army – which he had earmarked

Above: The bodies of German soldiers frozen in the snow drifts of the Russian steppe, a scene reminiscent of those west of Moscow between November 1941 and February 1942.

for Operation 'Saturn' – from Stavka reserve. Commanded by Lieutenant-General Malinovsky, it was one of the Red Army's most powerful formations. It contained three corps – 1st Guards and 13th Guards Rifle Corps with 2nd Guards Mechanised Corps – each with three divisions, mainly of elite guard status. Stavka deployed further Soviet reserves on the outer line of encirclement to secure the Stalingrad pocket. Lieutenant-General M. M. Popov, formerly deputy commander of the Stalingrad Front, took command of the 5th Shock Army. A powerful force of 71,000 troops, 5th Shock Army contained Major-General Rotmistrov's 7th Tank Corps and Volsky's 4th Mechanised Corps, in addition to five rifle divisions and 3rd Guards Cavalry Corps. It took up positions on the Chir with Trufanov's 51st Army on its left and Romanenko's 5th Tank Army on its right.

On 5 December Vasilevsky instructed Rokossovsky to devise new plans incorporating Malinovsky's 2nd Guards Army. On 8 December Malinovsky was present at Don Front headquarters and on 9 December Operation 'Koltso' ('Ring') was submitted to Stavka and Stalin. This operation proposed a sequence of three attacks designed to break up the pocket into smaller tactical pieces before systematically annihilating them. In the first stage, the Don Front would

Above: The burly Chuikov (front left) and other members of 62nd Army's command visit the famous Zaitsev, a member of 284th Siberian Division. It was a staged photo opportunity in January 1943.

Left: This Soviet sniper is perfectly clothed and equipped for the winter. Soviet troops could concentrate on fighting the enemy and surviving, rather than battling with the elements and starvation.

crush the four German divisions – 376th, 44th, 384th and 76th – beyond the river Rossosh in the northwestern corner of the pocket. In the second stage of the operation, Don Front troops would move southeast to meet Stalingrad Front's 64th Army coming north at Voporovno. This would confront German formations in the extreme west of the pocket, the Marianovka nose, with a choice of fighting withdrawal towards the city or annihilation as 64th Army destroyed German and Romanian divisions in the south. In the third stage, the unified forces of Don Front and Stalingrad Front would drive east for the Volga and splinter the remaining German divisions rather than attempting to encircle them, before completing the destruction of 6th Army. Stalin approved the plan on 11 December but insisted on the unification of the first two stages. German formations in the west and south were to be destroyed simultaneously before proceeding east to annihilate remaining German resistance. The operation was to be finished no later than 23 December 1942. However, as Stalin was confirming arrangements for the destruction of 6th Army, events were developing that would induce a dramatic revision of the Soviet timetable.

As Stavka considered Operation 'Koltso', Vasilevsky flew south-west to investigate reports of a significant

German build up on the Chir and at Kotelnikovo on the southern bank of the Don. On 1 December Manstein finalised Operation 'Winter Storm', designed to effect a junction with 6th Army. Manstein hoped to relieve 6th Army with a two-pronged offensive. The 48th Panzer Corps, 11th Panzer, 336th Infantry and 7th Luftwaffe Field Division would advance east to Kalach on the Don, while to its right, 4th Panzer's 57th Panzer Corps would move north-east from Kotelnikovo. Once contact had been established with 6th Army, 57th Panzer Corps – containing 6th Panzer, 23rd Panzer and 15th Luftwaffe Field Division – would open a supply corridor. Whether Operation 'Winter Storm' was designed to sustain 6th Army on the Volga or effect a breakout remained unclear. The codeword 'Thunderclap' would trigger a breakout but was dependent upon Hitler's exclusive authority.

However, on 30 November, Romanenko's 5th Tank Army attacked across the Chir on a front of 48km (30 miles) with 50,000 men, 900 guns and only 72 tanks, the majority of its armour having been transferred to the Don Front. In five days of bitter fighting, Army Abteilung 'Hollidt' held the line, but it was a close run thing. Major-General Balck's full-strength 11th Panzer Division, the cutting edge of 48th Panzer Corps, lost over half its strength as it performed tactical wonders to curtail 5th Tank Army. If the Chir line collapsed, the entire German operational position west of Stalingrad would implode, taking with it any hope of relief for 6th Army. Therefore, if 5th Tank Army's attack was a tactical failure, it forced a considerable revision of Operation 'Winter Storm'. It committed 48th Panzer Corps to the Chir, while the deployment of Popov's 5th Shock Army on 5th Tank Army's left, giving the Red Army a combined strength of 100,000 on the Chir, ensured that 'Winter Storm' would now consist of a single drive by Hoth's 4th Panzer Army.

As both Manstein and Vasilevsky realised, Major-General Trufanov's 51st Army was the weak link in the Soviet outer encirclement. It was deployed 97km (60 miles) south-west of Stalingrad with its back to the Aksai river and was only 34,000 strong, with three infantry divisions and 77 tanks represented by Colonel Tanaschshin's depleted 13th Tank Corps. Volsky's 4th Mechanised Corps, 51st Army's main strike force during Operation 'Uranus', had been shifted north to 5th Shock Army. An advance from Kotlenikovo possessed other advantages for Army Group Don. If it was further from Kotelnikovo to the pocket than from Kalach, the terrain, although crossed by the Aksai and Myshkova rivers, was more favourable. The rail junction at Kotelnikovo provided a useful springboard for the operation and would be vital in sustaining the supply corridor if, as was likely, Hitler refused to authorise a breakout. However, the operation was committed to a single line of advance and entirely dependent upon the German line on the Chir holding. Equally, even if 6th Panzer was at full strength, 23rd Panzer Division was damaged from fighting around Ordzhonikidze in the Caucasus. The situation was not helped by the failure of 17th Panzer to arrive before 'Winter Storm' began on 12 December. Vasilevsky had some warning but Operation 'Winter Storm' temporarily reclaimed the initiative for Army Group Don and forced a major revision in Soviet operational planning.

The 6th and 23rd Panzer Divisions, with 230 tanks between them and support from Lieutenant-General Pflugbeil's 4th Air Corps, made rapid progress against 51st Army. Trufanov's rifle divisions fell back on the Aksai as Vasilevsky and Yeremenko sought to buy time. A fast German breakthrough would threaten the rear of Tolbukhin's 57th Army on the southern side of

Right: An Italian soldier mans an anti-tank weapon overlooking the Don in December 1942. He is in a commanding position in common with the rest of the 8th Italian Army.

the inner encirclement. Naturally, Soviet commanders had to assume 6th Army would break out to meet 57th Panzer Corps, and their determination to sustain the siege of 6th Army dominated their actions over the next 48 hours. As 'Winter Storm' evolved, at 5th Shock Army's HQ on the Chir, Vasilevsky agreed with Yeremenko that 4th Mechanised Corps should form an improvised battle group with 13th Tank Corps. Volsky's 4th Mechanised was to blunt 6th Panzer, while 13th Tank Corps tackled the weaker 23rd Panzer. As Vasilevsky flew to Don Front's headquarters on 12 December he warned Malinovsky to prepare 2nd Guards Army to move south to block 'Winter Storm'. Yet Vasilevsky could not order 2nd Guards Army to abandon Operation 'Koltso' without Stalin's approval.

As Vasilevsky finally made contact with Stavka late on 12 December, Stalin reacted furiously to the suggestion that Operation 'Koltso' should be postponed and 'Saturn' drastically revised. Stalin refused to commit himself but at 0500 hours finally gave permission to move 2nd Guards Army to Yeremnko's Stalingrad Front. Stalin also ordered Vasilevsky to take personal charge of the Soviet counter-blow in the south while Marshal Voronov acted as the Stavka's coordinator of

Left: Sergeant Martinenkov, a hero of 39th Guards Division's struggle for the Red October Factory. This is a deliberately posed photograph, taken after he had survived the battle of Stalingrad.

Left: Sergeant Martinenkov, a hero of 39th Guards Division's struggle for the Red October Factory. This is a deliberately posed photograph, taken after he had survived the battle of Stalingrad.

As Malinovsky's 2nd Guards Army began its 193-km (120-mile) march across the open steppe through the blizzards of the Soviet winter, it was in a race against time to reach the River Myskova 48km (30 miles) south-west of Stalingrad. Its ability to win the race depended on the capacity of 51st Army to halt 57th Panzer Corp's advance over the Aksai south-west of Stalingrad. On 14 December, 57th Panzer Corps joined battle with 4th Mechanised and 13th Tank Corps. As 6th Panzer crossed the Aksai, it encountered Volsky's 4th Mechanised Corps at Verkhne Kumsky while 23rd Panzer confronted 13th Tank Corps. A swirling, confused battle developed, lasting three days, as 4th Mechanised Corps frustrated 6th Panzer's desire to advance quickly. By the time 6th Panzer secured Verkhne Kumsky on 17 December, bolstered by the arrival of 17th Panzer to the north-west, it was too late. On 19 December 17th Panzer and 6th Panzer, battling against dreadful weather, established minor bridgeheads over the Myshkova.

Malinovsky's 2nd Guards Army bore down on the Myshkova with the support of 6th Mechanised Corps. However, the victim of Trufanov's unsung 51st Army, 57th Panzer Corps, had missed its chance. Manstein reported to Hitler on 19 December 'it is impossible for the LVII Panzer Corps to establish a land link with

Operation 'Saturn'. Operation 'Koltso' was formally postponed at 2250 hours on 14 December. However, Rokossovsky and Yeremenko were 'to continue the systematic harassment of the encircled enemy troops by air and ground attacks, denying the enemy any breathing space by night or by day, pulling the encirclement ring ever tighter and nipping off any attempt by the encircled troops to break out of the ring.'

Below: Operations 'Winter Storm' and 'Small Saturn', Manstein's relief attempt and the Soviet offensive that forced him to abort it.

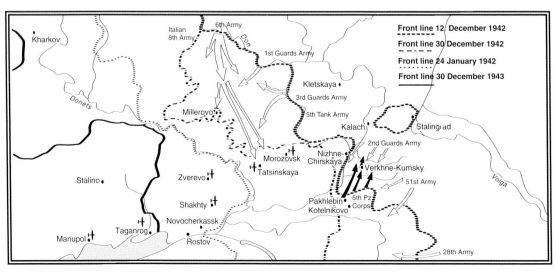

the 6th Army, to say nothing of maintaining the link. A breakout by the 6th Army to the southwest is the last alternative.' On 19 December a critical meeting took place within the cauldron at Gumrak, the site of 6th Army's headquarters, attended by Manstein's intelligence officer Major Eismann. At the meeting several participants advocated a breakout to 57th Panzer Corps. However, Major-General Schmidt argued that 6th Army did not possess sufficient mobility or strength to effect a breakout. In his opinion, breakout would be an acknowledgement of defeat and that if properly supplied, 6th Army could remain on the Volga until Easter. Paulus eventually concluded that a breakout was not possible and was in fact forbidden by Hitler. Manstein advised Paulus to send forces to meet 57th Panzer, not to abandon 6th Army's position, but to ensure resupply. A decision was essential, but neither Manstein nor Paulus would invoke 'Thunderclap' on their own initiative. The decisive point in the Stalingrad campaign had been reached: Hitler had a maximum of 72 hours to determine whether 6th Army should break out or remain on the Volga before 2nd Guards interposed decisively. On 18 December 2nd Guards Army forward detachments had moved into the Soviet line between 5th Shock Army on the Chir, and 51st Army on its left. Vasilevsky transferred 4th Mechanised and 4th Cavalry Corps from Trufanov's 51st Army along with the brand new 6th Mechanised Corps to 2nd Guards Army. Simultaneously, Stalin approved Vasilevsky's plan to concentrate Soviet forces for a massive counterattack on 4th Panzer Army beginning on 22 December. The attack was to be supported by 5th Shock Army attacking north-west into the heart of the German position on the Chir. On 21 December Manstein pressed Hitler

Above: Soldiers, wrapped in their winter clothes, trudge wearily through the wreckage of the unrecognisable city of Stalingrad. A more desolate scene can hardly be imagined.

to order 'Thunderclap' as 4th Panzer could not hold on much longer in face of the threat posed by 2nd Guards. Hitler's response was to suggest 6th Army did not possess the fuel to break out 48km (30 miles). Paradoxically, his indecision was decisive in condemning 6th Army to death, as the situation elsewhere forced Manstein to choose between 6th Army, the survival of Army Group Don, and the entire German position in southern Russia.

In his reaction to events, Vasilevsky never lost sight of the fact that the key to the destruction of 6th Army and the defeat of 'Winter Storm' lay on the Chir. In this context, his diversion of 2nd Guards Army from Don Front represented a flexible tactical evolution of his operational plan, not a total revision. The key to 'Winter Storm,' apart from Hitler's indecision, was the speed with which the Soviet high command reacted in forming the Aksai battlegroup and in re-deploying 2nd Guards Army. Vasilevsky recognised that the diversion of 2nd Guards and 5th Tank Army's containment on the Chir meant Operation 'Saturn' was beyond Soviet means. The deep operation south to Rostov moving through Army Group Don's operational rear would be vulnerable to counterattack if Soviet forces on the Don and Chir proved unable to break or fix German formations. However, the concept of a deep, though less ambitious, operation into the operational rear of Army Group Don remained valid. If successful, it could indirectly defeat 'Winter Storm' and regain the initiative for the Red Army, thus securing the isolation of 6th Army. This was the genesis of Operation 'Small Saturn'.

During 14 December Voronezh and South-Western Front received new orders relating to Operation 'Saturn'. It was to be replaced by Operation 'Small Saturn', in essence a smaller version of 'Saturn'. Indeed Stalin's orders stressed that 'the breakthrough will proceed in those sectors which were projected under Operation 'Saturn'. As in 'Saturn', 8th Italian Army on Army Group Don's northern flank was to be destroyed in a concentric attack from the north by Kuznetsov's 1st Guards, moving south to meet Lelyushenko's 3rd Guards moving west from its positions on the Don. This would trigger a deep operation as in 'Saturn' but, as Stalin pointed out, 'the revision lies in the fact that the main blow will be aimed not at the south, but towards the south-east in the direction of Nizhny Astahkov, to exit at Morozovsk ... breaking into the rear of the enemy forces facing Romanenko and Lelyushenko'. A key part of 'Saturn' was the fixing of German units on the Don-Chir line to permit the deep operation. On 14 December, 5th Shock Army forced the Germans to evacuate their bridgehead over the Don-Chir confluence at Niznhe Chirskaya. These attacks, with 5th Tank Army's repeated probes, ensured 48th Panzer Corps would play no part in 'Winter Storm'. On 18 December Vasilevsky again ordered 5th Shock to attack the Chir in coordination with 5th Tank Army in order to fix Army Abteilung 'Hollidt' and protect the deep operation as it moved south against Army Group Don's left flank and rear.

Right: Soviet infantry attacking to the south of Stalingrad from where Operation 'Winter Storm', the German attempt to cut a path through to 6th Army, came.

Left: The wreckage of battle in December 1942. Operation 'Small Saturn' got off to a sticky start on 16 December 1942 but within days South-Western Front had demolished the Italian-German position.

At 0800 hours on 16 December, 'Small Saturn' began disastrously. Fog prevented a targeted barrage and as the Soviet armies crossed the frozen Don in heavy snow, they met fierce resistance. By the end of 16 December, in the north, Kharitonov's 6th Army had advanced only 3.2km (2 miles) against the Italian Cosseria Division and 385th German Division. To the east, on the Don, Kuznetsov's 1st Guards struggled to make any impression on the Italian Ravenna and 27th Panzer Division. Vatutin attempted to secure a tactical breakthrough by committing tank corps designated to conduct the deep operation. It was a complete failure. As 17th, 18th and 25th Tank Corps moved forward, they blundered into an unmarked minefield, losing over 30 tanks in minutes. To the south on the upper reaches of the Chir, Lelyushenko's 3rd Guards made little progress. As they attacked across the frozen Chir, up the raised western bank, they were met by a storm of fire and counterattacks from the 62nd and 294th German divisions. Operation 'Small Saturn' had got off to a shocking start, notable only for its lack of cooperation between artillery, infantry and armour. However, a regrouping followed by improved all-arms cooperation reaped benefits on 17 December. By mid-afternoon the Italo-German line at the junction of 6th Army and 1st Guards began to creak as Soviet infantry and airpower attacked in conjunction with 17th, 18th and 25th Tank Corps. As dusk fell, Soviet armour penetrated the

Above: As the Red Army broke through, 8th Italian Army was encircled and annihilated. Soviet armoured forces rampaged virtually unopposed in the operational rear of Manstein's Army Group Don.

Italo-German line and Vatutin ordered 6th Army and 1st Guards to sustain their attack throughout the night. In bitter fighting, 3rd Guards Army clawed its way across the Chir.

By dawn on 19 December, 6th Army and 1st Guards had torn a hole 48km (30 miles) wide by 32km (20 miles) deep, while 3rd Guards was making steady, if bloody, progress west. In line with Triandafillov's theories on the deep operation, South-Western Front's exploitation forces were assigned key missions of disrupting Army Group Don's operational rear, severing German communications and withdrawal routes and blocking German reserves. On the western flank Poluboyarov's 17th Tank Corps was to take the key junction of Kantemirovka and head south with Bakharov's 18th Tank Corps to the main German supply base at Millerovno, 97km (60 miles) west of the Chir. To their left, Badanov's 24th Tank Corps and Pavlov's 25th Tank Corps were assigned the vital objectives of Tatinskaya and Morozovsk respectively. These were the principal airfields from which Richthofen's Air Fleet 4 was struggling to sustain 6th Army. They were also key rail junctions connecting Manstein's northern and southern wings and so natu-

rally their loss would represent a terrible blow to 6th Army and Army Group Don. Finally, on South-Western Front's eastern flank closest to the Don and Chir, Russiyanov's 1st Guards Mechanised Corps was to drive on Army Abteilung 'Hollidt's' left flank and rear before advancing on Morozovsk. These were ambitious operational objectives, but such was the pace of the advance on 19 December that Vatutin received Stavka's permission to expand 'Small Saturn' into the original 'Saturn'. On that same day, 19 December, Kuznetsov's 1st Guards met Lelyushenko's 3rd Guards moving west, completing the encirclement of 8th Italian Army. Without mobile reserves, the Axis position disintegrated. By 20 December the Soviet mobile groups were rampant as Hollidt struggled to contain 5th Tank and 5th Shock Army on the Chir. Pavlov's 25th Tank Corps battled with retreating Axis forces, while Badanov's 24th Tank Corps charged south to Tatinskaya. By 23 December, approaching Tatinskaya, 24th Tank Corps was 193km (120 miles) from its start

Left: As Soviet troops moved into the city from the west during January 1943 they made contact with Russian troops who had been isolated on the western bank of the city for several months.

line and short of fuel, support and ammunition. Nevertheless, at dawn on 24 December, the corps stormed Tatinskaya, taking the German garrison by surprise. Badanov's tanks marauded around, shooting up supplies, rail cars and the airfield. The German aircraft abandoned Tatinskaya and flew west.

The importance of Morozovsk and Tatinskaya to Army Group Don's operational position, 'Winter Storm' and, above all, the airlift, outweighed all other considerations for Manstein. Badanov's bold advance stung 48th Panzer Corps into action. On Christmas Day 1942, 11th Panzer, moving north-west from the Chir, trapped the exhausted 24th Tank Corps in Tatinskaya. The fate of the Soviet tank corps assumed great symbolic importance for Stavka. In the early hours of 26 December,

Stalin made Badanov the first recipient of the new Order of Suvorov, and renamed 24th Tank as 2nd Guards Tank Corps. As Vasilevsky informed Stalin that South-Western Front needed extra forces to complete 'Big Saturn', Stalin reminded Vatutin to 'remember Badanov, do not forget Badanov, get him out at any cost'. On 26 December, a small force cut through with fuel and supplies to Badanov, but remained trapped with him. To the north, German forces held off Pavlov's 25th Tank and Russiyanov's 1st Guards Mechanised Corps. Vatutin gave Badanov permission to break out, and at 0130 hours on 29 December, Badanov escaped to safety, having taken 11th Panzer completely by surprise. The Germans repossessed Tatinskaya, and they also held onto Morozovsk and resumed the airlift. As the tempo of the Soviet offensive declined, the Germans imposed some order upon the wreckage of Army Group Don's left flank.

The traditional analysis of 6th Army's fate focuses upon Hitler's reluctance to allow an early breakout, his insistence on an airlift, its failure, and his subsequent refusal to allow 6th Army to break out to meet 'Winter Storm' in December 1942. There is little doubt that denying an early breakout was a decisive and disastrous decision for 6th Army. However, apart from 62nd Army's epic struggle and Operation 'Uranus', the Soviet contribution to 6th Army's defeat is rarely considered. In particular, Vasilevsky's swift reaction to 'Winter Storm' and the implications of Operation 'Small Saturn' are often neglected. Operation 'Small

Below: Soviet infantry move quickly through the streets of Stalingrad looking for pockets of German resistance. By January 1943, the 6th Army's strength and morale had declined noticeably.

Right: A clearly staged photo opportunity for Chuikov and his commanders following their historic victory at Stalingrad. Chuikov's 62nd Army kept up the pressure on 6th Army until the latter's surrender.

Saturn' failed to capture and hold any of its specific objectives but was, nevertheless, an outstanding operational success. It played a key role in condemning 6th Army to its grave on the Volga. On 20 December Manstein cabled Zeitzler about the threat to Rostov and Army Group Don's operational rear. Significantly, he dispatched 6th Panzer north-west to the Chir as 17th Panzer and 23rd Panzer struggled towards the Myshkova. To all intents and purposes, by 24 December Manstein had effectively abandoned 'Winter Storm' for three reasons. First, because Hitler refused to authorise 6th Army's breakout, but secondly, because 'Saturn' forced him to sacrifice 6th Army to save Army Group Don and Army Group A. Thirdly, such was the operational success of 'Saturn' that it had already rendered the tactical success or failure of Operation 'Winter Storm' irrelevant.

In the face of the threat posed by 'Small Saturn', even if 4th Panzer Army had established a link with 6th Army, it is unlikely that 6th Army could have been sustained on the Volga, as neither Army Group Don nor the Luftwaffe had the capacity to supply it. Nor, in the unlikely event of Hitler granting permission, could 6th Army have successfully broken out. By the admission of Paulus and Schmidt, 6th Army was in a weak state. The men were starving and shattered, with sufficient mobility and fuel for only 24km (15 miles), but safety did not lie south-west of Stalingrad: it lay further west, beyond the Chir. In the face of Stalin's determination to destroy 6th Army, a weakened 6th Army and 57th Panzer Corps would not have survived the attentions of 2nd Guards Army and the Soviet armies surrounding Stalingrad. Equally, Soviet forces on the Chir would have been diverted to ensure the destruction of 4th Panzer and 6th Army. As the systemic power of Army Group Don lay in its operational rear – the area threatened by the deep operation of 'Small Saturn' – by 22 December, further direct or indirect assistance for 'Winter Storm' risked the operational destruction of Army Group Don and a major strategic threat to Army Group A. In such circumstances, German operational and strategic interests were now better served by 6th Army remaining on the Volga, tying down seven Soviet armies. Therefore, 'Small Saturn' was a decisive development in the Stalingrad campaign.

With secure lines of supply north and east of the Don, the Red Army could risk a temporary operational reversal of fronts, with Soviet forces operating west of the Don-Chir line towards Rostov, while German forces operated east of the Chir and south of the Don. The Wehrmacht could not; the capture of Rostov would trap Army Group A in the Caucasus, destroy the operational rear of Army Group Don, and isolate 6th Army and 4th Panzer. As 'Small Saturn' demonstrated, German supply lines in southern Russia were extremely vulnerable and the lack of correlation between German strategic ends and means ensured there were few reserves available to protect them. Army Group Centre was preoccupied with Operation 'Mars', while between Army Group Centre and the upper Don, 2nd Panzer Army and 2nd Army were already struggling to hold the German front together.

Therefore, Vasilevsky's swift reaction to 'Winter Storm' in conjunction with the operational success of 'Small Saturn' sentenced 6th Army to death. At 0800 hours on 24 December, having already resumed the assault on the Chir, 149,000 Soviet troops attacked 4th Panzer on the Myshkova. In 72 hours Soviet forces were advancing west along the southern reaches of the Don. The dual threat to Rostov from South-Western Front in the north and Yeremenko's Stalingrad Front from the east had dramatic implications for 6th Army. In the small hours of 28 December 1942, as the German position in southern Russia crumbled, Hitler authorised the withdrawal of Army Group A towards Rostov and the retreat of Army Group Don to a line 241km (150 miles) west of Stalingrad. Paulus and 6th Army were alone, without hope of rescue, dependent upon the Luftwaffe's airlift or a miracle. Stalin was determined there would be no escape.

CHAPTER 9

The Destruction of 6th Army

1 January to 2 February 1943

As 6th Army hoped for a miracle, Colonel-General von Richthofen prayed for a break in the miserable weather that had constantly undermined the Luftwaffe's airlift since its beginning on 25 November 1942.

The 24th Tank Corp's retreat from Tatinskaya and the successful defence of Morozovsk enabled the Luftwaffe to resume operations from these vital air bases. Yet it was a hopeless task, increasingly driven by the desire to alleviate 6th Army's death pangs. As predicted in November, the Luftwaffe was not capable of sustaining 6th Army. As the misplaced hopes invested in Operation 'Winter Storm' faded, and the cruel reality of their fate sunk into the starving and exhausted soldiers of 6th Army, between Christmas Day and New Year German morale deteriorated rapidly. In response, the Red Army began to finalise its plans for the much-delayed Operation 'Koltso'. The 6th Army was to be destroyed: there was no escape.

The Lutwaffe's airlift had been in trouble from the start, cursed by a lack of suitable aircraft, inadequate ground resources, the Soviet air force and the weather. The long, dark and cold winters of the Stalingrad region provided the worst conditions imaginable for sustaining a starving army the size of a small city. This is not to say the airlift could have worked had it been high summer – it could not – but the blizzard-whipped freezing steppe

Left: The 300,000-strong 6th Army had been humbled and destroyed. Some 91,000 men, including 24 of the rank of general, had surrendered to Soviet troops by 2 February 1943.

increasingly exacerbated the basic flaws in the operation. The weather imposed a fantastic strain on man and machine that the paltry depth of Air Fleet 4's resources struggled to overcome. In his study of the Luftwaffe's role in the Stalingrad campaign, Dr Joel Hayward quotes von Richthofen on 26 November, in the earliest days of the airlift, complaining of dreadful weather: 'Fog. Icing over. Snowstorm. No air operations, no supply possible.' Flying conditions for pilots on both sides were atrocious, but the Luftwaffe pilots, handling cumbersome, heavily laden transport planes in low cloud, fog and blizzards, cursed the conditions. A blind take-off and landing were the norm rather than the exception and this inflicted a steady toll which gradually assumed critical proportions. Hayward reveals Lieutenant-General Fiebig's despondency on 27 November: 'Communications with rear areas have disappeared ... we have one blizzard after another at Tatinskaya; a desolate situation.' A vicious circle developed; as 6th Army's need became greater, the Luftwaffe's ability to supply it lessened. The greater the demands on fewer pilots and machines, the more attrition was inflicted on diminishing assets which were already insufficient to meet even half of 6th

Below: The bodies of hundreds of German soldiers. This was the army that had marched across the steppe in the summer of 1942 supremely confident in its ability to destroy the Red Army.

Army's needs. The improvised nature of the operation and the hasty German retreat beyond the Chir, abandoning valuable winter equipment, ensured that the Luftwaffe did not possess sufficient ground facilities to deal with the cold. Thus, although ground crews worked long hours in freezing conditions, the lack of heated hangars, lubricants and cold-start facilities seriously undermined the efficient use of Air Fleet 4's scant resources. Several airfields did not possess sufficient – or indeed any – snow ploughs, reducing exhausted ground personnel to clearing runways with shovels in a region where 30cm (11.8in) of snow regularly fell in a day. Major-General Pickert recalled after surviving Stalingrad that inside the pocket: 'The cold caused unimaginable difficulties in starting engines, as well as engine maintenance, in spite of the well known and already proven cold starting procedures. Without any protection against the cold or snowstorms, ground support personnel worked unceasingly to the point where their hands became frozen. Fog, icing and snowstorms caused increasing difficulties which were compounded at night.'

The difficulties that Pickert and others encountered at night were largely the responsibility of the resurgent Soviet air force. Even with a massive influx of aircraft, Air Fleet 4 did not possess the resources to wage a war of attrition. Soviet accounts have exaggerated the number of German aircraft shot down by Soviet pilots

Above: The remnants of a once-proud city. In the last days of German resistance in the pocket, troops congregated in Stalingrad, awaiting their fate as the Soviet forces squeezed the pocket tighter and tighter.

Below: By February 1943 the city had been smashed beyond recognition, unfit for human habitation. This aerial photograph conveys some idea of the staggering destructiveness of the battle of Stalingrad.

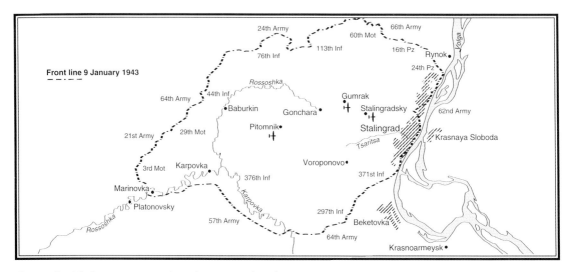

Front line 9 January 1943

24th Army

60th Mot

66th Army

113th Inf

16th Pz

Rynok

Volga

76th Inf

24th Pz

Rossoshka

64th Army

44th Inf

Gumrak

Baburkin

Gonchara

Stalingradsky

62nd Army

Pitomnik

Stalingrad

21st Army

29th Mot

Krasnaya Sloboda

Tsaritsa

3rd Mot

Karpovka

Voroponovo

371st Inf

Marinovka

376th Inf

Karpovka

Platonovsky

Rossoshka

57th Army

297th Inf

Beketovka

64th Army

Krasnoarmeysk

Above: The Stalingrad Kessel *in January 1943, showing the three airfields that were the pocket's lifeline.*

during the lift, but its improved performance played an important role in securing victory at Stalingrad. Colonel-General Novikov continued his strategy of night bombing, the aim being to wreck ground facilities and deprive German soldiers of sleep. In early 1943 Novikov created an air-defence ring around Stalingrad with a radius of 50km (31 miles). The ring was divided into five sectors patrolled by organised fighter groups who, instead of chasing German air-

craft around Stalingrad, took advantage of the predictable flightpaths the airlift imposed upon the Luftwaffe. It was far from watertight, but inflicted a steady toll on the transport planes on their journey to and from Stalingrad. The Red Army's flak units also capitalised upon the obvious supply routes so that a steady curtain of fire confronted Luftwaffe pilots as they entered and left the pocket. After a poor start in November, only once, on 7 December, did the Luftwaffe meet its daily target of 300 tons. However,

Below: A Soviet flag of victory flutters above Stalingrad, on the Mamayev Kurgan. It conveyed the simple, but stark message that, against all the odds, the Red Army had prevailed.

the 362 tons brought in were part of only 1055 tons the Luftwaffe managed to bring in between 1 and 9 December 1942. In the meantime, 6th Army lived off horsemeat and pitiful rations of bread.

The Soviet threat posed to Tatinskaya and Morozovsk by Operation 'Small Saturn' further undermined the airlift. On 20 December, Fiebig advised Richthofen to begin the evacuation of aircraft and personnel west to other airfields. This would ensure that the precious cold weather equipment and stores the Luftwaffe had managed to accumulate were not shot up or lost in a chaotic, last-minute evacuation. However, from Göring's point of view, it was unthinkable that the Luftwaffe should move away from the pocket at the same time as Operation 'Winter Storm' was advancing on it. On 19 December, even though he had no serious intention of allowing 6th Army to break out, Hitler ordered Fiebig to ensure it received 4000 tons of fuel and 1800 tons of rations, a figure regarded by Fiebig as simply impossible to accomplish. Hitler's chronic indecision (or deceit) over the ultimate purpose of 'Winter Storm' seriously compromised the airlift. If he intended to allow 6th Army to break out, then fuel had to be the priority, as well as ammunition and food. If, however, 6th Army was to stay on the Volga, whether or not

Below: In a pathetic scene soldiers of the 6th Army shuffle aimlessly around the ruins of Stalingrad. The brash, confident men of the summer of 1942, have been defeated by soldiers of the Red Army.

'Winter Storm' succeeded, then food and ammunition had to be the staple of the airlift. Hitler's inability (or unwillingness) to make a decision ensured that the airlift carried bulky fuel that 6th Army would never use. Meanwhile, German soldiers starved or faced Soviet attacks with virtually no ammunition.

With Soviet forces 24km (15 miles) away from Tatinskaya and Morozovsk, on 23 December Göring had issued a 'stand fast' order. Morozovsk and Tatinskaya could only be evacuated when Soviet forces began to fire directly on the airfields. Morozovsk never fell, but as Badonov raided Tatinskaya, aircraft flew in all directions, leaving behind tankers, spare parts and other equipment essential to sustaining the lift in such inhospitable conditions. A bitter Fiebig described it as incredible that he had only lost 46 of the 170 aircraft stationed at Tatinskaya. Yet he knew he was clutching at tactical straws from operational disaster. The lift resumed from Tatinskaya within days, but the damage in terms of lost aircraft capacity and support assets was done. In the week of 25–31 December 1942, the Luftwaffe delivered just over 900 tons of supplies to 6th Army – less than half described as the minimum daily average in November – to an army that had been starving for several weeks. The Luftwaffe commanders were desperate to return Tatinskaya and Morozovsk to something like full working order, not only because of their superior facilities but also because of their close proximity of approximately 160km (100 miles) to the pocket. The

Above: German commanders in Soviet captivity. Clearly some have spent more time in the field than others. Seydlitz is fourth from the left flanked by an utterly dejected Major-General Pfeffer.

consequences of flying from Novocherkassk and Salsk which lay 97–113km (60–70 miles) further west had become painfully apparent. Fuel took space from desperately needed supplies, while the increased distance and time exacerbated the risk of accidents and interception by Soviet planes. The greater turn-round time undermined overall capacity as fewer craft and pilots brought less into the pocket and fewer wounded out.

However, the return to Morozovsk and Tatinskaya was shortlived as events on the ground overtook those in the air. On 31 December, Hollidt informed Fiebig that he was abandoning them and withdrawing west to contain the threat posed by Stalingrad Front. The attack of 5th Shock and 2nd Guards Army down the northern and southern banks of the Don was impossible to contain unless the Germans withdrew. A dismayed Fiebig knew the airlift could not recover from this setback. Although the airlift continued until the last days of 6th Army's struggle, it had already failed where it could never have hoped to succeed. In the final days, a bitter Paulus reproached the Luftwaffe for the promises it had failed to keep. Yet, as Paulus knew, the reasons for 6th Army's destruction lay deeper than the Luftwaffe's failure to deliver Göring's sychophantic promises.

The climatic scenes described by Richthofen, Fiebig and Pickert, amongst others, help to define the memory of Stalingrad, yet they could easily have been commenting upon a scene west of Moscow in December 1941 or January 1942. The Wehrmacht's struggles west of Moscow were the product of deep strategic errors committed in August 1941 and the whole concept of the German *Vernichtungschlacht*. The problems of 6th Army and the airlift were symptomatic of a gross tendency to overestimate the power of the Third Reich and the tactical ability of the German armed forces. As on the ground, so in the air there was a chronic, almost criminal, lack of balance between ends and means. The very forces responsible for sustaining the trapped and starving 6th Army lived a hand to mouth, improvised existence. As at Moscow, the Luftwaffe's struggle with the weather was not the cause of their defeat, but the symptom of strategic decisions taken in July 1942. As 1942 drew to its close, the outlook for 6th Army remained unremittingly bleak. Defeat and disaster loomed.

Operation 'Small Saturn' breached the Italian and German line on 19 December and Marshal Voronov flew to meet Rokossovsky at Don Front headquarters. Stalin persistently harried Don Front to accelerate the operation. Eventually Voronov persuaded Stalin that a further delay was necessary, as well as reinforcements. However, the Don Front continued to labour under the false illusion that 85,000 German troops were in the cauldron. The plan was submitted to Stavka on 27 December as Don Front received 20,000 infantry reserves. It proposed one main attack from the west, to split the pocket in two, conducted by 65th Army with 21st Army on the right and 24th Army on the left, to be supported by the full weight of Lt-General Rudenko's 16th Air Army. The other armies in the Stalingrad region – 57th, 64th, 66th and 62nd – were to support the advance with subsidiary attacks which, in the words of Rokossovsky, 'were to pin down as many enemy forces as possible and deny him any opportunity of manoeuvring'. As Soviet infantry divisions remained weak, Voronov and Rokossovsky integrated the use of massed artillery fire to suppress German defenders and drive Soviet armies through the breach. However, the plan was criticised by Stavka for making insufficient use of Soviet armies in the south and north. Equally, the splintering of the pocket was condemned as encouraging diverging axes of attack. Stavka recommended three main points of effort, with a major assault by 57th Army in the south designed to link up with the westerly thrust by 21st and 65th Armies. Stavka also ordered a more powerful assault by 66th Army from the north of Stalingrad. This would be followed by a single advance west to destroy the remnants of 6th Army. The assault was to begin on 6 January 1943 and was to last between five and six days before Rokossovsky submitted his detailed plans for the second phase of Operation 'Koltso'.

However, Stavka did agree with Voronov and Rokossovsky's suggestion that Operation 'Koltso' should be undertaken by a single, enlarged Don Front, commanded by Rokossovsky, not a combined operation involving Yeremenko's Stalingrad Front. On 1 January 1943 the Stalingrad Front was disbanded. The 64th, 57th and 62nd Army were subordinated to the Don Front, which now deployed a total of 218,000 men on the inner ring of encirclement. The selection of Lieutenant-General Konstantin Rokossovsky to complete the destruction of 6th Army was ironic. Rokossovsky's career epitomises the fall, bare survival and eventual triumph of the professionalism of the Red

Above: The newly-promoted Paulus walks into captivity and a place in history. He was well treated by his Soviet captors, but was the first German field marshal ever to surrender to the enemy.

Army's officer corps in the face of the combined onslaught of Stalin and the Wehrmacht. Volunteering for the Imperial Russian Army in 1914, he rose from private soldier to junior officer by 1917. After serving as a Red cavalry squadron and regimental commander in the Russian Civil War, Rokossovsky rose with the Red Army as it developed in the 1920s and 1930s. He commanded 5th Cavalry Division in the early 1930s (with Zhukov as one of his regimental commanders) and, in 1936, took command of 5th Cavalry Corps. However, Rokossovsky was arrested on 17 August 1937 and charged with sabotage, being a Polish spy and unspecified crimes against the people. He was interrogated, tortured and subjected to mock execution, but escaped with a prison sentence that left him in jail until his release on 22 March 1940 within days of the Red Army's final, humiliating pyrrhic victory over Finland. As the commander of 9th Mechanised Corps in June 1941, Major-General Rokossovsky acquitted himself well, before distinguishing himself at Smolensk in July 1941. Commanding 16th Army at Moscow, he played a critical role in blunting the advance of 3rd and 4th Panzer Army but was badly wounded in March 1942, before taking control of the Don Front in late September 1942. Equally talented but more even tempered than Zhukov, he was respected by German commanders as a tough and able opponent. In contrast to many Soviet commanders, he was widely admired by his own troops and inspired a fierce personal loyalty among his officers.

While aggrieved at not being allowed to finish off the 6th Army, Yeremenko received command of the Southern Front. The Southern Front encompassed 2nd Guards, 51st Army, 5th Shock and 28th Army. It was already heavily engaged in driving 4th Panzer west along the Don, while Popov's 5th Shock continued to harass German forces on the southern Chir. As Stavka finally approved Operation 'Koltso', it simultaneously endorsed several other Soviet operational plans designed to complete the destruction of German forces in southern Russia. Golikov's Voronezh Front was to cripple the northern wing of Army Group B by destroying 2nd Hungarian Army. It was to follow this by an attack on General von Salmuth's 2nd German Army, west of Voronezh. Stavka's intention was to isolate Army Group B from its southern neighbour, Army Group Don, and destroy what was left of the sorely tried units of Field Marshal von Weich's command. Manstein's battered but resilient formations were to be destroyed by a further South-Western Front offensive

Below: The sheer enormity of 6th Army and Germany's catastrophe dawns on this German soldier. It was impossible to disguise the scale of the German defeat and the significance of the Red Army's victory.

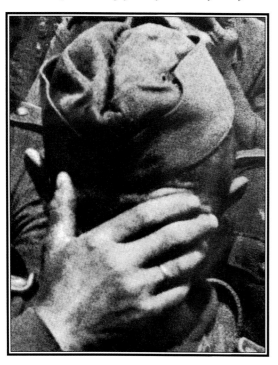

on Army Group Don's left, working in cooperation with 5th Tank and 5th Shock armies, which would simultaneously assault Manstein's right flank. These offensives incorporated the tactical principles of deep battle into operational planning. Once penetration had been achieved, German formations were to be destroyed as isolated, splintered groupings no longer capable of providing mutual support. This was preferable to destroying them as one massive whole in a *Kesselschlacht*, which might be capable of prolonged resistance, as 6th Army had demonstrated. Apart from the annihilation of 6th Army, the real prize remained Army Group A. Stavka instructed Yeremenko's Southern Front to race for Rostov, trapping Army Group A. The Southern Front was ordered to coordinate its operations with renewed activity by Tyulenev's Trans-Caucasus Front. On 4 January, the Black Sea Group – commanded by Petrov but part of the Trans-Caucasus Front – was ordered to undertake Operation 'Gory' (Mountain) and Operation 'More' (Sea). The aim of Operation 'Gory' was to destroy Ruoff's 17th Army south of Krasnodar and advance north into the rear of 1st Panzer Army. Operation 'More', conducted by Petrov's 47th Army, would simultaneously outflank 17th Army by conducting an amphibious landing at Novorossiisk. In the central Caucasus, Tyulenev's Northern Group was to assault 1st Panzer. It was to drive 1st Panzer north-west towards Rostov where it would be crushed between the north-eastern advance of the Trans-Caucasus Front and the westward march of the Southern Front.

Southern Front launched its westward drive on 7 January, but it confronted deep snow as well as increasing opposition as the left flank of the withdrawing 1st Panzer Army merged with the southern flank of 4th Panzer. Nevertheless, by 11 January, 2nd Guards and 51st armies had reached the river Manych, 241km (150 miles) east of Rostov. However, the Soviet offensive was hampered by adverse weather conditions. Petrov launched Operation 'Gory' on 16 January, but the attack was blighted by rain and flood. The rapid advance of the tempo required to corner 1st Panzer was out of the question. On 20 January, Petrov informed Vasilevsky that the use of armour in such conditions was impossible. The wooded, hilly terrain that had so frustrated 17th Army's advance on Tuapse during September 1942 now came to its rescue as German troops withdrew, secure in the knowledge that Soviet armoured corps could not outstrip them as they had done German forces in 'Uranus' and 'Small

both 1st and 4th Panzer armies would avoid complete disaster. Nevertheless, as they moved towards temporary sanctuary, they were a shadow of their former selves at the onset of Operation 'Blau' in June 1942. There was little to celebrate. They were being chased out of southern Russia, having failed to achieve their objectives. Where Stavka had failed in its ambitious attempt to annihilate Army Group A, elsewhere in January 1943, Soviet armies were on the rampage.

On 12 January Golikov's Voronezh Front had ripped into Jany's 2nd Hungarian Army, defending Army Group B's northern flank on the upper Don south of Voronezh. The aim was to destroy the Hungarians before attacking the exposed southern flank of von Salmuth's 2nd German Army in a successive operation. Golikov's forces deployed on a broad front with three designated zones of breakthrough. The purpose, as usual, was to undermine the depth and density of the Hungarian defences, dispersing their reserves, and permitting a rapid penetration of the line. In the north, Chernyakhovsky's 60th and Chibisov's 38th would fix 2nd German Army, while in

Saturn'. Operation 'More' floundered in rough seas that impeded both landings and regular supply. After a week of struggle, it became clear that Petrov's advance would be fitful and disjointed rather than the decisive deep operation which Stavka required. As Soviet forces slowed, 1st Panzer Army accelerated its withdrawal and the damage it inflicted to bridges, roads and communications conspired to frustrate the Trans-Caucasus Front further. Greedy for more success, Stalin drove on the Trans-Caucasus and Southern Fronts, but to no avail: the forces of nature proved stronger than his iron will. By 24 January it was clear, given the Germans' determination to hold Rostov, that

Below: German commanders were treated considerably better than their men. In time some, such as Seydlitz, co-operated with the Soviet authorities in denouncing Hitler.

the centre, Moskalenko's 40th Army would smash through the Hungarian lines to meet Rybalko's 3rd Tank Army coming north. The 2nd German Army had two corps of seven divisions, while 2nd Hungarian, supported by one German infantry division, was over 150,000 strong. The southern end of the line was held by the remnants of Gariboldi's 8th Italian Army. The three divisions of the Italian Alpine Corps had not been savaged during 'Small Saturn', and Gariboldi also commanded 24th Panzer Corps, containing a panzer division and two infantry divisions. The Axis divisions were understrength, but held defensive positions they had occupied since the early days of 'Blau' in July 1942 and, in some cases, for nearly a year. A Soviet reconnaissance in force began on 12 January, followed by the main assault over the next 48 hours. By 15 January, 2nd Hungarian's defences had been penetrated in several areas and were in utter disarray. As 3rd Tank Army rushed through the breach, it linked up with Moskalenko's 40th Army and, on 18 January 1943, encircled 2nd Hungarian, the majority of the Italian Alpine Corps, and elements of 24th Panzer. By 27

Above: As the Don Front advanced east in January 1943, it crushed all resistance. All roads to Stalingrad were littered with the bodies of German soldiers as the Red Army destroyed the 6th Army.

January it had taken 86,000 prisoners and destroyed 2nd Hungarian. On 28 January, Moskalenko's 40th Army moved north against 2nd German as Pukhov's 13th Army, from the Bryansk Front, moved south to trap von Salmuth's forces, which were pinned to the east by the 38th and 60th Armies. However, Hitler had temporarily learned his lesson and the forward elements of 2nd German had already begun to withdraw from Voronezh. In the event, only two of von Salmuth's three corps were encircled, but 2nd German had received a savaging, and was barely fit to hold the line.

The German position on the upper and middle Don was deteriorating by the day. By the end of January 1942, Army Group B had ceased to exist as an effective operational command, leaving a gaping 322-km (200-mile) hole in the line. To the south, Army Group Don's flanks were under attack with no anchor as Army Groups A and B withdrew, pursued by Soviet

Right: German survivors shuffle into captivity. Their battle for survival was far from over; through a mixture of malnutrition, cold, casual Soviet neglect and brutality many prisoners would not survive.

forces. In an impressive series of successive and simultaneous deep operations, the Red Army had destroyed the German position in southern Russia. In summary, the Stalingrad campaign had produced a dramatic reversal of fortune: all that remained for Stalin was to administer the killing blow to 6th Army.

However, on 3 January Voronov and Rokossovsky dared to ask Stalin for another delay, of four days, to Operation 'Koltso', scheduled for 6 January. Stalin was furious, insisting to Voronov that 'you'll sit it out so long down there that the Germans will take you and Rokossovskii prisoner'. Nevertheless, for all his sound and fury, in contrast to Hitler, Stalin heard out Voronov and granted Rokossovsky's request. Stalin also gave permission for Rokossovsky to offer Paulus the opportunity to surrender. In his memoirs, Rokossovsky recalled that the idea sprung from New Year celebrations at Don Front headquarters attended by Voronov, Vasilevsky and Novikov. Soviet intelligence was aware of the decline in German morale following the failure of 'Winter Storm' and probably thought the moment propitious. Equally, unlike many Soviet commanders, Rokossovsky was keen to avoid unnecessary casualties and saw little sense in the pointless slaughter of starving, surrounded German soldiers. In propaganda terms, Stalin and the Red Army had much to gain from the surrender of the once mighty 6th Army, rather than its wholesale annihilation. Furthermore, the release of Soviet forces around Stalingrad to support other operations in southern Russia would be of massive benefit. On 7 January Voronov and Rokossovsky sent an ultimatum to Paulus, who refused to meet Soviet emissaries. The ultimatum, addressed to Paulus directly via the radio, stated: 'You as the commander, and all the officers of the encircled forces, fully realise that you have no real possibility of breaking the ring of encirclement. Your position is hopeless and further resisitance can serve no purpose whatever.' In the event of surrender, German officers could retain sidearms, the wounded and frostbitten would receive medical aid, while all would receive normal rations. Paulus rejected the offer, as he did on 9 January when it was made again. The ultimatum ended with the promise that if 6th Army rejected the Soviet offer, it would be wiped out and the German command would be responsible.

Below: The weapons of the dead and living piled together following the German surrender. The Red Army destroyed or captured huge amounts of German equipment.

Above: Soviet soldiers celebrate victory and survival at Stalingrad. To have fought at Stalingrad was a hallmark of great prestige that veterans of the battle carried with them until the end of the war.

At dawn on 10 January 1943 Rokossovsky made his way to the command post of Batov's 65th Army. He recalled how, 'At the appointed time, 0805 hours, signal flares soared into the sky, and our artillery, mortars and rocket launchers opened fire. The artillery preparation lasted 55 minutes, after which a rolling barrage accompanied our infantry and tanks attacking the enemy positions. The attack was also supported by air strikes. All the troops along the whole perimeter of investment rose simultaneously to the attack.'

This crushing bombardment of 7000 guns had a devastating impact on the German defenders who, summoning fantastic reserves of courage, continued to resist desperately. As Rokossovsky points out, in some areas, Soviet troops 'literally had to gnaw through the enemy defences'. Soviet forces advanced from all sides of the pocket, infantry riding aloft on tanks with Red Army banners waving. In the west, 65th Army tore into the German lines, supported on its left by Galinin's 24th Army and, on its right, by Christyakov's 21st Army. In the north, Zhadov's 66th Army pinned down and drove back 60th Motorised and 16th Panzer, while on the southern side of the pocket, Shumilov's 64th

Army assaulted 297th Division and 20th Romanian Division. By 12 January 1943, the Don Front had destroyed the German position west of the Rossosh river and eliminated the Marinovka salient. In the process, the Don Front had virtually annihilated 44th Division, 29th Motorised and 376th Division in the south-west. As 3rd Motorised withdrew from its exposed position in the Marinovka salient, 6th Army staggered eastwards towards the city, where Chuikov's 62nd Army skirmished with German troops. The scale of the Soviet attack and the fanatical resistance of German troops appalled German and Soviet commanders.

On 13 January Rokossovsky regrouped his forces and switched the main effort to 21st Army. The intention was to capitalise on superior Soviet mobility to break up the German defences as quickly as possible. The next tactical objective, Pitomnik, was the most significant position within the Kessel. Pitomnik was the main airfield within the pocket used by the Luftwaffe to supply 6th Army and by which Paulus's army maintained physical contact with the outside world. At this late stage of 6th Army's agony, in the early days of 1943, Hitler had instructed the Luftwaffe's Inspector-General, Field Marshal Erhard Milch, to oversee and increase the effectiveness of the airlift. Milch was an able individual who set about his task with his customary drive but unsurprisingly failed

Right: Nikita S. Khrushchev, the future General Secretary of the Soviet Union. A senior political commissar at Stalingrad, he is celebrating the surrender of the city to the Russians in February 1942.

to transform a failing airlift into a successful one. In common with Soviet and German officers, he understood that Pitomnik's loss would be the final nail in 6th Army's coffin. All roads to Pitomnik from east and west were strewn with the wreckage and bodies of a dying army. German soldiers retreated across the steppe in temperatures of -20°C as wounded men screamed for aid. Huge, frozen clumps of disfigured and dead German soldiers littered the landscape. Soviet armies advanced relentlessly towards Pitomnik, and dreadful and harrowing scenes developed as wounded German soldiers fought each other to secure a miserable chance of survival. German commanders began selecting officers to fly out of the pocket to rebuild their shattered division so that their units might live on in memory of their dead, fallen at Stalingrad. Pitomnik fell on 16 January and all hope disappeared for 6th Army. The end was in sight: by 16 January, eight German divisions – 3rd Motorised, 44th, 60th Motorised, 76th, 113th 297th, 376th and 29th Motorised – had already been destroyed as effective fighting formations.

On 17 January the Soviet army commanders asked Rokossovsky to order a pause so that they could regroup for a final push to the Volga. However, Rokossovsky ordered them to press their advantage. As he recalled later, 'the enemy suffered considerable losses in the fighting, but in spite of the hopelessness of his position he still continued to put up a fierce resistance'. Equally, after interrogating a senior German officer, Rokossovsky understood for the first time the sheer size of the pocket. After Pitomnik fell, German soldiers without ammunition and hope had begun to lose the will to fight. Rokossovsky did not want to give any respite and risk a bloody, sacrificial last stand in Stalingrad, led by fanatically committed officers like Schmidt. To many in the pocket, Schmidt seemed to be in charge as Paulus reflected on his fate. While the Soviets moved east, the situation deteriorated at Gumrak, the last usable airstrip, now little more than a bomb blasted field, and doctors attempting to treat the wounded in freezing outdoor conditions or filthy, infested cellars and rooms. On 23 January Gumrak fell, bringing the airlift and lingering German hopes to an end. The moment of reckoning approached as 100,000 German officers and soldiers crowded into the city of Stalingrad to await their fate.

Rokossovsky's forces drove west along the banks of the Tsaritsa as 6th Army and 4th Panzer had done in the early days of September 1942. However, Rokossovsky was not trying to encircle and destroy the German troops west of the city in a cauldron battle of

Left: A Soviet soldier waves the Red Flag. Stalingrad was a shattered, virtually unrecognisable city, but it was an unconquered city. It had defied the Wehrmacht to the bitter end.

annihilation. On the contrary, in line with Soviet ideas on deep battle, Rokossovsky sought drive into the heart of the German positions and break them up into smaller, isolated groups. On 24 and 25 January the Don Front crushed everything in its path, and at dawn on 26 January the forward detachments of 21st Army and 65th Army made contact with Rodimstev's 13th Guards north of the Mamayev Kurgan, and split the pocket in two. It was the first time that any officer or soldier from Chuikov's 62nd Army had made contact with another Soviet army since 4th Panzer Army had shouldered 64th Army aside on 14 September 1942. The northern German pocket coalesced around Stalingrad's factories, while to the south, a larger group of smashed German forces came together between the Mamayev Kurgan and the Tsaritsa. On 26 January Russian troops cut the last links between the two pockets. The 6th Army was forced to stop the pitiful rations to the 25,000 wounded in the city as the able-bodied began to collapse in the street from malnutrition, exhaustion and incessant Soviet attacks. On 29 January Rokossovsky's troops split the pocket into three. Strecker's 11th Corps was trapped in and around the Dzerzhinsky Tractor Factory. On their left, Heitz's 8th and Seydlitz's 51st Corps were isolated between the Mamayev Kurgan and Stalingrad-1 railway station. To the south, 4th Army Corps (without Major-General

Janicke, who had been evacuated) and 14th Panzer Corps (now commanded by Schlomer, as Hube had been flown out) awaited the final curtain.

Meanwhile Hitler sang the 6th Army's praises, proclaiming that 'Sixth Army has made an historic contribution to Germany's greatest struggle'. On 31 January he raised Paulus to the rank of field marshal, ostensibly as a reward for his stoicism in adversity, but in reality because, as Hitler knew, no German field marshal had ever allowed himself to be taken prisoner by the enemy. By this promotion, he was signalling to Paulus that he should kill himself.

The reduction of the pockets continued as Soviet troops penetrated right to the heart of the mangled city of Stalingrad. German commanders openly discussed suicide or surrender while the fanatical Schmidt spoke of fighting to the bitter end in the hope that 6th Army's famous sacrifice would inspire Germans for years to come. As Soviet soldiers probed the ruins and cellars and flushed them out with hand-grenades and flamethrowers, Rokossovsky ordered continuous artillery fire on the German lines. German soldiers began to surrender while thousands died fighting or of

Below: Italian prisoners of war march off into captivity. They are clearly in better shape than their German counterparts. Their relief at an end to the fighting on the Don is abundantly clear.

Left: German soldiers march away from Stalingrad. After weeks of starvation and fighting, to some surrender was a relief, but few retained the strength to endure such marches.

wounds, starvation and exhaustion. To the end some remained loyal to Hitler, but Paulus, the Führer's willing servant, rejected his master's invitation to kill himself. As Soviet artillery fire rained down and Soviet tanks and infantry closed in, Paulus surrendered on 31 January to a Russian lieutenant. In a matter of hours, he was driven away to meet Voronov and Rokossovsky at Don Front headquarters some 80km (50 miles) away at Zavarykino. Paulus had not ordered 6th Army to surrender but all over the city German troops began to capitulate. Yet with the remnants of six smashed divisions, Strecker, a fervent German nationalist, if not a committed Nazi, refused to give in. Angered by this unnecessary prolongation of Stalingrad's agony, Rokossovsky concentrated the Don Front's artillery on the pocket to annihilate 11th Corps with a density of up to 300 guns per kilometre. By the morning of 2 February, 11th Corps' resistance had been smashed and its soldiers surrendered. An exhausted calm settled over the wrecked city. At 1600 hours on 2 February 1943 the Don Front formally suspended military operations. The battle of Stalingrad was over and the Red Army had won it.

Below: A scene to send a shiver down Hitler's spine had he ever been exposed to the brutal reality of 6th Army's defeat. German prisoners stumble along what, for the majority, was a road to nowhere.

CHAPTER 10

The Aftermath

After Stalingrad, there was no way back for Germany. Bar her failed offensive at Kursk in 1943, the remainder of the war saw the inexorable advance of the vengeful Red Army towards the very heart of the Reich: Berlin.

In the last days of August 1942, List's Army Group A and Weich's Army Group B drove dispirited and defeated Soviet Armies before them. Hitler's Germany appeared to be on the verge of the decisive victory that had eluded the Wehrmacht in 1941. However, by February 1943, the situation on the Eastern Front had been transformed. The Wehrmacht had suffered a series of defeats at the hands of a resurgent Red Army. German losses are uncertain, but inside the cauldron alone, 60,000 had died since 23 November with over 130,000 captured, 91,000 of those on 2 February 1943 alone. The combined German losses of 6th Army and 4th Panzer were over 300,000 men. If the losses of Army Group A, Army Group Don and other German units of Army Group B during the period 28 June 1942 to 2 February 1943 are included, German casualties were well over 600,000.

In addition, the German defeat at Stalingrad made it clear to Germany's allies such as Finland, Hungary, Italy and Romania that the Soviet Union was likely to survive and look for revenge upon those who aided and abetted Hitler's ideological crusade in the east. The Hungarian leader, Admiral Horthy, admitted to Hitler that 2nd Hungarian's losses were 80,000 dead and 63,000 wounded. The 8th Italian Army lost 84,830 killed, missing and captured between 11 December 1942 and 31 January 1943, with another 29,690 wounded or frostbitten. Marshal Ion Antonescu, the Romanian leader, also informed Hitler that the Romanians had suffered 158,854

Left: Head in hands, a German artilleryman sits on the remains of his knocked-out gun at the battle of Kursk in 1943, the last major offensive launched by the Wehrmacht on the Eastern Front.

dead, injured or missing in the entire Stalingrad campaign. In total, Germany's allies had incurred 494,374 casualties in a matter of months.

The Romanians returned to the fray in 1943 and 1944 but the Hungarians and Italians had little to offer Germany as effective allies after Stalingrad. Italy's losses seriously undermined Mussolini's domestic position. In September 1943, as the Allies prepared to invade southern Italy, Mussolini was removed from power. Italy officially surrendered to the Allies but German occupation ensured two years of bitter fighting on Italian soil. As Soviet forces invaded Hungary in 1944, German and Hungarian troops fought alongside each other, but Hungary could not actively support the Wehrmacht on the Eastern Front during 1943. Axis troops had played a key role in enabling German units to take the offensive in 1942 by manning dormant sectors of the front. However, in 1943 their absence would stretch German manpower resources to breaking point. As

Above: Soviet tank men survey the ground at Kursk. Their care to avoid detection is noticeable. The Germans entirely underestimated Soviet armoured reserves at Kursk.

Below: German soldiers pass the time waiting for the next Soviet assault. Their sullen, resigned expressions indicate their mood and situation, despite the contrived air of relaxation.

Above: German armour moving up to confront the Red Army. Kursk saw thousands of tanks in combat, often without respite, for days on end. Both sides suffered heavy casualties.

the failure of Operation 'Barbarossa' denied the Wehrmacht the means to conduct simultaneous offensives by all three German army groups in 1942, so the disastrous Stalingrad campaign ensured German offensive operations in 1943 were limited to the area of Kursk in July 1943. Therefore, as the war entered 1943, the imbalance between German ends and means – an imbalance that had been there from the start of the war in June 1941 – was beginning to reach critical proportions. Furthermore, an Anglo-American invasion of western Europe in 1943 was a distinct possibility, if not a probability, ensuring that German forces in the east could not rely upon reserves transferred from the west.

At Stalingrad, of the 91,000 prisoners marched off into Soviet captivity, including 22 German generals, only 5000 would ever see German soil again. Survival was in many respects a random combination of luck and the will to live. It was also dependent upon rank, for while over 90 per cent of German soldiers died, along with just over half the 6th Army's junior officers, only five per cent of senior officers succumbed. Senior officers received better treatment by the Soviet authorities, but were also in better health at the time of the surrender. The British journalist, Alexander Werth, who visited Stalingrad in the days following the German capitulation, was surprised at how well German commanders appeared – with the significant exception of Paulus – in contrast to their undernourished soldiers. Soviet mistreatment of German prisoners was not systematic, but the Soviet government made little effort to protect German soldiers from incompetent administration over food and medical aid. In a state where ordinary people starved and millions of Soviet soldiers died fighting a horrific war started by Nazi Germany, the welfare of German soldiers was not a significant Soviet priority. German prisoners suffered at the hands of guards and interrogators keen to extract revenge for the slaughter the Wehrmacht had brought down upon Stalingrad and Mother Russia. Thousands of German soldiers died in camps or in transit through neglect and disease, but also because of the cumulative impact of the malnutrition and hardship they had endured in the pocket since 23 November 1942. Whereas a fit and healthy army would have struggled to cope with conditions in Soviet camps, the 6th Army soldiers were already in a state of starvation and physical collapse. The Soviet authorities did, however, put a great deal of time and effort into persuading embittered German generals and officers to denounce Hitler.

The League of German Officers, with Seydlitz as its president, began working with the Soviet regime to destabilise the Wehrmacht and prompt the officer corps to overthrow Hitler. However, although Seydlitz received support from several generals, including Korfes, Lattman, von Daniels, Drebber and Schlomer, the majority of captive officers shunned active cooperation with the Bolsheviks. Seydlitz was condemned in a court of honour by other imprisoned officers, and in April 1944 was publicly condemned in Germany as a traitor. The verdict was overturned in 1956 by West German courts, but Seydlitz, the hero of Demyansk in spring 1942, would be ostracised, indeed hated, by many Germans following his return to Germany in 1955. The propaganda leaflets dropped on Wehrmacht lines angered and worried the regime in Berlin, but they had little impact upon the field army. Paulus did not cooperate with Seydlitz, but in August 1944 he finally agreed, along with 29 other captive German generals, to put his name to an appeal to Army Group North to surrender. Paulus had aged rapidly and his son Alexander had been killed at Anzio, in Italy, during February 1944. A broken man, he was tortured by the memory of 6th Army's destruction, and saw his duty as involving anything that would shorten the war. In 1946 he appeared as a witness at the Nuremberg trials and returned to live in East Germany until his death in 1957.

As Operation 'Koltso' completed the annihilation of 6th Army in January 1943, Stalin and Stavka, well aware of the significance of the Stalingrad victory, sought to capitalise on it by launching a series of successive operations in southern Russia and the eastern Ukraine. The aim of Operation 'Gallop', undertaken by Vatutin's South-Western Front, was to move west into the eastern Ukraine and reach the lower Dneipr along the northern coast of the sea of Azov. To the north, Golikov's Voronezh Front was to launch Operation 'Star', which envisaged the capture of Kharkov and a move into the Ukraine on South-Western Front's northern flank. The overall operational objective was the destruction of Manstein's Army Group South, an amalgamation of the pieces of Army Groups Don, A and B. There was little time for sustained preparations as Stavka gambled on the Red Army's ability to smash the German line once again. Furthermore, as the Stavka became prey to an infectious, almost irrational optimism, Zhukov and Vasilevsky planned a huge operation that envisaged a major offensive against Army Group Centre.

After finishing off 6th Army, Rokossovsky's Don Front – by then renamed Central Front – was to attack 2nd German and 2nd Panzer Army in conjunction with the Bryansk Front and the left wing of Western Front. It was to move north from the Kursk

Below: Soviet infantry attack at Kursk, having just destroyed a German self-propelled gun. Soviet anti-tank gunners played a critical role in the Soviet victory, inflicting heavy losses on German armour.

region into the rear of Army Group Centre at Smolensk, where it would meet the right wing of Western Front and the Kalinin Front, trapping and destroying German troops in the Rzhev salient. This was essentially a combination of the failed Operation 'Mars' and Operation 'Jupiter', driven by Zhukov's desire for revenge upon Army Group Centre. It was an extraordinarily ambitious concept, in fact too ambitious, as the events of spring 1943 would reveal. Stavka underestimated the resilience and skill of the Wehrmacht and overestimated the stamina and power of tired, worn-out Soviet fronts. Thus, as with so many German offensives, so with the Red Army's operations of February and March 1943 there was a distinct lack of correlation between ends and means.

As German forces withdrew into the Donbas area, north of Rostov, they also concentrated previously dispersed combat power. Still furious and stunned by the Stalingrad debacle, Hitler gave Manstein a relatively free hand in preparing a devastating counteroffensive. As German reserves arrived, including the lavishly equipped and full strength 2nd SS Panzer Corps, Operation 'Gallop' and 'Star' got off to a racing start. By 15 February, Soviet forces were approaching Kharkov and Kursk, while Rokossovsky's Central Front, although late in arriving in

Above: Stalingrad saved the Soviet peoples while Kursk paved the way for the defeat of Nazi Germany. Soviet and Polish soldiers pose in celebration of victory, complete victory. This is Berlin in May 1945.

the Kursk region, tore into 2nd German Army. However, Manstein calculated that Soviet forces in the south were operating on dangerously extended lines of supply and trying to achieve too much with too little. He deliberately encouraged the Red Army to believe Operation 'Gallop' and 'Star' were more sustainable than they really were by conceding Kharkov, a major rail and road junction. The Red Army swallowed the bait. On 20 February 1943, led by 1st Panzer, 4th Panzer and 2nd SS Panzer Corps, German armoured forces counterattacked. By mid-March 1943, South-Western Front and Voronezh Front had been given a severe mauling. The Red Army was driven out of Kharkov and only a spring thaw saved the Soviet forces in the south from further setbacks. Manstein's brilliant counteroffensive also played a key role in curtailing the offensive of Rokossovsky's Central Front. In the last days of February 1943, Rokossovsky's forces had made deep inroads into 2nd German Army, advancing further west than any Soviet force had done in the winter of 1942–43. Yet, in response to Manstein's counter offensive, Soviet reserves were diverted south to prop up the Soviet position on the Donets river rather than reinforcing Rokossovsky's success. The Central Front's advance faltered and, in March 1943, came to a halt, forcing the abandonment of the proposed offensives by Kalinin and Western Fronts.

Manstein's counteroffensive was a highly impressive demonstration of the German's residual tactical prowess. It was a severe setback for the Red Army but its significance needs to be put into a proper strategic context. As the spring thaw descended upon the Eastern Front, German forces were in positions they had occupied at the beginning of Operation 'Blau'. In other words, even though the Kharkov counteroffensive was an operational success, it could not disguise the fact that the Stalingrad campaign had been a catastrophic strategic failure. In the words of Dr H.P. Willmott, 'the reality after November 1942 was that Germany was fighting at best a defensive war, at worst a war that was lost'.

The Red Army had suffered for its triumph. If measured from the creation of the Stalingrad Front under Timoshenko on 12 July 1942, the Stalingrad campaign cost the Soviet forces approximately 1.1 million casualties, 485,751 of them fatal. However, the disparity between Soviet and German casualties was nothing like as great as in 1941. In the various operations undertaken between 19 November 1942 and 2 February 1943 by Vasilevsky's Fronts, Soviet losses were 154,885 dead and 330,892 wounded. Although shocking in itself, this rate of loss, given the scale of Soviet strategic and operational success in this period, reflects the substantial improvement of the Red Army since 1941 in the hands of superior commanders such as Vasilevsky, not withstanding the disaster of Operation 'Mars'.

By February 1943, the Red Army was far from the finished article as a war machine, but nor was it the blundering colossus that it was between June 1941 and September 1942. At Kursk, in July 1943, the Red Army would defeat the Wehrmacht's last significant offensive on the Eastern Front and begin its march on Berlin. In April 1945, it was perhaps appropriate that Chuikov's 62nd Army was in Berlin as the Red Army stormed the Reichstag.

The origins of the Red Army's victory in World War II lay in the stupendous struggle on the Volga conducted between 13 September 1942 and 2 February 1943. As Alexander Werth wandered about the shattered city of Stalingrad in February 1943, in the days following 6th Army's annihilation, he stood in awe at the scale of the destruction: 'Trenches ran through the factory yards; through the workshops themselves; at the bottom of the trenches there still lay frozen green Germans and frozen grey Russians and frozen fragments of human shape, and there were tin helmets, German and Russian, lying among the brick debris, and the helmets were half-filled with snow. There was barbed wire here, and half-uncovered mines, and shell cases, and more rubble, and fragments of walls, and torturous tangles of rusty steel girders. How anyone could have survived here was hard to imagine.' The 6th German Army commanded by Colonel-General Friedrich Paulus had not survived: it had been destroyed.

On 3 February 1943 the news of 6th Army's defeat was released to the German people. Although Hitler's régime acknowledged that 6th Army had been beaten, it refused to admit that many German officers and soldiers had surrendered rather than fight to the death. An official communiqué, as misleading as it was revealing, stated 'The supreme command of the Wehrmacht announces that the battle of Stalingrad has come to an end. True to its oath of allegiance, the Sixth Army under the exemplary leadership of Field Marshal Paulus has been annihilated by the overwhelming superiority of enemy numbers.' Stalingrad was not simply a military defeat; it was a catastrophe. The eyes of the world had been fixed upon the drama unfolding on the Volga, and the Wehrmacht's aura of invincibility was shattered forever, as the scale of the German defeat became apparent. Two German armies, Paulus' 6th Army and Hoth's 4th Panzer Army, had been destroyed and Richthofen's Air Fleet 4 brought to the point of collapse. In Germany, three days of national mourning were declared and a deep-seated conviction in the superiority of German arms was replaced by a profound, if rarely acknowledged, fear of defeat. To the peoples of the Soviet Union, Stalingrad was the first moment of triumph in a bitter war for survival, replacing dark nightmares of defeat at the hands of the Nazis with the conviction that victory, although it would not come easily, would eventually come. Although the war was far from over, it had taken a decisive turn against Nazi Germany.

Right: The Mamayev Kurgan: a memorial to the Red Army soldiers who died in the struggle on the Volga. The battle of Stalingrad shattered the Wehrmacht's aura of invincibility.

Order of battle

RED ARMY

STALINGRAD FRONT (Yeremenko)

28TH ARMY
34th Guards, 248th Rifle Divisions
6th Guards Tank Brigade
52nd, 152nd, 159th Special
Brigades

51ST ARMY
15th Guards, 91st, 126th, 302nd
Rifle Divisions
254th Tank Brigade
38th Special Brigade
4th Mechanized Corps
4th Cavalry Corps

57TH ARMY
169th, 422nd Rifle Divisions
90th, 235th Tank Brigades
143rd Special Brigade
13th Mechanised Corps

62ND ARMY
13th Guards, 37th Guards, 39th
Guards, 45th, 95th, 112th, 138th,
193rd, 196th, 244th, 284th, 308th,
10th NKVD Rifle Divisions
84th, 137th, 189th Tank Brigades
92nd Marine Infantry Brigade
42nd, 115th, 124th, 149th, 160th
Special Brigades

64TH ARMY
36th Guards, 29th, 38th, 157th,
204th Rifle Divisions
13th, 56th Tank Brigades
154th Marine Infantry Brigade
66th, 93rd, 96th, 97th Special
Brigades

FRONT RESERVE
330th Rifle Division
85th Tank Brigade

8TH AIR ARMY

DON FRONT (Rokossovsky)

24TH ARMY
49th, 84th, 120th, 173rd, 233rd,
260th, 273rd Rifle Divisions
10th Tank Brigade
16th Tank Corps

65TH ARMY
4th Guards, 27th Guards, 40th
Guards, 23rd, 24th, 252nd, 258th,
304th, 321st Rifle Divisions
121st Tank Brigade

66TH ARMY
64th, 99th, 116th, 226th, 299th,
343rd Rifle Divisions
58th Tank Brigade

16TH AIR ARMY

SOUTH WEST FRONT (Vatutin)

1ST GUARDS ARMY
1st, 153rd, 197th, 203rd, 266th,
278th Rifle Divisions

5TH TANK ARMY
14th Guards, 47th Guards, 50th
Guards, 119th, 159th, 346th
Rifle Divisions
1st Tank Corps
26th Tanks Corps
89th Cavalry Corps

21ST ARMY
63rd, 76th, 96th, 277th, 293rd,
333rd Rifle Divisions
4th Guards, 1st, 2nd Tank
Brigades
4th Tank Corps
3rd Guards Cavalry Corps

FRONT RESERVE
1st Guards Mechanised Corps

2ND AIR ARMY

17TH AIR ARMY

GERMAN ARMY

6TH ARMY (Paulus)

4th CORPS
297th, 371st Infantry Divisions
29th Motorised Infantry Division

8th CORPS
76th, 113th Infantry Divisions

11th CORPS
44th, 376th, 384th Infantry
Divisions

24th PANZER CORPS
16th Panzer Division
3rd, 60th Motorised Infantry
Divisions

51st CORPS
14th, 24th Panzer Divisions
71st, 79th, 94th, 100th, 295th
305th, 389th Infantry Divisions

MAJOR ARMY TROOPS
4th, 46th, 64th, 79th Artillery
Regiments
54th, 616th, 627th, 849th
Artillery Battalions
49th, 101st, 733rd Heavy
Artillery Battalions
51st, 53rd Mortar Regiments
2nd, 30th Nebelwerfer Regiments
6th, 41st Pioneer Battalions

LUFTWAFFE GROUND TROOPS
9th Flak Division

AIR FLEET 4
VIII Air Corps

Chronology

1941

22 June Operation Barbarossa, the German invasion of the Soviet Union, launched.

1942

28 June German summer offensive begins in the Kursk sector.

30 June German 6th Army begins its offensive in the Belgorod sector.

6 July Voronezh on the Don captured by German forces.

9 July German offensive in Kharkhov sector begins.

21 July The German Army crosses the Don at Rostov.

23 July Rostov-on-Don captured by the Germans.

26 July Army Group A launches its offensive into the Caucasus.

28 July Soviet High Command at Stalingrad issues a directive: 'Not one step backwards.'

4 August Germans cross the Aksay, and start drive on Stalingrad itself.

6 August Germans cross the Kuban near Armavir.

7 August German 6th Army attacks near Kalach.

9 August Krasnodar and Yeysk, a port on the Sea of Azov, are captured by the Germans.

14 August Germans cross the Kuban at Krasnodar.

19 August Sixth Army ordered to attack Stalingrad by von Paulus.

22 August German advance into the Caucasus halted.

25 August Stalingrad declared to be in a state of siege.

1 September German and Romanian troops cross the Kerch Straits and advance into the Taman Peninsula. Bridgehead on the Terek established by the Germans.

3 September German troops attack the centre of Stalingrad.

6 September Novorossiysk on the Black Sea captured by the Germans.

15 September Russian attack on Voronezh.

24 September Germans advance towards Tuapse.

6 October Germans capture Malgobek in the Terek salient.

9 October Military commanders given sole authority in the Red Army.

14 October Hitler brings the summer offensive to a close, ordering that all German Army Groups must 'consider their present lines springboards for a German offensive in 1943 and hold them at all costs.'

18 October German drive on Tuapse halted.

25 October Fresh German offensive in the Caucasus.

1 November Alagir in the Caucasus captured by the Germans.

2 November Ordzhonikidse in the Caucasus taken by the Germans.

19 November Operation Uranus launched by the Russians, breaking through the Romanian forces north of Stalingrad.

20 November Second part of Operation Uranus launched south of Stalingrad. Manstein appointed commander of Army Group Don.

22 November Russian forces meet at Kalach, encircling 6th Army.

25 November German airlift to Stalingrad begins.

12 December Launch of Operation Winter Storm, an attempt by 4th Panzer Army to relieve Stalingrad. Hitler continues to refuse 6th Army the opportunity to break out.

16 December Russians launch Operation Little Saturn, an offensive aimed at Rostov. Italian 8th Army retreats in disarray. Attack on Tuapse called off by the Germans.

21 December Relief attempt for Stalingrad halted on the Myshkova.

23 December All attempts to relieve Stalingrad called off.

24 December Russian attack towards Kotelnikovo. Romanians retreat in disorder.

28 December German Army Group A receives orders to retreat from the Caucasus.

1943

1 January Germans begin retreat from the Terek.

5 January Milch ordered to ensure the Stalingrad airlift succeeds.

8 January Surrender ultimatum sent to 6th Army.

10 January Rokossovsky leads Russian attack to liquidate the cauldron.

12 January Hungarian and Italian lines broken by Russian troops on the Don. Germans in Caucasus retreat to the Kuban bridgehead.

13 January Germans retreat from Terek to the Nagutskoye-Alexsandrovskoye Line.

14 January German Army General Staff propose to strengthen the Eastern Front by force, conscripting people from the Baltic States for army or police duties.

17 January German panzer corps surrounded on the Don.

24 January Russian Trans-Caucasian Front halted at Novorossiysk-Krasnodar.

25 January 6th Army at Stalingrad split in two by Russian attacks. Germans retreat from Armavir and Voronezh.

31 January Paulus surrenders in the southern pocket at Stalingrad.

2 February Northern pocket surrenders. The battle for Stalingrad is over.

Index